Dempsey and Tunney
in the Roaring Twenties

ALSO BY LEW FREEDMAN
AND FROM MCFARLAND

*Hoyt Wilhelm: Life of a Knuckleballer* (2024)
*Chuckin' Charlie Conerly and the New York Football Giants* (2023)
*Johnny Mize: A Biography of Baseball's "Big Cat"* (2022)
*Caught by Don Hutson!: A Biography
of Pro Football's First Modern Receiver* (2022)
*Lightning Strikes Twice: Johnny Vander Meer and the Cincinnati Reds* (2021)
*Buffalo Bill Cody: The Man Who Shaped the Wild West Legend* (2020)
*Cy Young: The Baseball Life and Career* (2020)
*Ernie Banks: The Life and Career of "Mr. Cub"* (2019)
*Connie Mack's First Dynasty: The Philadelphia Athletics, 1910–1914* (2017)
*Baseball's Funnymen: Twenty-Four Jokers, Screwballs,
Pranksters and Storytellers* (2017)
*The Boyer Brothers of Baseball* (2015)
*Joe Louis: The Life of a Heavyweight* (2013)
*George Altman: My Baseball Journey from the Negro Leagues
to the Majors and Beyond* (George Altman with Lew Freedman, 2013)
*DiMaggio's Yankees: A History of the 1936–1944 Dynasty* (2011)
*The Day All the Stars Came Out: Major League
Baseball's First All-Star Game, 1933* (2010)
*Hard-Luck Harvey Haddix and the Greatest Game Ever Lost* (2009)
*Early Wynn, the Go-Go White Sox and the 1959 World Series* (2009)

# Dempsey and Tunney
# in the Roaring Twenties

Lew Freedman

McFarland & Company, Inc., Publishers
*Jefferson, North Carolina*

ISBN (print) 978-1-4766-9555-6
ISBN (ebook) 978-1-4766-5573-4

Library of Congress cataloging data are available

© 2025 Lew Freedman. All rights reserved

*No part of this book may be reproduced or transmitted in any form or by any means, electronic or mechanical, including photocopying or recording, or by any information storage and retrieval system, without permission in writing from the publisher.*

Front cover images: Gene Tunney and Jack Dempsey from a poster promoting their fight at Soldier Field on September 22, 1927, in Chicago, Illinois (Underwood & Underwood)

Printed in the United States of America

*McFarland & Company, Inc., Publishers*
*Box 611, Jefferson, North Carolina 28640*
*www.mcfarlandpub.com*

# TABLE OF CONTENTS

*Preface*   1
*Introduction*   5

**1** Jack Dempsey   9
**2** Gene Tunney   16
**3** Enter Doc Kearns   22
**4** A Changing Country   26
**5** Tunney Progresses Slowly but Surely   33
**6** Boxing's Treatment of Blacks at Its Worst   38
**7** The Champ   43
**8** The NFL Comes into the Picture   52
**9** Tunney's Learning Curve   57
**10** Radio and All That Jazz   60
**11** Life Gets Complicated Outside the Ring   66
**12** The Babe Saves Baseball   70
**13** Parlez Vous Knockout?   75
**14** Where Can a Guy Get a Drink? Everywhere   80
**15** Tunney Goes to School   86
**16** Dempsey, Kearns and Shelby, Montana   90
**17** Baseball, God and Moving Pictures   100
**18** Meeting Harry Greb   106
**19** Horses and Other Heroes   111
**20** A Champ at His Leisure   120

| | | |
|---|---|---|
| 21 | The Craziest Fight of All Time | 123 |
| 22 | The Serum Run | 131 |
| 23 | This Guy Greb Won't Go Away | 137 |
| 24 | Tennis, Anyone? | 144 |
| 25 | Doing Everything but Fighting | 151 |
| 26 | Red Grange and Notre Dame Meet the Nation | 157 |
| 27 | Dempsey Finally Defends—Tunney Rising | 165 |
| 28 | Dempsey and Tunney Fight at Last | 170 |
| 29 | Let's Do It Again—Maybe | 179 |
| 30 | Charles Lindbergh | 185 |
| 31 | Dempsey–Tunney II Is On | 190 |
| 32 | The Long Count | 195 |
| 33 | That's All, Folks | 202 |
| 34 | Things Unravel | 208 |
| 35 | Dempsey and Tunney Together Forever | 213 |
| *Chapter Notes* | | 221 |
| *Bibliography* | | 227 |
| *Index* | | 229 |

# Preface

From the end of World War I, on November 11, 1918, to the stock market collapse that ignited the Great Depression in October 1929 on Black Tuesday, America lived out one of its most distinctive decades.

The country's high-speed, helter-skelter existence seemed to jump-start drunkenness despite Prohibition, provoke barely rational acts that jitterbugged across the national stage, introduce a new age of the heroic, larger-than-life sportsman and violent crime bosses running wild in the streets while seeking respectability.

Corruption crept into the White House and Hollywood movies generated household-name stars. Radio began penetrating living rooms and cars began filling roadways between cities.

What else? Everything else. Sacco and Vanzetti. Charles Lindbergh flew across the Atlantic Ocean. King Tut's tomb was dug up in Egypt. The books of F. Scott Fitzgerald and Ernest Hemingway were being read. Moonshine was the beverage of choice and moonshine agents even became celebrities. The Ku Klux Klan's radical racism sought to destroy the country and nearly subsumed Indiana completely.

After the bitterness and bleakness of "the war to end all wars," which was perhaps the most optimistic statement ever uttered in international politics when the armistice was signed, there was a massive exhale of relief in the largest American cities and across the globe in countries that emerged from havoc comparatively unscathed.

Many called it "The Jazz Age," when frolicking to music became an "in" thing, a free thing encouraging the body to let loose. Women gained the right to vote in the United States, and apparently the right to smoke in public, too.

"The Roaring Twenties was an age of iconic events and people, of talismanic names and episodes that have entered our consciousness more like myths—or morality tales—than historical occurrences," it was written in the book *Anything Goes: A Biography of the Jazz Age*.[1]

With the guns thankfully silenced, now it was time to frolic, make money and make merry. That was the attitude prevailing across the United States. Times were no longer so tough and men and women had earned the right to play.

People also gradually began to appreciate, more than ever before, they had the right to applaud the greatest players among them. While baseball was still king, the National Hockey League was founded in 1917 in Montreal and the National Football League was established in 1920. In each of these sports, fans learned to appreciate the great individual talent, the man who stood above the crowd (and it was mostly men) through his skill and individual personality.

This era gave us Babe Ruth, even today the most famous and perhaps the greatest baseball player of them all. Barely an American alive is unfamiliar with his slugging exploits.

America went crazy for Red Grange as a college and then professional football icon with the University of Illinois and the Chicago Bears. "Big Bill" Tilden introduced booming, dominating tennis for the masses. Women—Suzanne Lenglen and Helen Wills—enraptured those tennis fans, too. Bobby Jones practically invented golf. Johnny Weissmuller swam like a dolphin.

There was also Knute Rockne and Notre Dame as a powerhouse in college football, which told us all to "win one for the Gipper" someday. A star of few words—make that no words—of the era was the Thoroughbred horse Man o' War.

And then there was a duo, linked together, almost as one. The men who helped define the era were boxers, fighters, heavyweight champions, titans of their sport whose two encounters nearly a century ago still resonate with the American sports fan, and especially the boxing fan, as among the most intense, highly publicized sanctioned sporting wars of all time.

The man known as Jack Dempsey, but who wasn't really officially named Jack Dempsey, won the heavyweight crown and the image that attended it as "the toughest man in the world" early in this quixotic period in American life.

The man known as Gene Tunney, who accidentally, then on purpose, fooled the many into thinking of him as a man of privilege, but whose background really was as a tough-as-nails, hardwired, single-minded fighter, stamped himself as the spoiler, the man whose determination and ego would not let him rest until he lifted the crown.

Then after he got it, he seemed to lose interest in it almost immediately when he could have capitalized on its worth. He fought Dempsey again, defended the title once more and retired to marry an heiress and enter business. Thereafter, the man who had regularly quoted

Shakespeare to sportswriters was as often seen wearing a tuxedo as shorts.

"He didn't look like a prizefighter," wrote the *New York Times'* John Kieran. "He didn't talk like a prizefighter. He didn't act like a prizefighter."[2] Outside of the boxing ring, that is.

Dempsey, "The Manassa Mauler," was originally from Colorado. He once described his skill in the ring this way: "I can't sing and I can't dance, but I can kick any man's ass."[3] That was not Shakespearean patois.

Although Dempsey possessed a high-pitched voice, this was the type of stuff the heavyweight champ was supposed to verbalize. Indeed, he may have borrowed his phraseology from John L. Sullivan, the bareknuckle champion known as "The Boston Strong Boy" who some 40 years before would regularly rise from a chair in a saloon or some such locale and roughly proclaim, "I can lick any son-of-a-bitch in the house."[4] And he could make good on the vow.

Dempsey and Tunney met twice in a boxing ring, in Philadelphia in 1926 and in Chicago in 1927. Both times the heavyweight championship belt was at stake. With the exception of automobile racing, the Indianapolis 500 in particular, and some stock car races, the turnouts for the two bouts were among the largest sporting events in American history.

A century later they remain so, the crowds flocking to see these men at the pinnacle of the boxing world nearly overwhelming the facilities. One of the two fights included one of the most controversial critical moments in any American sporting event, a moment that well may have rewritten history. This so-called "long count" battle has never been forgotten by those who know the fight game.

Nor has the rivalry between the men who seemed so different but at heart may well have been more similar than many suspected. As the most directly violent of any major sport, boxing sets itself apart for the one-on-one nature of the competition. The four American major professional sports leagues—Major League Baseball, the NHL, the NFL and the National Basketball Association—are all team endeavors.

One man can make a difference in the result, but the winners and losers are teams. In boxing, one man's hand and arm are raised to the sky, proclaiming him the victor. Rivalries are notable in various sports, from New York Yankees–Boston Red Sox to Green Bay Packers–Chicago Bears and Boston Celtics–Los Angeles Lakers. But the most intense rivalries in boxing are more personal, more visceral. It is probable that the greatest boxing rivalry of all time is Muhammad Ali–Joe Frazier, and perhaps the greatest sports rivalry of them all.

Yet despite its comparatively ancient dating, Dempsey–Tunney, from 100 years ago, still rates near the top of any such evaluations. Their combined glitter captured the minds of and elicited roars from fans of the sport in the 1920s and the spotlight has never really worn off.

# Introduction

The United States was late into World War I, the conflagration that began in 1914, when it joined on the side of the Allies in 1917.

By the time hostilities ceased in late 1918, approximately 17 million people, nine million of them in the military and eight million civilians, were dead and some 23 million were wounded.

The long-standing Turkish Ottoman Empire had been shattered, much of Europe was in ruins and the seeds were planted for the hatred and violence in Germany that would come to pass in two decades with the poisonous arrival of World War II.

U.S. president Woodrow Wilson was in dire health physically and politically weakened when he left office in 1921, and he died in 1924 with much of the body politic averse to his idealistic League of Nations. A powerful strain of isolationism ran through public discourse.

As a comparatively unscathed nation, the United States itself had risen to an apex of power internationally, even if its citizens had no taste for further war and a distaste for the Russian communist revolution beginning in 1917. World War I and its awful consequences

Jack Dempsey, who brought glamour to the heavyweight boxing division during the Roaring Twenties, poses showing off his muscles (Library of Congress).

displaying such newfound horrible ways for man to kill man as trench warfare and chemical weapons were a scar America bore. Even worse, it seemed, was witnessing so many of the country's youthful soldiers coming home shell-shocked.

Peculiarly, at this time, it seemed two very different major developments were approved, one greatly expanding freedoms for millions of Americans and one greatly reducing freedoms for adult Americans. Decades of lobbying and politicking went into each significant adjustment.

In 1920, the women's suffrage movement bore fruit, with the female portion of the population being granted the right to vote in a chauvinistic nation. That same year, Prohibition, the banning of the sale, creation and drinking of alcoholic beverages, took effect, lasting into 1933. The first represented a milestone of human rights. The latter proved to be a boneheaded law that was absurdly enforced, created more problems than it solved and might well have been the most shortsighted public policy ever imposed on the American people.

Future heavyweight champion Gene Tunney, who grew up in the Greenwich Village part of New York City, shows off his jabbing form as part of a workout (Library of Congress).

Americans got used to women voting. They never got used to being told they could not have a beer at the corner saloon or a glass of wine with dinner. It might be said, snidely, yet accurately, given the context of the Roaring Twenties, that Americans mostly danced around Prohibition, except for how it helped create new tiers of criminals, from Mom and Dad in the dining room of the home to Al Capone ruling the streets with blood and guts.

When the nation was at war, people were too worried about limitations from rationing and worrisome reports from the front. When peace reigned, the economy boomed and such phrases as "leisure time," heretofore pretty much unknown, took hold. This became a marvelous period for spectator sports, for those who admired the best athletes of all to loosen their purse strings and become something known as the ticket-buying public.

As if on cue, a new generation of great athletes seemed to arrive on stage simultaneously, showing off skills previously unimagined. Baseball was one of the old standbys. The National League was established in 1876 and Major League Baseball officially dates its origin to that year.

By 1920, all-time greats such as Ty Cobb, Cy Young, Napoleon Lajoie and Christy Mathewson—later honored as Hall of Famers in Cooperstown, New York—were all household names. However, before it could rise, become freshly embraced and take hold of the American psyche all over again, baseball had to reach its nadir.

In 1919, the Cincinnati Reds won the World Series by defeating the heavily favored Chicago White Sox. In a shocking series of events, it was concluded that gamblers had tampered with Americans' trust by paying off White Sox stars to fix the result of the World Series. It was a cheating scandal of such power it could have wrecked the game for good, destroyed any faith in fans whose goodwill was necessary to perpetuate the sport's success.

In a true case of baseball rising from the ashes, the mighty swats of one man lifting his heavy wooden bat and blasting the ball for home runs revolutionized the game, re-excited the populace and made him perhaps the most famous American athlete in history. George Herman Ruth, "The Babe," demonstrated baseball could be played another way altogether, not simply by laboriously pushing across runs one at a time, but in a cluster with a single swing. It turned out the followers of the game liked that and were so enthusiastic they might show up at a ballpark 50,000 at a time to prove it.

Whether it was due to the violent but conclusive nature of the contest, or its roots in mano-a-mano competition, boxing, the most elemental of sports, had always had a firm grasp on the American consciousness. There was nothing subtle about it. Any casual observer, even one who had never attended a fight before, could comprehend the basic rules, and certainly the results, if just one man was left standing while the other was prone on the canvas.

As the largest of the combatants among the men who wore gloves into the ring as one of eight weight classes from flyweight, or 112 pounds, on up, the conceit of the holder of the heavyweight championship is that he was called the toughest man in the world.

For decades it was said that boxing was received by the public at large and the sports fan in general based on this phrase: "As the heavyweight championship goes, so goes boxing." The heavyweight champ was one of the most recognized athletes in the country and across the world. He was the man atop the mountain, the symbol of fisticuffs for all, with the title perceived as being the greatest individual prize in sport.

While still young, by this era, the Marquis of Queensbury Rules, published in Great Britain in 1867, were codified and established. They shepherded the sport from the bare-knuckle stage into the use of leather gloves.

By 1919, there had been a universally recognized lineage of heavyweight titleholders, beginning with John L. Sullivan in 1885. He was followed by James J. Corbett, Bob Fitzsimmons, Marvin Hart, Tommy Burns, Jack Johnson and Jess Willard. That year, Jack Dempsey became the heavyweight champion when he knocked out Willard in the fourth round.

Dempsey had fought his way to the top in the ring, but he had not fought in World War I, a fact that detractors used to insult him as a slacker. Gene Tunney, who became nicknamed "The Fighting Marine," developed his boxing talents while in the service during World War I.

It seemed crazy to suggest Dempsey, the man admired for his toughness, was a coward, but that was a subliminal text of this scorn.

# 1

# Jack Dempsey

**I**F HE SLUGGED YOU JUST RIGHT, you went down. The fighter with the fists of iron so powerful his punches to the jaw could pulverize just about anyone he stood toe-to-toe with in the ring was born William Harrison Dempsey on June 24, 1895, in Manassa, Colorado.

Not Jack. "Jack" could not be found on the birth certificate his father, Hyrum Dempsey, and his mother, Mary Celia, agreed with but was acquired only later. At home they called this youngster Harry. He was the ninth of 13 children. While contemporary writers refer to Dempsey's father as "Hiram," when he wrote his autobiography, Jack spelled it "Hyrum."

While Dempsey's mother was pregnant with him, one day a door-to-door salesman stopped at the house trying to peddle some wares. He was older and clearly flirting with exhaustion and coping with the cold weather. Celia, as she was most often called, let him into the house to warm up, fed the man some hot food and a hot drink, loaned him a blanket and watched as he dozed off by the fire. When he awoke, refreshed, the man insisted for her kindness that Celia take anything of her choosing from his stash of goods.

Mrs. Dempsey did not covet anything she was shown, but she was an avid reader, so she plucked a dust-covered book from the salesman's items. It turned out to be the autobiography of John L. Sullivan, the first official heavyweight champion. Although Celia was no fight fan, when telling the story to her young son, she said she read it through more than once. Mother took it as a sign Harry would grow up to be very strong and "you could be just like him."[1]

Call it an oddity of foreshadowing, or a family myth, but the unborn child did grow up to become very much like this former heavyweight champion.

In boxing circles, when one of the most famous boxers of all time began his journey to the heavyweight title, Dempsey was called "Kid Blackie." Then, one day in 1914 when his brother Bernie could not fulfill

Jack Dempsey (left), one of the most famous heavyweight champions of all time, spars before a crowd of onlookers (Library of Congress).

a fight commitment and his brother stepped up to replace him on a card, he pretended to be someone else who was already pretending to be someone else.

The Dempsey boys followed the fights and were fans of the middleweight John Edward Kelly, Irish-born but an American later, as he won that championship in 1884. Kelly first made the Dempsey name well-known, even though that was not his real name either. He called himself Jack Dempsey and gained the nickname "Nonpareil." During this era, it seemed, boxers had more aliases than criminals on wanted posters.

Kelly was born in Curran, County Kildare, in Ireland. Before emigrating, the Dempsey family had its roots in Ireland, as well, both on Dempsey's father's side and his mother's side.

Kelly's claim for posterity occurred under the name Jack "Nonpareil" Dempsey. He was the first acknowledged middleweight champ and felt to be unbeatable, hence the somewhat stilted nickname. Perhaps half the fight crowd didn't even understand what *nonpareil* meant, but overall, it meant that he was pretty darned good. Dempsey/Kelly was unbeaten between 1883 and 1889.

The Dempsey clan—there were five brothers—thought highly of this Dempsey, and when Bernie began fighting in small Western towns and in mining camps, as the family moved around with Dad seeking work, he paid homage by employing the Jack Dempsey name. By then, the Nonpareil was dead, into his grave, just shy of 33, partially due to tuberculosis and partially due to alcoholism, so he wasn't going to object.

On the day Harry pinch-hit for Bernie and borrowed the Jack Dempsey moniker, no one felt it would stick. Harry proved to be the better fighter, though, and when he kept winning his rough-around-the-edges bouts in formidable fashion, this new Jack Dempsey hung on to the name.

At one point, some years later, Dempsey simplified his explanation of his shift to "Jack," saying, "It was only when they found out I could fight the best, that I got to be Jack."[2] Not quite, but close enough no one really disputed that.

It was like the second coming of a Babe Ruth, it might be said, but while the original sort-of Jack Dempsey was spectacular in his own way, with 51 victories, four losses and 11 draws, the second-time-around Jack Dempsey eclipsed the Nonpareil's fame and reputation.

While the heavyweights were always representing the largest weight class among boxers, the heavyweights of more than a century ago were smaller humans than the athletes of today. Many of the finest fighters weighed 200 pounds or less, light compared with more recent heavyweight champions.

When Muhammad Ali (who at that moment was still fighting as Cassius Clay, his birth name) captured the heavyweight crown from Sonny Liston in 1964, he weighed 210½ pounds and Liston weighed 218. Riddick Bowe later fought a title match at 252 pounds. Lennox Lewis fought at around 245 pounds. Both men stood about six-foot-five.

Dempsey was six-foot-one and his general fighting weight was mostly in the low 190s. In 1920, the average American adult male was 5–8¼ tall. Genetics matured in the 50 to 80 years in between the measurement of those other heavyweight boxing specimens. If Dempsey was ultimately viewed as great by the American public, it took time for him to gain that stature.

Young Harry/Jack's family moved around. He was born in Colorado and spent some time in West Virginia before the Dempseys moved on to Utah. He was not someone who was going to go to college and study for the bar. He was a physical man who worked by spending sweat and by slinging his fists. He aspired to be a great boxer, but mostly his opportunities came at the lowest levels of club boxing where the pay was low and the atmosphere was far from glitzy.

It was by happenstance that Dempsey was born in Colorado and received that "Manassa Mauler" nickname because his earliest days as a professional fighter where records were kept were in Salt Lake City. In a routine matter for the time period, but virtually unheard of now, many of Dempsey's early contests were registered as no contest—no winner or loser.

At Bernie's suggestion, Jack ate pine gum, supposedly to strengthen his own jaw, soaked his hands in brine to make them stronger and lathered his face in beef brine with the goal of toughening his skin so he would not bleed so readily when struck.

"It was hard work," Dempsey said years later. "The training was tedious. But it didn't bother me. I loved fighting."[3]

At the beginning, as Dempsey learned his trade, learned to keep his hands up at all times for defense, learned how to jab, learned his footwork, learned that his uppercut could temporarily separate an opponent from his senses, Dempsey's base was Utah.

Dempsey's first official fight on his lifetime record of 58–6–9 took place on November 30, 1914, at the Garrick Theatre in Salt Lake City. In his debut, setting the tone for the fierce nature of his knockout style and record, he KO'd Billy Murphy.

Dempsey stayed busy after that, mostly at the Garrick. He won his next four bouts there, as well, one by decision and the other three by knockout, before he dropped the first fight of his career to Jack Downey on a decision on April 4, 1915.

During those early days, Bernie and other brothers trained in a home-fashioned gym shaped from a chicken coop. Bernie was the older leader, though Dempsey said he never made it big in boxing because he had a glass chin (which is a long-standing phrase in the game indicating a fighter cannot take a punch to the face). Dempsey devoured the *Police Gazette* reports on fights and was itchy with youth to move up and move on, reach another level in the sport.

Dempsey engaged in that Bernie-supervised training when he was still a youngster, really, and it was a big deal in his house when he graduated from eighth grade. Mom may have loved reading books, but the children of the Dempsey household were not much for pursuing formal education. Dempsey felt he was ready to join the workforce, to go make money and make a mark on society.

By the age of 16, Dempsey had his first hard-labor job, in a copper mine in Utah. This was the type of work that had broken the backs of immigrants who came to the United States with great dreams but never became wealthy enough to lift family members above the poverty level, or at least the lower-class work level.

Dempsey's assignment involved descending underground 3,000

feet, shoveling coal and loading an ore car. One day, a smartass began tossing dirt at Dempsey and refused to cease when warned to stop. This confrontation ended with a fight, which naturally Dempsey won quickly. That burnished his local reputation as a tough guy and led to Dempsey's first minor celebrity status.

He spent five years switching mining camps, working at outfits bringing up gold, silver and copper from the earth. Between gigs, Dempsey signed up for pro cards wherever he worked. The venues changed, even within Utah, but also spilled across regional borders for fight stops in Reno, Ely and Tonopah, Nevada.

That was Dempsey's life once he turned pro and he kept busy with his fists throughout 1915 in mining towns where the workers appreciated a good man who could punch, who displayed his toughness. Sometimes, Dempsey rode the rails of freight trains between locations, hardly the safest mode of travel and hardly the best preparation for a bout. But he had no money to spend on travel splendor, to relax in the comparatively cushy seating that showed off the scenery of the West through windows, not at track level.

Dempsey was essentially running his own show, booking himself into these low-level bouts and hopefully absorbing the type of experience that would one day pay off with gaining a broader reputation and making more money. Inwardly, he set a lofty goal—to one day become the heavyweight champion of the world. He believed he had the power to make that come true in his brine-roughened hands, but he had no connections, no links to promoters, especially those in the East, who built the names and fame of the ranked fighters, who gave them their shots at glory, who featured them on cards that highlighted the best men.

This was a test of Dempsey's faith in himself, yet that faith never wavered during these lean years. One way (something that would likely never have been recommended by a savvy handler) he tried to build his own reputation was to emulate John L. Sullivan, after all. If Sullivan was well-known for challenging anyone in a given bar or drinking establishment, Dempsey copied him by waltzing into gyms where the fighters of a neighborhood gathered to work out and proclaim he could lick any one of them. Yes, shades of Sullivan in bravado.

While this may have seemed like a keen idea to him, once Dempsey began attempting this trick, it garnered little response. It was not clear if most of the fighters thought he was just being silly, or they had management partners who refused to let them indulge in such impromptu bouts.

Dempsey shouted that he was willing to take on "anyone." But "anyone of decent standing was not willing to have anything to do with me. A few who had nothing to lose agreed to take me on, and I arranged a few quick fights and made a few bucks."[4]

When Dempsey finally acquired a manager, they took off for New York City, a new attempt to put Dempsey's name on the map. His own description of how he appeared to the masses at 42nd Street and Broadway mentioned he was carrying a cardboard suitcase and wearing shabby-appearing clothing. To him, everything about New York looked big, bright and shiny. In a sense, he was trying to live up to the song "New York, New York," with its lyrics of if someone could make it there, they could make it anywhere. That may have been the thinking, even though the song was not written until 1977.

Dempsey was out of his element in New York then. When it came to boxing regulations, New York rules were in a state of flux and many bouts were termed "newspaper decisions." Rather than results be decided by judges and a referee, a fight that went the distance was evaluated by sportswriters choosing who was the winner.

Still naive, Dempsey was gobbled up by the big city, had a parting with his manager and fled after a handful of fights in the Bronx and Harlem. Dempsey was still a popular fellow in Utah, though, and he returned there to resume his career. He had met a woman, older, harder and more opportunistic than he was, fell in love and got married to Maxine, a move that haunted him for some time.

One plus of Dempsey's roaming and fighting in the West that seemed to work to his benefit later was crossing paths with a guy who hoped to one day become a famous writer—and did so. When Dempsey emerged on the national scene, one newspaperman ahead of the curve in his knowledge of the up-and-comer was Damon Runyon.

Runyon, who became part of the core group of the most influential of New York sportswriters during the 1920s and eventually gained even greater renown by writing the legendary story *Guys and Dolls*, was basically in Dempsey's corner for decades.

Dempsey credited Runyon as bestowing the nickname "The Manassa Mauler" on him and he liked it. "It was to stick to me for the rest of my life," Dempsey said. "I was very proud of it."[5]

For a time, Dempsey moved on to San Francisco, perhaps thinking he could break into a different territory. A new manager, Fred Windsor, got him some fights and dragged him around to the sports departments of newspapers at a time when such big cities had many papers.

A writer named Scoop Gleason, another who remained supportive of Dempsey for many years, wrote a story about him in the *San Francisco Bulletin*. Dempsey, who had been stuck trying to sell himself for years, said this tour of newspapers, as limited a success as it was, taught him the value of publicity. "This was my first encounter with the grand art of ballyhoo," he said.[6]

Things didn't last in San Francisco and as the new year turned to 1917, the United States, so determined to remain removed from the worldwide battles raging across continents, could no longer do so. The U.S. entered the war on the side of England and France against Germany, Austria-Hungary and the Ottoman Empire.

Rather than enlist immediately, Dempsey took a critical-industry job, going to work in a shipyard in Tacoma, Washington, as fighting spread across Europe, the Middle East and into Africa and some areas of Asia. For Dempsey, this was a pivotal moment. For decades, some would assign him the description of a slacker because he did not cross the ocean to fight and chose an acceptable way to show his support for the American war effort.

"They needed men badly," Dempsey said of the shipyard. "The European war was expanding and preparedness was uppermost in men's minds. Patriotic in my own way, I figured that working in the shipyard would be a useful thing to do."[7]

Dempsey filled out government forms for a draft deferment, which was granted, saying he was the sole support of his family. Eventually, in 1918, he tried to enlist in the navy, but then the war ended.

Trying to kill a week's worth of time in Tacoma, where he knew no one, Dempsey said he wandered into a bar not to drink, since he did not, but to mix with other people. A fight broke out, he did honor to his fists, then left the scene. He overheard that the entire brawl had been the fault of some guy named Jack Kearns.

After working at the shipyard, Dempsey got emergency word from his mother that his brother Bernie was dying after being stabbed. Dempsey raced back to Utah but was too late to see his brother before he passed away. While he was there, though, a letter found him. It was from the same Jack Kearns he nearly met in Washington. Kearns was a boxing manager who knew of Dempsey's prowess and said he wanted to represent him.

This turned into one of the most fateful, important and meaningful relationships of Dempsey's life, leading to riches, fame and accomplishment, even if it ended in bitterness.

# 2

# Gene Tunney

Another Irishman by heritage, James Joseph Tunney, another prominent sports figure who became famous with a different first name from his given one, was born May 25, 1897, roughly two years after Jack Dempsey, who became his legendary dance partner in the boxing ring.

Tunney's parents, mother Mary Lydon and father John Tunney, were both from Ireland but met in New York City after emigrating. The fighting Tunney was one of seven children, the oldest of the brood, who as a youngster was bullied by older and stronger toughs in his West End neighborhood called Greenwich Village, or the west side of Lower Manhattan. This was not to be confused with Greenwich, Connecticut, where Tunney resided later in life.

John, Tunney's father, became absorbed by the sport of boxing in Ireland, where he rooted from afar for John L. Sullivan. For a brief period, before moving to the United States, he competed in some bare-knuckle bouts. But he was not seriously tempted to engage in the individual battles himself in terms of a moneymaking job.

Later, following Sullivan's retirement, John Tunney became a fan of another heavyweight champ, James J. Corbett. By all accounts, he was a passionate fan, but his life's work as a longshoreman was physical enough labor for him. He might gain pleasure from watching club fights outside the ring but had no desire to strap on the gloves in America or, originally, for his oldest boy, James Joseph, to do so either.

Even as an elementary school student, the boy who became better known as Gene was a reader. The application of the name *Gene* stemmed from younger sisters having difficulty pronouncing James.

Tunney would have been at a loss for activities if not for his library card, and he often brought piles of books home to peruse. Being a bookworm, however, and being slight enough of stature to be nicknamed "Skinny" did not help the younger Tunney make friends, nor did it provide much of a defense against those who harassed him on the streets.

Worried about his son's well-being, John Tunney invested in a pair

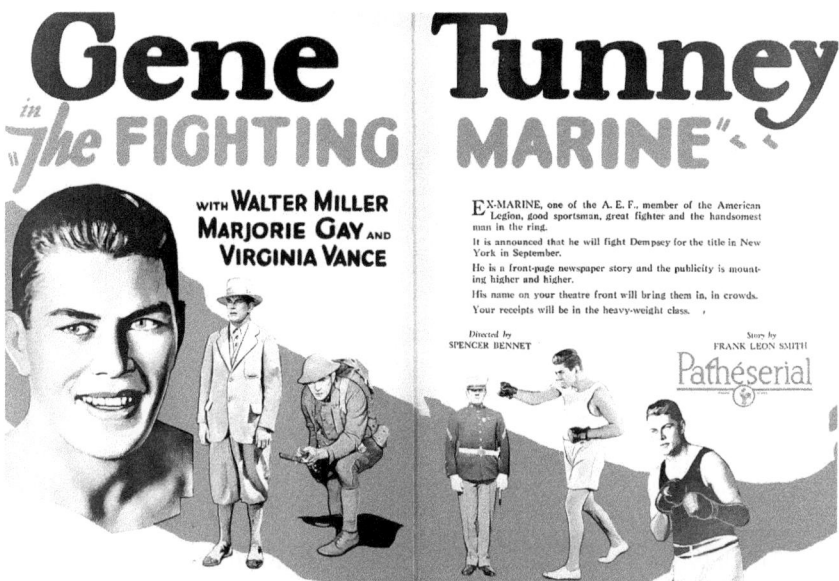

A poster produced in 1926 advertising a movie about Gene Tunney, who developed his boxing prowess in France during World War I while serving in the military.

of boxing gloves, and when Gene turned 10, his dad began teaching him the art of self-defense. One topic Gene followed through newspaper reports was the local boxing scene, so he harbored a burgeoning interest in the game. Neither of his parents wished to steer the young Tunney to a career in the ring. They wanted him to become a priest.

Not that someone who was a fourth grader was ready to commit to either the Lord or fisticuffs as a way to make a living. The primary object was that if Tunney could learn to punch and move, he might no longer come home bleeding from the nose and mouth. His younger brothers got into the spirit of this new home activity and began swinging away, too.

This introduction to boxing instruction struck a spark in Tunney. He wanted to not only protect himself and defuse the local hoodlums' nastiness, but he also wanted to see how good he might become. Tunney became a regular visitor to the Villagers Athletic Club, where he sparred with friends. He was no longer easy meat for the bad boys of the neighborhood.

From the standpoint of history, it is somewhat humorous Tunney the reader as a young boy was also inspired to build up his physique by the utterings and writings of President Theodore Roosevelt. Roosevelt, a champion of physical fitness, was a sickly lad as a youth and committed to making himself more robust. He preached the value of exercise, pushed for physical fitness programs and boxed himself, though not professionally.

At one point, after he had been bullied, TR's father brought in a former professional boxer named John Long to tutor him. Ultimately, Roosevelt, if never to approach the accolades in the ring as Tunney did, though obviously achieving in other realms, won a minor boxing tournament.

During his time in the White House between 1901 and 1909, Roosevelt kept up his boxing regimen by staging fights for workouts. During one session, Colonel Daniel T. Moore landed a shot to the eye on the president. According to research conducted by *USA Today*, "Teddy Roosevelt regularly staged boxing matches in the White House, taking on anyone he could—including professional boxers. He only stopped boxing when his eyesight was permanently damaged by a punch from his military aide."[1]

The boy whose parents sought to shape him into a priest was an industrious youngster. Tunney took on part-time jobs as a youth. He worked for a butcher shop and delivered meat. He then became an office boy for the Ocean Steamship Company. One reason his wages were important to the family was the $45 cost of his attendance at Catholic parochial school instead of public school.

Taking the president's preaching to heart, or at least doing what felt right to him, Tunney could be seen running through his neighborhood to aid his physical condition. For amusement and challenge, he pressured himself to keep up with the pace of the Fifth Avenue bus on foot, using its stops to pick up and discharge passengers to gain an advantage.

One might think Tunney was training for the Boston Marathon, not for sparring stints at the local gym. Still, as most people are aware, especially those who watched the movie *Rocky*, the legs are critical to a boxer's stamina, so his version of cross-country running did help his boxing conditioning.

When he was 16, Tunney climbed into the ring to spar for three three-minute rounds with a seasoned pro from the area named Willie Green, who was 10 years older and more experienced. Green pushed Tunney around and cut his mouth. Tunney knew he was in over his head, saying, "I learned by this experience that I was but a child in the hands of a professional."[2]

Most fighters who are growing into themselves and spend all of their time training virtually beg their management to get them a real fight. Their curiosity burns with the desire to measure themselves against another contestant for real. Tunney was not like that as a teenager. He was not in a hurry to battle for real. Eventually, in July of 1915, he committed himself to appearing on a card for a 10-round bout against a boxer named Bobby Dawson.

This was actually absurd matchmaking. Tunney was 18 and weighed 140 pounds, far from being the heavyweight he became. In the early stages of their careers, beginning boxers fight four-round pro matches, then sixes. They don't jump into the ring for a 10-rounder. Still, Tunney proved himself worthy. Exhausted, worn down, arm heavy, he managed to pile up points, and when Dawson did not come out to the middle of the ring off his stool for the eighth round, Tunney was declared the victor. His purse for the bout was $18.

By 1917, when the United States was entering its own fight, Tunney was on the sidelines. He was coping with an injured left arm that kept him out of the ring and saddled him with serious pain. It was unclear just what was wrong with this essential piece of machinery, and after the arm was placed in a cast it just kept atrophying.

Unable to fight for himself in gyms, Tunney decided he should fight for his country, inspired by a recruiting poster that read "A Marine is a two-fisted fighting man!"[3] While the sentiment touched Tunney, at the moment he was only a one-fisted fighting man and he could not pass the physical.

After some time passed, Tunney managed a single bout for the bucks, then got a job at an engineering firm. Someone recommended a doctor who specialized in electrical treatments. The doc diagnosed neuritis and he cured Tunney. Tunney enlisted on May 2, 1918, and was sent to Parris Island in South Carolina.

This development seemed likely to end, if not seriously interrupt, Tunney's boxing career. Instead, as he was sent to France for some real fighting, Tunney was about to stumble into a circumstance that accidentally made him as a boxer.

All of Tunney's years of training in New York paid off in the marines. The quirk in his life path took its first turn when he was attending a boxing show at a base YMCA in France. One combatant was a no-show, so instead of a main event, the other fighter was given a walkover, the winner by default. The captain told the crowd there was a new champion and, given what had occurred, he would be willing to fight anyone in the house, regardless of that person's size.

Tunney was exhorted into stepping up by some of his fellow marines—and was promised by a superior he could skip guard duty the next day if he participated. Tunney was skeptical, had not trained and was even wearing regular boots instead of boxing gear, but he accepted the challenge and won the match. Tunney's boss, a.k.a. the commanding officer, then insisted on making a match between Tunney and a fighter who had been a pro and the professional champion of Montana. Tunney had three days to prepare.

When he won, Tunney began evolving into a mini-celebrity on base. More tournaments were scheduled and Tunney was entered. The higher-ranking officers were proud of his deeds, but someone commented that Tunney was getting hit too often by inferior boxers. Tunney said he was better than that, but because he spent so much time doing guard duty, he could not properly train for the fights. It was a clever retort, with a sly undercurrent of basically, "What's in it for me?"

Soon enough, as the war was winding down with an Allied victory in the offing, Tunney was sent to rings for various service tournaments to defend the honor of his fellow marines. He never got near the front when explosions were going off and rifles were being fired. It was during this stretch of time in the service, boxing on behalf of his companies, battalions and divisions, that Tunney established a reputation overseas. No one was passing out medals to a soldier who did not fight the enemy, but Tunney earned the nickname in France that stuck with him during his professional boxing career. Tunney was dubbed "The Fighting Marine."

While still in France in 1919, Tunney met Billy McCabe, secretary and athletics director of the Knights of Columbus for France. McCabe told Tunney, "Live as a man, as the same clean boy you are now, and you'll see the day that you'll become the heavyweight champion of the world."[4]

Essentially, while Tunney had harbored a burning ambition to succeed in the ring, he had been on a road to nowhere before joining the marines, and being borrowed from the ranks by his commanding officers to spend his allotted time fulfilling service obligations this way best served him.

Unlike Jack Dempsey, with whom he would be paired in conversation for decades, Tunney was a different kind of fighter. Dempsey was the prototypical killer in the ring who battered opponents into unconsciousness.

Tunney applied his experience in these tournaments to make himself into more the boxer than the puncher, the clever defensive stylist who could stay out of trouble rather than battle his way out of difficulty. By the time Tunney was discharged from the marines, he had embraced his grand goal in life. He was a close friend of Eddie Eagan, who had been a boxer but even more remarkably had won gold medals for the U.S. in both the Summer Olympics as a fighter and the Winter Olympics in the four man-bobsled. Impressed by Tunney's intellect more than his jab, he urged his marine friend to join him in studies at Yale University.

Tunney's response represented the clarity of his thinking. "Eddie," Tunney said, "I won't have any time for Yale. I am going to win the heavyweight championship of the world."[5]

It was pretty obvious by then that Gene Tunney was not going to become a priest.

# 3

# Enter Doc Kearns

**O**VER THE COURSE OF THEIR LIVES together, Jack Dempsey called Jack Kearns by many names, not all of them complimentary, but early in their association he anointed him "Doc" and that was the one that stuck.

The man born John Patrick Leo McKernan in 1882 took on the name "Young Kid Kearns" when he began boxing. Dempsey chose to call him "The Doc" once their association started, and Doc it was over time to the public and the rest of the fight world.

Kearns was born in Waterloo, Michigan, to a farm couple, German on his mother's side and Irish on his father's side. The farm life would be too sedate for Kearns, who emerged from anonymity to build and promote Dempsey into the most famous fighter in the world.

He understood promotion, or ballyhoo, as the publicity game was often referred to during this era, and while he helped Dempsey earn riches, and very much enriched himself on the road to glory, too, Kearns engaged in numerous adventures as he grew up and older.

Although Kearns ended up being inducted into the International Boxing Hall of Fame in 1990, years after his 1963 death, there was little doubt he was somewhat of a scoundrel, too. In 1989, he was described as one of sport's greatest con men. As much as Kearns did for Dempsey after that introductory letter he wrote, care of the fighter's parents in Utah, Dempsey grew to despise him and the feeling became mutual.

What began as a beneficial business partnership disintegrated into a bitter divorce, one that, due to the love-hate nature of things, seemed to gain the most for lawyers, not participants.

In the beginning, however, it was all so grand. Dempsey had ridden those rails, hitchhiked his way great distances, played the rental fighter on the bottom of boxing cards, and hardly anyone knew his name. He couldn't get a break and he couldn't make a breakthrough.

Kearns had seen Dempsey along the way, in that Washington bar, in small bouts, and he identified what no one else saw—potential. By then, Kearns had seen a lot on his own, in and out of the boxing game.

## 3. Enter Doc Kearns

After his birth in Michigan, Kearns's family moved to North Dakota, then on to Washington state. He was just 14 years old when he took a run at the Alaska Gold Rush, heading to the Yukon by way of jumping on a freighter pointed north. When Kearns, like so many others who did not successfully pan for gold, struck out, he returned home.

For a while he worked as a ranch hand. Or perhaps that was a loose description because some say Kearns was rustling cattle.

He also took on less-reputable forms of making a living. Kearns became a dog-napper and helped a group smuggle Chinese residents across the Canadian border into the United States. No one ever accused Kearns of having too much principle or conscience to land on the side of the law when there was a choice to be made.

Kearns said his first pro fight took place in Billings, Montana, and asserted he competed in more than 60 bouts as a welterweight. The official record is a bit shy on detail. Once, when he was still in his late teens, Kearns said a promoter asked him if he could actually fight and Kearns responded with this comment: "Stick out your chin and find out."[1] That may have boldly exaggerated Kearns's skills in the ring, but it buttressed any argument that he was quick to open his mouth with timely retorts, true or not.

Kearns started his own boxing club and saloon in Spokane, Washington, but drifted away from that. Then he gravitated to San Francisco, where he became a promoter.

Kearns began managing fighters in 1909 and wasn't really making a mark yet. In 1916, one of Kearns's fighters, Joe Bonds, took on Dempsey and lost a decision. Much later, when he and Dempsey were on the outs, Kearns said his first impression of Dempsey was of him being as "thin, ragged and run-down. His face was gaunt and hollow-cheeked and you could have played his ribs like a xylophone. I got him going. But before I came along, he was a bum."[2]

Dempsey's pride would not allow him to accept that analysis quietly. He responded by saying, "Sure, I rode the rods," Dempsey said. "Sure, I was a hobo. But Kearns has the facts dead wrong. I was a hobo all right. But I was never a bum."[3]

Of course, that was long after the falling-out and with Kearns harassing Dempsey with specious lawsuits. In the beginning, the men were good for each other. Kearns sent Dempsey a train ticket in Utah and included meal money. Dempsey said he was definitely hungry and could use the bucks for food. When he climbed off the train at the station in San Francisco, Kearns did see a skinny guy.

Rather than rush Dempsey into immediate training, Kearns moved him into his own mother's house in Oakland. She mothered Dempsey, made sure he was well-fed, made sure he got enough sleep, advised her son to take good care of him. There was a getting-to-know-you period between Dempsey and Kearns. Back then, they trusted one another, Dempsey said. They needed one another. Kearns needed a hot property to manage and Dempsey needed a savvy boxing expert to guide him into the big time.

"Jack Kearns was not the type of guy to sit still and watch the world go by," Dempsey said. "He tackled just about anything, whether it was acceptable or not. He was a crafty alligator, a real slicker, as expert at making a fortune as losing one. He was a man who connived for success and any way was good enough as long as it worked."[4]

Young Dempsey was naive. He had no familiarity with quid pro quo arrangements or how to make his own entrée into the big time without someone's guidance, either through dubious or honest means. Kearns knew how to work the edges.

So, Dempsey's career was put into the hands of Doc Kearns and it reached the kind of heights both men dreamed of but might never have truly imagined would come to pass. Dempsey was fattened up and firmed up and began fighting West Coast bouts for Kearns—and winning them.

Until then, Dempsey's career had included some losses and draws against some fairly nondescript competition. It was time to more adroitly exploit his power, to arrange better matches and to uplift his profile. It was up to Dempsey to whack out the men put in front of him and it was up to Kearns to tell the world how good Dempsey was—and was going to become.

Once the men hooked up to work together, things began clicking. Dempsey's competition was upgraded. He defeated veterans Gunboat Smith, Bill Brennan, Billy Miske and Battling Levinsky, thinning the herd of contenders who stood in line for a chance to take on incumbent heavyweight champion Jess Willard.

"I worked damn hard in the ring and Doc worked his tail off outside it," Dempsey said. "Our goal was to force people to recognize me as the leading contender. When I read about myself in the papers, I had the eerie feeling I was reading about someone else, someone who was fighting, staging exhibitions and selling Liberty bonds."[5]

Dempsey's fortunes improved, alongside those of the United States, as World War I concluded. The Americans who had been deployed around the world were on their way home, to make new lives for themselves, to reestablish their identities.

Dempsey was in the midst of fighting in earnest, but America no longer was. When President Woodrow Wilson announced the armistice ending the war, he in part wrote, "Everything for which America fought has been accomplished."[6]

The announcement was actually made in the middle of the night. Wilson was optimistic a Rubicon had been crossed, that with the United States essentially in charge of the modern world, the country and world were embracing long-term peace. Oh, how naive he was. For the time being, however, Americans could focus on issues, political or not, sporting or not, and daily life simplified by not worrying if the boy next door was going to get blown to bits.

# 4

# A Changing Country

After World War I ended, fulfilling a common cause with the United States being on the winning side, it seemed all Americans had different dreams to pursue starting in 1919. Could everyone get what they wanted?

Jack Dempsey dreamed of becoming the heavyweight boxing champion of the world. Gene Tunney dreamed of becoming the heavyweight boxing champion of the world.

President Woodrow Wilson wanted ratification of the Treaty of Versailles to ensure the United States' preeminent position in world affairs and peace on earth for mankind. Nice try, but Wilson's wishes were deflected by his own U.S. Senate and he died in 1924 after becoming a sickly man and not knowing of the horrors to be unleashed on the world stage in coming years with more destructive weapons than had been employed in World War I.

For many optimistic young American families with more modest ambitions, it would be possible to gain ownership of one of Henry Ford's fancy automobiles as they rolled off the assembly line by the millions. As long as they could come up with the scratch, those Americans could obtain greater freedom of the roads, such as they were long before an interstate system. By 1920, Hank's family-owned company—still—was producing a million cars per year and revolutionizing travel.

It took only about 145 years for the United States' American Revolution to grant women the right to vote, affirming and preserving the life work of Susan B. Anthony, Elizabeth Cady Stanton, Lucy Stone and Frances Ellen Watkins Harper.

Decades of lobbying and lawsuits, pursuing legislation and constitutional alteration led to the ratification of the 19th Amendment to the Constitution in 1920 granting women the right to vote. For a nation that was supposed to be the most liberal, Democratic and forward-thinking beginning in 1776, this was one example of slow-motion progress.

It took blood, sweat, tears and zeal to reach this landmark moment in history, though in the century since, probably because Americans do not wish to look backward to realize how disenfranchisement appeared, it has seemingly been forgotten as a major milestone. Most women in the 2020s, glancing at comparative pay scales for men and women in the workplace, would probably say the battle for women's rights continues.

As early as 1872, Anthony showed up to vote in her hometown of Rochester, New York, and then was arrested for doing so. She went to trial and was convicted but refused to pay the fine levied. Anthony fought for this major change in the American way of life until she died in 1906, 14 years too soon to see the women's right to vote implemented.

Women of the late 1800s and early 1900s who banded together to create a movement in the United States to argue and lobby for passage for that major change in the electorate also tended to back the Women's Christian Temperance Union.

The Temperance Union, founded in 1874, tied the notion of religion together with refraining from drink. Its announced purpose was to create "a sober and pure world," equating drinking alcohol with sin. The women involved in the Temperance Union played a helpful role in gaining women's suffrage but also in forcing adoption of Prohibition.

Looking back from the vantage point of 100 years, Americans of the 2020s must think the people inhabiting the country then were nuts to even propose the outright banning of liquor.

Glancing about the neighborhood and reviewing menus at family restaurants that sell drinks, where the tables encircle bars, where a stop to purchase a snack is in the same quickie convenience store where six-packs of beer are sold, at a time when it seems every other television commercial during a sporting event advertises a different brand of beer, living in a world where alcohol was forbidden seems unimaginable.

The most remarkable thing about the failed 18th Amendment to the Constitution was that it lasted as law as long as it did, from 1920 to 1933, before being repealed. Mishandled, misapplied, poorly overseen and scoffed at by multitudes from the start, Prohibition of booze may have been the most misguided constitutional amendment ever passed.

While it was not necessarily the habit of Jack Dempsey or Gene Tunney to down a frosty cold one after a workout (though that did seem to be Babe Ruth's mode of behavior) or during a night out on the town, the average 1920 American did not feel much like a lawbreaker by pouring a glass of wine with dinner.

As an indication of what a failure Prohibition and the Volstead Act really were, Will Rogers, America's foremost humor commentator-social critic, observed, "Prohibition is better than no liquor at all."[1] There were so many holes in the laws, in the enforcement, they made Swiss cheese look like a clean sheet.

What was really behind the passage of forcing the entire country to go dry was a morality play tinged by racism and anti-pluralism. "Beyond the debate on the rights of reformers to regulate social behavior by force, restricting individual freedom in the name of better health, morality and godliness, Prohibition was the rearguard action of a still dominant, overwhelmingly rural, white Anglo-Saxon Protestant establishment," one historian observed. These people feared being overwhelmed by the rising immigrant population who were "beer-swilling and wine-drinking."[2]

There were exceptions to the no-alcohol rules, as in the use of industrial alcohol and alcohol prescribed for medicinal purposes. The latter proved to be a hoot for drinkers who had friendly doctors to write favorable prescriptions. There were well-off Americans who spent lavishly to stockpile their favorite beverages, some of them even renting warehouse space for their stashes of booze. The night of January 16, 1920, the day before the Volstead Act took effect, was essentially an American drink-a-thon, a nationwide party of imbibing, a second New Year's Eve. There were many who doubted whether the law would stand for very long, many hoping it would soon go away.

Probably no one, the bamboozled Congress or the law enforcement community, likely envisioned what a serious mess had been birthed, with the rise of gangsters and how criminalized the drinking world would become. Speakeasies may have sounded innocent, but the men behind the booze supply were no innocents. They controlled the supplies and distribution by force. This peculiar decade of supposed restraint instead made people like Al Capone into some of the most famous and infamous crime bosses in American history.

The transition from wet to dry took place as the presidency transitioned from the austere Wilson to Republican Warren Harding. Harding was a newspaper publisher from Ohio who became his party's nominee at a divided convention.

Known as a poker-playing man of great bonhomie, Harding appointed some greatly admired men to his cabinet when he took office in 1921 and some greatly reviled men who were revealed as scam artists after Harding died in office in 1923. Everyone liked Harding and he was a good-natured man, apparently just not a strong leader.

Harding was popular when he lived in the White House and his image was dramatically tarnished after his death when scandals perpetuated during his reign were unveiled, such as the infamous Teapot Dome event.

It was said—and described in books about him—that Harding was guilty of participating in numerous extramarital affairs and having at least one child out of wedlock. Love letters he wrote outside of marriage were released in 2014. The friends he placed in high offices in the U.S. government took advantage of their freedom and power in the cabinet and might well have embarrassed him right out of office if he had lived long enough to run for reelection.

Harding himself seemed to realize his own limitations for the highest office in the land, once quoted from a golf-course discussion as saying, "I don't think I'm big enough for the Presidency. I can't make a damn thing out of this tax problem. I listen to one side and they seem right and then I listen to the other side, and then God, they seem just as right, here I am where I started. I know somewhere there is a book that will give me the truth, but hell, I couldn't read the book!"[3]

There was no book out there with instructions on how to handle Prohibition because no other government anywhere had ever tried such a social engineering program before—except, perhaps for totalitarian states, and Harding was no dictator. He was more of a fun guy. He loved to drink whiskey and there may have been a Volstead Act in effect outside his office, but his White House office was well-stocked. And no one ever died of thirst at the poker games Harding hosted while president.

Harding was only 57 years old when he passed away on a road trip to the North and West in early August of 1923. Harding, accompanied by his wife, First Lady Florence Harding, embarked on a summerlong, meet-the-people trip across the United States. In June of that year, he became the first president to visit Alaska. Purchased from Russia for $7.2 million in 1867 in a deal wangled by Secretary of State William Seward, Alaska was still a territory, not accepted as a state until 1959.

It was Mrs. Harding's idea to visit Alaska, and after taking a train across the country to San Francisco, the Hardings sailed north. They stopped in the Native village of Metlakatla and were entertained by local musicians. They sailed on to Ketchikan and were given fancy gifts.

In Juneau, Governor Scott Bone, who had been appointed to his job by Harding, hosted the first couple at a dinner for 500 people and a night of dancing. Then it was on to Seward, named after the Great Land's purchaser, by July 13. While it was somewhat common knowledge in Washington, D.C., that Florence Harding was the power behind the throne, it became evident to new audiences on this trip that it was true. The Hardings were also seen arguing off and on throughout the journey.

Over one stretch of railroad track, between Wasilla and Willow, about 25 miles, Harding actually drove the Alaska Railroad engine. The train stopped in Nenana, which is about 53 miles south of Fairbanks on the current-day Parks Highway, and a formal ceremony took place. This was the designated highlight of Harding's visit to Alaska. He drove the golden spike that connected the northern and southern ends of the railroad, officially completing the railroad on July 15, 1923.

The party continued to Fairbanks and then drove by automobile on the rudimentary (but since very much spruced-up) Richardson Highway to Seward and began the voyage south, back to the United States. Before the trip even began, Harding had complained about not feeling well. During the journey, Mrs. Harding often commented that her husband was not a well man. On board this ship, sailing through Cordova and Sitka, Harding began complaining about a stomachache and eating bad shellfish was blamed. However, others in the group had eaten from the same batch of shellfish with no issues.

Sailing onward, there was a stop in Seattle, and in Vancouver, British Columbia, Harding gave an address to 40,000 people despite feeling ill. Back in San Francisco, the president feeling worse all the time, the Hardings checked into their hotel. No one expected the serious nature of the drama that quickly ensued.

The following was the lead to a Ketchikan, Alaska, newspaper story reviewing the history of what happened next. "On Wednesday, August 1, 1924, First Lady Florence Harding locked herself and a very ill President into the bedroom of the posh presidential suite of San Francisco's historic Palace Hotel and refused to admit anyone into the room—including the president's five attending physicians. It wasn't until the next day, August 2, that she opened the door and left the room to announce that the president, her husband of more than 30 years, Warren Gamaliel Harding, was dead. The headstrong first lady refused to allow an autopsy, and the body was prepared for the lengthy trans-continental funeral-train trip back to Washington D.C."[4]

For many years, Alaskans in a way blamed themselves for Harding's death, or claimed credit, depending on how one read comments made such as, "You know, Harding died in Alaska." He did not. But he may have been poisoned in Alaska and there was even suspicion his wife, Florence, perhaps infuriated by his gallivanting, played a role in his demise.

Harding was transported from California to Washington, D.C., by a funeral train with many thousands of Americans paying tribute as the train passed through their communities on his sad eastern trek. Before he arrived back in Washington, Harding had been succeeded in office by his vice president, Calvin Coolidge.

It was Coolidge who inherited the aggravations of Prohibition and also presided over the flare-up of the scandals the Harding administration left behind as the new chief executive changed out most members of the cabinet.

Coolidge, a sterner man, and much less of a party dude than Harding, once referred to Prohibition as being one of the greatest social experiments undertaken by a government. Coolidge was not a teetotaler but was not regarded as a serious drinker. Still, one author who chose to analyze the presidents by their favorite beverages did come up with the recipe for Coolidge's drink of choice.

"'Silent Cal' drank very little, but he was very fond of Tokay wine," author Mark Will-Weber claimed in his book *Mint Juleps with Teddy Roosevelt: The Complete History of Presidential Drinking*. "The Coolidge Cooler was concocted by Vermont Spirits on Cal's birthday: one-and-a-half ounces of Vermont White vodka; a half-ounce of American whiskey; two ounces of orange juice; club soda."[5]

Did President Coolidge forgo the "Coolidge Cooler" completely during Prohibition? Probably not. He did ban wine from state dinners at the White House to save money, though.

As further illustration that strange things happened during Prohibition in the world of alcohol, there is a drink even today that is called the "Gene Tunney." One source suggests a bartender invented the drink during Prohibition in homage to the fighter's fame and popularity and said the contents include bourbon, sweet vermouth, orange bitters and Angostura bitter.

That is one recipe. On its website, Absolut gives the following information about a "Gene Tunney" drink. That version contains "one-and-a-half parts gin; half-part dry vermouth; one dash lemon juice; one dash orange juice; one whole maraschino berry."

A website called MinuteBartender.com offers its own recipe—and viewpoint on how the drink came into existence. "The Gene Tunney cocktail, named after the legendary American boxer, is a classic drink that has stood the test of time. This delightful concoction has a fascinating history and origins that make it a favorite among cocktail enthusiasts."

In addition, "The Gene Tunney cocktail is believed to have been created during the Prohibition era in the United States, a time when the production, sale, and consumption of alcoholic beverages were banned. This period led to the rise of speakeasies, secret bars where people could enjoy a drink in secrecy. It was in one of these hidden establishments that the Gene Tunney cocktail is said to have been born."[6]

Later in its dissertation, the site gives Tunney credit for his taste.

"Gene Tunney, a renowned heavyweight champion of the 1920s,

was not only famous for his boxing skills but also for his refined taste in cocktails," the MinuteBartender.com said. "Legend has it that he frequented a speakeasy where a talented bartender crafted this drink specifically for him."[7]

Then comes discussion about the variances in the drink's contents.

"The exact recipe for the Gene Tunney cocktail may vary," according to the site, "as is the case with many classic drinks. However, it typically combines a harmonious blend of spirits and mixers to create a balanced and refreshing taste. The precise combination of ingredients remains a well-kept secret, adding an air of mystery to this beloved cocktail.

"The Gene Tunney cocktail has a reputation for being smooth and sophisticated, much like the boxer himself. It is often described as having a subtle sweetness with a hint of bitterness, making it a perfect choice for those who appreciate a well-rounded flavor profile."

Almost strangely, as time has passed and Tunney in some ways has faded from public consciousness outside of the boxing world, the site said the drink is evermore popular and is a worthy tribute to the fighter.

"Over the years, the Gene Tunney cocktail has gained popularity and has become a staple in many cocktail bars around the world," MinuteBartender.com said. "Its timeless appeal and association with a legendary figure have contributed to its enduring status. Whether you're a boxing enthusiast or simply a fan of classic cocktails, the Gene Tunney is sure to impress with its rich history and delightful taste."[8]

# 5

# TUNNEY PROGRESSES SLOWLY BUT SURELY

JACK DEMPSEY ACQUIRED DOC KEARNS as a key figure to guide his career, as iffy and testy as their relationship turned out, but after coming out of the marines, Gene Tunney was searching for any type of reputable management to guide him.

As he began learning the ropes before entering the marines, and after leaving the corps, Tunney seemed to switch managers as often as some playboys change girlfriends. Between 1915 and 1918, as a beginner, his manager was Billy Jacobs. In 1919 and 1920, Tunney listened to the advice of Billy Roche and Sammy Kelly.

Offering somewhat more assistance after that was Frank Bagley between 1920 and 1922. Ironically and coincidentally given Kearns's nickname, Bagley also had the nickname of Doc. Between 1923 and 1928, covering his prime as a heavyweight, Tunney's manager was Billy Gibson.

Unlike Dempsey, who had always sought good representation, sometimes it seemed as time passed Tunney was pretty much his own manager, making key decisions. But that was mostly later in his career.

Honed by his military service, Tunney became widely known as "The Fighting Marine" after he returned to the general U.S. population. It was an appendage that did not do him any harm, especially among supporters prone to like him anyway.

When Tunney finally began appearing on fight cards as he tried to begin his climb through the championship ranks following his military discharge, he and Roche had difficulty getting bouts. When Tunney at last started appearing on undercards, he might take home $150 or $200 per fight. It beat his original $18 payday, anyway.

Tunney had a long way to go, both in terms of gaining experience and building his mental toughness in the ring. Yet he began making an impression. Although Tunney was always known as more of a boxer and

Before he captured the heavyweight championship, Gene Tunney bested Georges Carpentier of France for the light-heavyweight title on July 24, 1924, at the Polo Grounds in New York.

a defensive expert, he did pack enough of a punch against other young unknowns. That was the way to get noticed amid an anonymous group of young pugilists.

For a time in late 1919 and 1920 after returning to the United States from France, Tunney found work in smallish arenas sprinkled around northern New Jersey. He appeared on shows in Bayonne, Newark and Jersey City, with a few stops across the state line in the latter stages in New York and Staten Island.

Before those fights occurred, however, strange as it may sound given boxing's place of prominence in New York City and Madison Square Garden in the ensuing years, the sport was illegal in New York through 1919, which was why Tunney was taking ferry rides to New Jersey so often.

Flamboyant Jimmy Walker, soon enough to become mayor of New York City in 1926, was the force behind the legalization of professional boxing in New York while serving in the New York State Senate. He sponsored what was called the "Walker Law." Walker is a member of the International Boxing Hall of Fame in Canastota, New York, and it is not because he ever went 15 rounds with Tunney.

## 5. Tunney Progresses Slowly but Surely

Part of Walker's district was the Greenwich Village neighborhood Tunney called home. Whether it was coincidental or intentional for Tunney's benefit, the change in the law definitely helped him by boosting his hometown-hero image.

During the post–World War I era, Tunney buffered his reputation by knocking out nine straight opponents. On December 29, 1919 (Happy New Year!), Tunney blasted novice Bob Pearce unconscious with a single punch to the jaw. The men faced off at light-heavyweight, with its 175-pound ceiling. That lifted Tunney's overall record at the time to 20–0–2.

Staying busy and keeping one's name in front of the public and the sporting press and piling up knockouts were all key ways to polish his reputation and set himself apart from the pack of other aspirants who wished to become champions.

One of the more rugged guys that Tunney faced during this build-up stretch of time was Al Roberts of Staten Island. Tunney immediately took control, starting with a first-round knockdown, and he ultimately knocked Roberts down six times, including three times in the seventh round. But Roberts brought more savvy to the ring than many of Tunney's other opponents. Roberts concluded his career with a 36–10–1 mark and with 23 knockouts himself.

It sounded one-sided but was not completely so. Roberts was not nearly as slick as Tunney, but he had some thunder in his fists and he unleashed a solid right to Tunney's chin in the second round that staggered him. A Tunney biographer wrote, "Tunney was hurt. His eyes glazed, his knees buckled, and he reeled back on rubbery legs. One more solid clout and the Greenwich Villager would certainly have hit the canvas."[1]

One thing that separates champions from good fighters is their resilience. No matter how terrific a fighter is, sooner or later he is going to get tagged by an opponent. Sometimes the punch will be the perfect shot and nothing can be done except to try to bounce back from it. Sometimes it can be shrugged off. And sometimes the finest of fighters will be hurt and yet, through instinct and inner fortitude, may rebound, outlast the moment of weakness and respond through his own will.

By that point in his career, Tunney had taught himself will in the ring. Roberts possessed the power to put Tunney down, if not out, but when he conked him with that critical blow in their February 2, 1920, bout, Tunney wavered but did not collapse.

Instead, he called upon a lesson from a recent bout. Tunney was up against Whitey Allen in a New Year's Day match in 1920 in Bayonne. Since Allen was knocked out with a left hook, leaving his lifetime record at 6–11, this may not have seemed an important moment in Tunney's career. But he later said it was.

He had entered the ring that night with uncertainty. While those outside of the fight game sometimes half believe the best of the best are supermen of sorts and carry an aura of invincibility with them into matches, that is not always true regardless of what they have accomplished.

When the bout against Allen began, the opponent rushed at Tunney with the obvious intent of knocking him aside quickly. Tunney's slipperiness made Allen miss a big right. After a clinch, Allen repeated his attempted assault. Tunney made him miss again. A round later, Tunney tattooed Allen with punch after punch and ended the fight in the second round.

From afar, Tunney fans might have been saying, "There was never anything to worry about." Yet Tunney had worried. He decided from then on that he would not harbor such fears again. "I decided for the future that no matter how uncertain the outcome of a match might be, I would shut the doors of my mind to the possibility of defeat. This process of mental training I started the moment Whitey Allen was knocked out."[2]

Talk about your power of positive thinking.

At this point in their fight lives, while Dempsey had likely never heard the name *Gene Tunney*, Tunney had started to become obsessed with Jack Dempsey. Tunney, who frequently fought at a weight of around 165 pounds overseas and worked his way into becoming a regular light-heavyweight in the 175-pound division, seemed from an early date to fixate on winning not that world championship but the big one, the heavyweight title.

Not that he planned to skip over the light-heavyweight class altogether. He was happy to pick off that championship belt as he filled out, built muscle and eyeballed the heavyweight crown. It was more or less an "I'll take it" kind of thing, almost with a shrug. It has ever been thus in the boxing world. The heavyweight title is magnified in riches and fame by a great deal over ownership of the light-heavyweight title.

A key reason Tunney became so focused on Dempsey was that after his very long and winding road and gradual march through the other contenders, Dempsey had reached the top. On July 4, 1919, he crushed Jess Willard to take the big man's heavyweight crown. The hard labor of Dempsey was vindicated. The creative planning of Doc Kearns brought opportunity to Dempsey's doorstep. Tunney watched from afar and plotted his own rise. One day, he told others and constantly thought, "That is going to be me."

There was no guarantee whatsoever by the time Tunney matured into a heavyweight contender and established his status that Jack Dempsey would still be boxing, that Jack Dempsey would still own the heavyweight title. But that was how Tunney thought and believed and what motivated him.

The fighter with a literary bent, who read voraciously, also studied boxing scientifically. To raise his stature and improve his chances as he fought the comparative nobodies and somebodies, Tunney not only studied the talents and skills of those he faced in the ring but he also observed the habits of the heavyweight king Jack Dempsey to learn as much as he could about Dempsey's own skills and tendencies.

It was almost crazy to think that way because the future was unwritten and, as always in the boxing world, was uncertain. Yet Tunney was able to stay grounded and take care of his own business and make the progress he needed for positioning his own career just the right way.

# 6

# Boxing's Treatment of Blacks at Its Worst

THE DISGRACEFUL RACIAL HATRED that followed Jack Johnson before, during and after his reign as boxing's heavyweight champion hounded him into prison and forever made him an abject example of American society at its worst and also tainted the sport and its ensuing champs.

Johnson was the first Black heavyweight champion, and his achievement threatened and enraged racist followers of the sport to an alarming and extreme degree. They could not abide the notion of a Black man being anointed the world's toughest man, and even worse, Johnson's flamboyant personality, flaunting his superiority and seemingly rubbing it in their faces by marrying a white woman, poisoned the sport for years.

The man who generated the odious desire of fight partisans to find a "Great White Hope" to defeat him was born John Arthur Johnson in Galveston, Texas, on March 31, 1878, and he became heavyweight champion by besting Tommy Burns in Australia in 1908. Johnson retained the crown into 1915.

While champion, James J. Jeffries refused to battle Johnson and retired instead. Johnson took on and bested former champion Bob Fitzsimmons, but new titleholder Burns ducked Johnson. Burns was a Canadian and Johnson dogged him at various stops in his career, taunting him into a meeting. Eventually, Burns agreed to fight Johnson as long as the champ was guaranteed $30,000. The bout took place in Sydney, Australia, and was stopped by police authorities with Johnson beating up Burns, showing racial attitudes seemed about the same as they were in the United States.

Often enough, when Johnson fought, race riots followed. The white boxing community devolved into a frenzy as Johnson bested every contender seeking the title. Jeffries emerged from retirement, he said at the time, to show that a white man could beat a Negro. They met on July 4, 1910, in Reno, Nevada, and Johnson was the master during the bout, knocking Jeffries down for the first two times in his career.

When it was over, Jeffries was contrite, admitting Johnson was the better fighter. "I could never have whipped Johnson at my best," he said. "I couldn't have hit him. No, I couldn't have reached him in 1,000 years."[1]

Johnson was subsequently pursued for violation of the Mann Act, transporting women across state lines for sexual purposes, but after he was convicted in 1912, Johnson fled the country. He boxed overseas for seven years before surrendering to U.S. authorities and serving time in jail.

Jack Johnson was harassed and tormented because as a Black man he won the heavyweight championship of the world.

In 1919, those pushing the search for a Great White Hope to take on and defeat Johnson seemingly found their opponent. On April 5, 1919, on a steamy day in Havana, Cuba, Jess Willard, who at six-foot-six and 245 pounds dwarfed Johnson, stopped Johnson in 26 rounds. There are some who suggest Johnson ultimately just yielded to Willard, not rising from the canvas when he could have, but that was not proved.

By authoring history, showing off his skills and beating all of the best of his time, Johnson was verbally tortured and harassed for years. And one of the biggest impacts, beyond his becoming a symbol of American racism, was that in the following years, into and beyond the 1920s, the finest African American contenders for the heavyweight title could not obtain an opportunity to compete for the big prize.

Promoters, even the biggest of them, such as Tex Rickard, refused to give men like Harry Wills a shot at the crown. They did not wish to deal with the backlash that might attend the arrival of another Black champion. These top fighters were shut out because of racism, shunted to the side instead of having matches made that might have put them first in line to fight the titleholder.

This was even at a time when there did not seem to be many available worthy contenders. Wills, born in New Orleans in 1889 and a participant in 111 fights between 1911 and 1932, desperately wanted a chance. He pined for a shot at Jack Dempsey, before and after Dempsey won the crown. The best he could muster from the sport was a half-hearted recognition as the "World Colored Heavyweight Champion," which was no true title at all. That was like attending a segregated school and calling it good.

It seems that sanctioning officials and promoters had learned from the Jack Johnson experience. Just maybe Black fighters were too good to take the risk with since they might actually win the heavyweight crown.

As a demonstration of how restrictive and absurd the situation became, Wills fought the great Sam Langford, another Black boxer, 22 times, because they could not get other equivalently talented fighters to sign on for matchups. Langford was born in Nova Scotia but moved to Boston, Massachusetts, and used that as his base. Langford was a smaller man at 5-foot-6½, but he would fight at any weight, including heavyweight. In another era, he likely would have focused on lightweight or perhaps welterweight divisions, but Langford never was allowed a shot at a real belt.

That was despite, in future years, *The Ring* magazine ranked him as the second-hardest puncher across all weight classes of all time. Langford fought a remarkable 314 fights, 210 of them victories, 43 of them losses, 53 of them draws and eight considered no contests.

Before he took over Dempsey's management, Doc Kearns actually had arrangements with Wills and Langford and promoted one of their fights against each other, though given the frequency of their combat, who hadn't?

Johnson was not shy or retiring and did not kowtow to white men. He possessed an incandescent smile, shaved his head and was boastful. He was inclined to have a good time, and he did. Having made the grievous error of pounding out white men, he compounded it by acting ostentatiously. A Johnson–Dempsey bout would have been intriguing, but the Black heavyweight of the hour was Wills since Johnson was otherwise indisposed trying to stay out of prison.

It was inescapable that as he polished off every other possible contender on his rise to the title, Dempsey would be asked about a match

## 6. Boxing's Treatment of Blacks at Its Worst

with Wills. He did not duck the question, but his answer, at various times, seemed to contain at least some initial equivocation.

"It's the public that runs boxing," Dempsey said. "If the people want me to fight Willis, I'll make the match."[2] It was a diplomatic response. Dempsey did not make matches, of course. He was a bit down on the hierarchy, below the promoter who sold the tickets, and generally yielded to Kearns's thinking. At that point in his career, before he had the title, he was definitely not making those types of decisions guiding his next steps. From a fighting standpoint, he probably wouldn't have minded facing Wills because Dempsey figured he could beat anyone out there standing in his way. So, why not? The more directly involved businessmen, though, made the matches.

In the 1920s, when Dempsey was champ and spent a few years more or less goofing off away from the ring, Wills gained a newspaper following clamoring for him to get his opportunity. A biography of Tex Rickard, the preeminent promoter of the time, dealt with the controversy Dempsey became embroiled in by avoiding making the match.

The reasoning was not that Rickard was racist, but he didn't want the aggravation that would accompany a Wills fight because of the Black-versus-white nature. "Rickard still remembered the strain on his nerves from the controversy over Jack Johnson's reign as heavyweight champion," this book said. "The Wills controversy was one piece of ballyhoo that Rickard would have preferred to do without."[3]

He defended himself as previously showing he had supported lightweight champion Joe Gans and Johnson. Also, citing the Johnson experience, he did not believe there was money to be made by pitting Wills against Dempsey during Dempsey's climb up the ladder. If a Black man won the crown again, Rickard said, "then the championship ain't worth a nickel. That's what Johnson taught us."[4]

Later, after Dempsey and Gene Tunney met twice, there was speculation Wills would get a shot at becoming either the No. 1 contender or get a championship match. The New York State Boxing Commission pressured Rickard into giving Wills a chance, but Rickard did not make such plans. Before that, when Dempsey was champ and mostly idle, he said he would not face Wills. It might have been possible for a match to be made in some city out of the Northeast, but Rickard was wary of the finances anywhere.

Never mind Wills and Langford. When Johnson got out of prison after doing time at Leavenworth, he wanted to return to the ring and he wanted a piece of Jack Dempsey. That was never going to happen because he was viewed as too controversial a figure and boxing's new licensing commissions could deny him permission to fight.

Johnson still had to make a living and he sought out more permissive locales that would allow him to box, but he was not then a real headliner in terms of boxing's big picture. In the 1920s, and into 1931, Johnson fought in Montreal, Mexico, Indianapolis, Kansas City, Oklahoma, and Wichita. By then, he was 51 years old.

During the Chicago World's Fair, Johnson boxed exhibitions for $1 apiece—with children. Later, he granted interviews where he analyzed the crop of current heavyweight contenders for the price of someone paying for his dinner.

White society had gone all out to marginalize Jack Johnson and his accomplishments, and it succeeded, except in the eyes of history. Historians routinely recognize the raw deal he received.

Those who made movies telling his story, *The Great White Hope*, with the estimable James Earl Jones playing Johnson in 1970, and then the Ken Burns documentary *Unforgivable Blackness: The Rise and Fall of Jack Johnson* in 2005, educated later generations, explaining the beatings handed to Johnson that did not occur in the ring.

Whatever consolation it may be to a long-dead Johnson, who died in 1946 at 68, he is well-remembered.

When he was being persecuted, Johnson understood precisely why. "I'm Black," he said. "They never let me forget it. I'm Black, alright. I'll never let them forget it."[5]

# 7

## The Champ

While Jack Dempsey always possessed fists of thunder with a bazooka's knockout capacity, when he was hustling bouts on his own early in his career, he sometimes showed up for fights weighing in the 160-plus-pound range.

Even when Doc Kearns began promoting Dempsey, they would periodically show up at a venue after making a commitment on a fight card and have the promoter seek to rebuff him, claiming he was too small and he would get clobbered by a real heavyweight.

Those promoters did not believe Dempsey would pass the eye test for the crowd. They felt fans would look at him and see a blown-up middleweight, not a for-real heavyweight, and either boo from the get-go or convince themselves they were being suckered into paying for a mismatch.

The reality was that Jack Dempsey could always hold his own. In those days there were eight boxing weight classes. More than a hundred years later, the number of divisions has expanded. There was no cruiserweight class back then. When the cruiserweight class was created, the limit was 190 pounds. Currently, it is 200 pounds.

The existence of the cruiserweight division and the expansion of its size reflects the growth of human beings over this past century. During Dempsey's day, light-heavyweights were maxed out at 175 pounds and it was not uncommon for heavyweights to enter the ring weighing under 200 pounds.

In recent years, one heavyweight champ, Riddick Bowe, six-foot-five, hit 271 pounds. Lennox Lewis was also six-five and weighed as much as 249 pounds. Tyson Fury, the World Boxing Council heavyweight titleholder in 2024, stands six-nine and has weighed in at 262 pounds.

Jack Johnson was six feet tall and weighed 201 pounds. James J. Jeffries stood 6-1½ and weighed 225 pounds. Bob Fitzsimmons, who won titles at three weight classes, fought at about 168 pounds even when campaigning as a heavyweight.

Jack Dempsey—shown smashing his opponent in the face—began his seven-year reign as heavyweight champion of the world by lifting the crown from much bigger Jess Willard in Toledo, Ohio, in 1919 (Library of Congress).

Occasionally, an enormous heavyweight rose through the ranks. Along came one of the occasional early behemoths who towered over his contemporary champion heavies. Known as the "Pottawatomie Giant" because he referred to Pottawatomie, Kansas, as his hometown (though it was possible people just liked to say the tongue-twisting word), Jess Willard had been a cowboy into his 20s and did not take up boxing until he was 27. As the paranoid, frantic search continued to find some white man who might be able to defeat Johnson, Willard rose to the top of the rankings.

Willard seemed a likely foe and threat to Johnson because of his comparatively massive size. Willard had modern dimensions, standing 6-foot-6½ and weighing 245 pounds. His sheer size scared some opponents and, given that he didn't really defeat many fighters of note to earn the spot, his bulk gave legitimacy to his shot at the title.

Under a fiery sun in Havana, Cuba, Willard toppled Johnson in the 26th round on April 5, 1915, to become heavyweight champ. For a time, there was some question about whether the bout was on the up-and-up, though evidence from the film itself indicated it likely was. In the end, Willard put a period on Johnson's reign. Sometimes the bigger they are, the harder they don't fall easily.

Willard appeared to be a champion proud of holding the belt, but not of showing an inclination to actually defend the title. For nearly a year, Willard did not fight, then on March 25, 1916, he took on Frank Moran at Madison Square Garden in New York with a defense occurring in Tex Rickard's inaugural New York promotion.

Moran, called "The Pittsburgh Dentist," compiled a record of 36 wins, 13 losses, 16 draws and one no contest. Moran was a pretty good power puncher, knocking out 28 opponents and apparently rearranging their bridge work. Still, there was a belief Willard would readily overpower him.

Originally, there was an attempt to stage the fight in New Orleans, but that fell through. This was a title defense determined by newspaper vote since New York state still had archaic rules in place. The fight went the distance and Willard received some criticism for his failure to KO Moran. Willard said his right hand was too broken up with injury, though post-fight examination showed a single hairline fracture. Technically, because of New York's cockamamie guidelines of the time, there was no true winner and the 10-rounder was declared a no-decision. That was pretty much like playing a baseball game to a tie score.

Willard promptly went back into boxing hibernation. America had its mind more on World War I than little private, in-ring wars, but still, Willard turned invisible in terms of showing why he deserved the title. Being heavyweight champ had its perks but also its responsibilities. Willard hoarded the title, failed to show it off and sought to reap any possible benefits that might accrue without putting the crown up for grabs.

Willard was determined to make the most of what opportunities came to him. He wanted to establish financial security for himself and wife Hattie. He got involved with Buffalo Bill's Wild West, though just as it went through management changes, shifted to the 101 Wild West Show and spent time touring with the circus.

Financially, this proved valuable for a time, but boxing fans became irate at Willard over his inactivity in the ring. Sometimes, he answered such questions from the press in this manner: "In time I will meet all my challengers," Willard said, "picking out the real contenders first. They need not worry, for as long as they are not colored, I shall not bar any of them."[1]

Of course, that meant there would not be a rematch with Johnson (no one ever thought there would be), nor would Wills get a shot as far as Willard was concerned. As it turned out, once Willard eliminated Moran from consideration, it seemed he never could find any contender worthy of meeting him.

Willard did not fight again until July 4, 1919, more than three and a quarter years after polishing off Moran. At last, after his years of struggles, Jack Dempsey woke up and found out his turn had come.

The highest approximate weight Dempsey fought at during his prime was 192 pounds, but sometimes he fought at a lesser weight. That meant at the least he was giving away more than 50 pounds to Willard. Perhaps that made Willard overconfident, but he would have been better off sticking with the circus than agreeing to a showdown with Dempsey.

Willard was a big, strong man of impressive size. Dempsey was a smaller strong man of great aggressiveness and with a killer instinct, as well as surprising dynamite in his fists. In 1918, as he worked himself into becoming a serious contender, and as Willard was entertaining fans of lions and tigers and elephants, Dempsey was cleaning the floor with all opponents.

Dempsey boxed 21 times that year. He knocked out Gunboat Smith, Carl Morris and Battling Levinsky and he outpointed Billy Miske. He lost once, by decision to Willie Meehan. Dempsey was a handsome man of mostly relaxed disposition when he was not in the ring, but he could wear a veil of viciousness when putting men on the canvas. Many could not readily figure out how this man packed so much strength in his blows.

"It's not about how much you weigh," Dempsey said, explaining leverage. "It's about getting your body weight in motion. That's what a punch is, isn't it? Body weight exploding into motion."[2]

George Lewis Rickard was the real name of one of the greatest sporting promoters of the 20th century, though no one called him that.

## 7. The Champ

He was much better known as "Tex." Rickard was born in Kansas City, moved to Texas as a toddler and was already in Alaska when the Klondike unveiled its riches in gold in 1897.

Rickard and a pal staked a successful strike and he opened a saloon but lost all his money gambling before moving on to Nome on the Bering Sea coast, where he befriended Wyatt Earp, who was operating his own saloon there. Rickard followed the money, relocating to gold fields in Nevada, and did some boxing refereeing.

In 1910, Rickard was co-promoter of a Jack Johnson title fight won over James J. Jeffries. While making six-figure profits on his biggest bouts, Rickard took a break from boxing anyway. He headed to Paraguay and started a cattle ranch, no small operation at something like 300,000 acres. Before losing a million bucks due to political controversies in Latin America, Rickard accompanied former president Theodore Roosevelt on a scientific expedition.

After all of his wanderings, Rickard found himself in New York, where he founded the New York Rangers of the National Hockey League, guided the building of a new Madison Square Garden and ended up with a 10-year deal to promote fights in what he helped turn into a famed sports palace.

He got serious about boxing, and after Willard eliminated Johnson from the picture, Rickard rushed in to secure an agreement to defend the title for $100,000. Willard even surrendered the right to veto an opponent.

Even as Dempsey wangled his way to a higher status with his repeated pummeling of foes, Rickard still harbored some of that old doubt about Dempsey being big enough. When Dempsey and Doc Kearns (who was already unconscionably taking 50 percent of Dempsey's purses instead of the customary 33 percent) showed up at Rickard's office on 23rd Street in New York to agree to terms, Rickard backtracked slightly.

"Willard is a big, strong man," Rickard said. "You look small." "I strip big," Dempsey retorted. "Every time I look at you, you get smaller," Rickard replied. "I'm afraid if I put you in the ring with Willard, you'll get killed. I'm afraid Willard will kill you."[3]

In an oddity, Rickard, a grand hustler on the big stage, and Kearns, a hustler for his man, had met in Alaska during the Gold Rush years and developed a dislike for one another. Yet they were capable of putting feelings aside for the common good, that being piles of greenbacks.

Rickard came around but told the Dempsey party the contract could not be signed in New York. He was going to rent a ferry and bring the sportswriters out onto the water and cross into New Jersey.

Dempsey signed the contract in Weehawken and he was guaranteed just $19,000.

The location for this sports spectacle was Toledo, Ohio. If it could not be held in New York, Rickard wanted to maximize the opportunity for big spenders to attend and the community was a railroad crossroads. Rickard put construction men to work building an 80,000-seat stadium.

During this period, pennies were like dollars of today and the kinds of paydays and salaries offered by professional sports teams in no way approached the reality of the 2020s. Rickard had apparently set some kind of record with the $270,755 paid gate for his own Johnson–Jeffries promotion in Nevada. He felt this fight could certainly exceed that—and by a goodly amount.

Rickard suggested a likely gate of more than $400,000, "give or take some change," was a realistic prospect. After all, as he hyped the event, "Willard–Dempsey shapes up as the greatest bout and the richest event in the history of sport."[4] There were elements of truth in the gab and elements of hyperbole.

Rickard was not the only fight man who wondered if Dempsey could stand up to Willard's gigantic size. In the lead-up to Dempsey–Willard, Ring Lardner and Grantland Rice, two giants of the sports writing fraternity during the era, debated their opinions. "I think Willard," Lardner said. "I think size. Willard is immense. I've bet $500 on him." But Rice demurred. "I think you've made a mistake, Ring," Rice said. "An ox cannot defeat a tiger."[5]

Especially if it did not take its foe seriously. Willard did not train very hard for the fight, did not even bring his trainer into camp. Ignoring the track record, he seemed to view Dempsey as some kind of shrimp who could never hurt him. Just too small was the attitude Willard brought into the fight.

Even before they agreed to meet, Willard made his feelings known about what easy pickings Dempsey would be for his own fists. "Men like Dempsey were especially made for me," Willard confidently boasted. "So, tell the people in the north to save Dempsey for me. Don't let some second-rater brush him off."[6]

Willard had busied himself with show business rather than boxing, but with the war diverting public attention and the first hits from the influenza disease causing trouble, it was difficult to arrange any kind of meaningful fight. The fact that Rickard was finally able to do so was a testament to his acumen.

Dempsey was boxing matches for charities but still very much had his eye on the real prize he had long coveted. Before the real deal was signed, Willard and Dempsey almost faced one another in a boxing carnival for charity, but fear of the spread of the flu halted that event.

Now the men were getting ready to rumble. Fireworks of more than one type were scheduled for Toledo on Independence Day.

Grantland Rice had been a foreign correspondent in France in 1917 and 1918 covering the war rather than being a sportswriter over that period. In 1919, he was back at his usual haunts and that meant covering boxing as one of the major sports on the block. The night before the Dempsey–Willard fight, he and another sportswriter stopped in to see Willard.

The way Willard behaved compared with what came to pass was something Rice wrote about years later. "Willard looked on Dempsey as a little boy," Rice said, using 250 pounds for Willard's weight and 180 for Dempsey's (although Dempsey said he was 187 that day). Willard said he would outweigh Dempsey by 70 pounds. "He'll come tearing into me. I'll have my left out. And then I'll hit him with a right uppercut. That'll be the end."[7]

If Rickard's boast of the fight being the biggest sporting event of all time needed some factual support, it did not receive it from the attendance, which with a crowd of about 20,000 left acres of empty seats, a little peculiarly mostly those in the cheap $10 range rather than the $60 ringside seats.

Yet about 400 sportswriters came and the paid gate did set a record with receipts of more than $450,000, a little bit more than what Rickard projected.

Willard, who had killed a man in the ring, asked Rickard to indemnify him in case he killed Dempsey during the fight. Dempsey laughed when he heard of the request, saying Willard was so fat he couldn't hurt Dempsey's father in the ring.

One thing that was unanticipated and unfriendly on the day of the fight was the 110-degree temperature for the opening bell. Although the betting odds were 6–5 Willard, Kearns demonstrated the ultimate confidence in his charge by placing $10,000 at 10-to-1 odds that Dempsey would KO Willard in the first round. That would have earned him a $100,000 payout.

For most of his life, especially as he aged, those who met Jack Dempsey summed him up as a gentleman and a person of a polite and gentle nature. That was on the street. The ring, however, was his cage and boxing was his performance art. Any pugilist foolish enough to take him on risked all.

Willard may have been contemptuous of the smaller Dempsey, but Dempsey was a hunter, a killer, an aggressor who pounced from a semi-crouch when an opponent got near, who unleashed harmful power when his large hands delivered a blow. He was a no-mercy guy who understood that the law of the ring was that the other guy was out to get you, so you'd better be out to get him.

Dempsey was not a jab-and-move fighter. He was a come-at-you guy. The ring size at the time was most often 24-foot square. To accommodate that large number of sportswriters, Rickard shrunk it to 20 feet square. When told, Dempsey snarled that he didn't care, and it was OK with him if it was reduced to 15-feet square. The saying "You can run, but you can't hide" was not coined until later, but it might as well have been uttered for Dempsey. He did not need much room to maneuver.

Willard may have been a large dude, but Dempsey didn't care about his size, what he brought to the game or whether the big man was coming after him or not. In the following minutes after the opening bell, in the following days and the following years, what Dempsey did to Willard in grabbing the heavyweight title in the 12-round scheduled bout was termed a massacre by many.

Think Chicago Bears 73, Washington Redskins 0, in a later National Football League title game. The Dempsey dismantling of Willard was one of the greatest high-profile sports slaughters of all time and the result helped solidify Dempsey's long-term reputation.

Dempsey wore white trunks and Willard wore blue. Briefly, when Willard pulled off his robe and Dempsey got a close-up of his opponent's physique, he had a moment of fear. But he stifled it quickly. "I thought I was going to be sick to my stomach," Dempsey said.[8]

The fight began at 4:09 p.m. and by about 4:10 Willard was in dire straits after landing a couple of ineffectual left jabs. Stalking began and then Dempsey delivered a brutal flurry of right and left hooks to Willard's body, a short right to the face and a devastating left hook that crushed Willard's cheekbone. It was broken in 13 places and Willard went down for the first time, only to rise at ref Ollie Pecord's count of six. That was the first test of Pecord's arithmetic capability.

Terrible things happened to Jess Willard, inflicted by Dempsey's fists. There are many phrases applied to such beatings in conversation, such as "He beat the crap out of him" to the more vulgar and "It was total destruction from start to finish."

Dempsey hit Willard with overhand rights, uppercuts, hooks, jabs, whatever was at his disposal and knocked Willard to the canvas seven times in the first three minutes. Willard was already a bloody mess when the first round ended. Indeed, Kearns, with his monstrous, daring bet threatening to pay off, thought initially Dempsey had notched that first-round knockout, earning him the bonus 100 grand.

## 7. The Champ

By the fifth knockdown, it was obvious Willard did not realize where he was. He seemed dizzy and disoriented. For the seventh knockdown, Pecord read off a 10-count, which should have ended the fight. Only there had been confusion at the start with a malfunctioning stopwatch that had not been corrected. The timekeeper waved off the knockout, saying the round had ended seconds earlier. Call it "The Short Count."

As Kearns was mentally counting his money and telling Dempsey he was the champ as he left the ring, Willard, still down, was actually being saved by a whistle, not a bell, because the bell had malfunctioned, too.

Willard was barely aided to the stool in his corner and doused with ice water. Somehow, he pulled himself together sufficiently to come out for the second round. Dempsey had to scramble back through the ropes. Willard remained on his feet through round two, but Dempsey caught up to him again in the third round and finished him off.

Championship reign concluded, Willard was a bloody mess with his shattered cheekbone, teeth knocked out, broken ribs and an eye swollen shut. Dempsey had done all but rearrange Willard's molecules.

In the immediate aftermath, Willard said, "I was fairly beaten and thoroughly beaten. Will I try to recover the championship? I will not because I could not. Dempsey is a great fighter. I know that now."[9]

Happy, but not exuberant, Dempsey returned to his hotel and, rather than celebrate with a party, went to sleep. However, he woke up in the early morning hours woozy from a nightmare, wondering what was real. He went out into the street and encountered a newsboy selling copies of the *Toledo Blade* with its gigantic headline being about him.

"Who won the fight, son?" the disoriented Dempsey asked the boy. The boy recognized Dempsey and said, "You did, ya big jerk. Look at the paper."[10] Dempsey gave the newsboy $1 for what was likely a nickel paper and felt the tip was a worthwhile investment.

Jack Dempsey's dream had become reality and he had done his bit to kick off the crazy times of the Roaring Twenties by becoming one of the symbols of the era and his generation with a brilliant fisticuff performance.

# 8

# The NFL Comes into the Picture

The National Football League as we know it was birthed in an automobile showroom in Canton, Ohio, and as another way to add to the sports landscape, took the field in 1920. Not hardly the same as it is now, but it was a rough-edged version of pro football the owners felt the public was ready to embrace.

Although it took years to become fully appreciated and raise its stature, those founders were right about the basic premise that there was room for the opportunity to play beyond college and there was interest in watching it.

Football at the college level was a mess in the early 20th century. The flying wedge and restrictive rules led to players being killed in games with regularity. Football might have been said to be as violent as boxing. President Theodore Roosevelt convened a White House summit conference with some leaders of the sport and demanded implementation of new approaches so parents sending their boys off to college did not receive them back home in coffins as if they had been to war.

This led to opening up the game somewhat with the introduction of the forward pass. Roosevelt and the other manipulators of the game would be amazed at just how often quarterbacks throw the ball in the 2020s and how wide open it has become.

Pro football's beginnings are basically dated to 1892 when William "Pudge" Heffelfinger was paid a fee to suit up for the Allegheny Athletic Association. He was known as the first pro. Over the following couple of decades, football gained in popularity through semipro teams sprinkled through the East and Midwest, attached to towns and businesses.

The Green Bay Packers' founding dates to 1919 and one of the men who started the team was Curly Lambeau, a legendary coach with longevity for whom the current stadium is named.

That optimistic gang of money men who gathered in Ohio to start

## 8. The NFL Comes into the Picture

the NFL (albeit for a year it was called the American Professional Football Association) included George Halas. Halas was a unique character in NFL history. The eventual member of the Pro Football Hall of Fame won 324 games as a coach and was instrumental in shepherding the passage of new rules that gave spark to the game as a member of the competition committee. Sometimes, employing overall fairness, Halas voted for policies that aided weaker teams rather than his own strong team.

A former University of Illinois athlete, Halas briefly patrolled right field for the New York Yankees before Babe Ruth took his job. Halas ran the football team as the Decatur Staleys, a starch company, before it was bequeathed to him by the firm and he changed its name to the Chicago Bears while presiding over its operations for decades.

George Halas, former player, in 1922, in the earliest days of the Chicago Bears and the National Football League.

Among the charter league teams were the Akron Pros (winners of the first title), the Dayton Triangles, the Chicago Cardinals (still around today as the Arizona Cardinals), the Rock Island Independents and the Canton Bulldogs. The first commissioner of the new league was Jim Thorpe.

Between 1912 and 1920, Thorpe was pretty much the most famous athlete in the country, if not the world, after he won two gold medals at the Summer Olympics in Sweden in the 1912 Games. The champion in the pentathlon and decathlon was proclaimed the world's greatest athlete.

Thorpe had been a two-time football All-American for the Carlisle Indian Industrial School in Pennsylvania and then starred for Canton. On the football field, Thorpe could outrun and outkick anyone, was a devastating tackler and could hardly be tackled by a single man. Thorpe, though, was designated as the commissioner because of his name value, not his administrative skills.

The six-foot-one, 185-pound Thorpe also dabbled in Major League Baseball, batting .252 over six seasons with the New York Giants. This was due to the recruiting of famed Giants manager John J. McGraw, who saw potential in Thorpe and was willing to pay well (for the times), giving him $6,000 as an untried prospect.

This was also at roughly the time Thorpe was being abused by the International Olympic Committee and his track and field medals were withdrawn because of the assertion he was a professional, having been paid a minimal amount for playing baseball before.

"McGraw has now the best advertised athlete in the world," one contemporary account noted. McGraw retorted, "I hired Jim as a baseball prospect, pure and simple, not as any advertising freak."[1]

That was humbug really. He wanted to attract more fans by appealing to ethnic heritages, though he definitely wanted a supremely talented athlete to fill this mental quota. At a time in American history when prejudice of many forms was rampant, McGraw was essentially free of it. Thorpe was a Native American and subject to discrimination. McGraw spent years searching for a Jewish superstar to attract those patrons to the Polo Grounds in New York, missing out on Hank Greenberg. After he died in 1934, John J.'s wife revealed McGraw kept a list of talented Black players handy whom he would have liked to sign if only his sport would allow him to buttress his roster in that manner.

Thorpe's was not a bad performance considering baseball was pretty much no more than his third-best sport. During his last season, in 1919, he batted .327 in 60 games. In midcentury, Thorpe was named the greatest athlete of the 21st century to that point.

Long after Thorpe passed away, his Olympic medals were restored in the record books. In 1920, though, the fathers of the NFL were mostly interested in Thorpe's football reputation. Thorpe made quite the impression at Carlisle under famed coach Pop Warner.

In a big game against Brown University, won 32–0 by Carlisle, Thorpe scored three touchdowns and kicked two field goals. Fading back to punt into his own end zone, Thorpe faked the kick and took off running. He notched a 110-yard TD. "I've seen the greatest football player ever," said the referee of the game. "[He] was a tornado."[2]

Halas had played against Thorpe before stepping fully into coaching and front-office work and admired Thorpe's defensive prowess, too. He once said, "His tackling was as unusual as his running style—he never tackled with his arms and shoulders. He'd leg-whip the ball carrier. If he hit you from behind, he'd throw that big body across your back and damn near break you in two."[3]

There was no greater promoter of, and believer in, professional

## 8. The NFL Comes into the Picture

football than George Halas. It used to steam him to hear what now would be considered quite ludicrous comments about how the college players were better than the pros. He loved any opportunity to show the facts to slow learners.

When the Chicago Charities College All-Star Game was established in 1934 by *Chicago Tribune* sports editor Arch Ward, Halas relished any chance that came his way for his Bears to face the collegians. The game pitted the defending NFL champion against All-Stars headed to their pro training camps. When that game was initiated, Halas mentioned the college-versus-pro debate's existence, but it was always clear where he stood.

The early years of the NFL may have provided an extra boost of entertainment to those Roaring Twenties spectators with leisure time and extra money, but the growing pains of the league were sometimes brutal. For every Bears, Cardinals and Packers franchise, all of whom struggled for ticket buyers, the stars-in-their-eyes founders tripled the financial beatings.

It took more than a decade for the teams to shake out. So many of the original and early NFL teams from that decade are not even memories except for historians. Who recalls the Rochester Jeffersons, the Massillon Tigers, the Muncie Flyers or the Pottsville Maroons?

It was important for the new league to establish itself in New York for credibility, even as these smaller towns were falling by the wayside. The football New York Giants were formed in 1925. Tim Mara, a bookmaker (who actually later tangled with Gene Tunney over a specious legal matter), was able to buy into the league for $500 and he kept ownership of the club until his death in 1959. The Giants are still owned mostly by the Mara family.

Halas was inducted into the Pro Football Hall of Fame in Canton, Ohio, where the league got its start so long ago, enshrined in its charter class in 1963. Even then, more than 40 years had passed since the meeting in that automobile showroom. This was a day for Halas to reminisce, though. "On my trip down here," Halas told the listeners at his induction ceremony, "my memory was stirred back quite a few years when I think of the wonderful men who did so much to develop football in this area and through the country." He mentioned 1921 through 1939 and added, "You may be sure some of those years were pretty tough."[4]

The Great Depression was about as tough as it got, and Halas and his Bears worked their way through that challenge later in the 1920s into the 1930s and the Second World War, too, before anyone put the sweat in to build a Hall of Fame for the sport. It is likely no accident at all that the Hall of Fame itself is located on George Halas Drive.

The NFL has progressed from featuring players without helmets to players without face masks to super-conditioned, highly paid, extra-large athletes cheered by millions of people on television every week. Along the way, it surpassed baseball as the United States' most popular sport. That would have been difficult to foresee in the 1920s, except perhaps by anyone not named George Halas.

## 9

## TUNNEY'S LEARNING CURVE

THE FIRST TIME JACK DEMPSEY and Gene Tunney met it wasn't at a weigh-in. Nor was it during the formulation of a boxing card. It happened purely by accident in one of those chance encounters average members of the public occasionally notch with a celebrity.

During the spring of 1920, Tunney and his then-manager, Billy Roche, were riding the New Jersey–Manhattan ferry. Tunney was still very much an unknown to almost all fight fans. Tunney and Roche were aboard the ferry because they had just signed a contract for his next fight—with championship boxing still illegal in New York City.

Also riding on the boat was a much more visible and recognizable Dempsey. He was in his prime, handsome and dark, with very dark hair, in need of a shave, it seemed, perhaps just five-o'clock shadow. Not so long before, Dempsey had beaten Jess Willard to become the heavyweight champion.

When the incident was described by some writers, it was not mentioned that Dempsey was being mobbed by admirers, as he well might have been, and certainly would have been in other locations in the soon-to-be-coming years.

Tunney, then 23, seemed almost like a starstruck fanboy in one description, even as Roche teased him and suggested he wait until that day in the future he had predicted, when he took on Dempsey for the title. But no, Tunney would not be swayed. He wanted to meet Dempsey in person right now.

Unbothered by any multitudes, Dempsey was quietly reading a newspaper when Tunney approached and introduced himself to the champ and made clear he was also a boxer. Then Tunney engaged Dempsey in a chat about a problem he was having. He told Dempsey that he had injured a knuckle in a match when he was still in France and it just wouldn't heal.

Almost as if he was a doctor checking over a patient, Dempsey took Tunney's hand in his own and examined the sore spot. It was inescapable for Tunney to notice Dempsey's powerful hands were much larger than his own. Dempsey gave Tunney some healing advice and the conversation ended.

Tunney seemed almost giddy about the meeting, much like a citizen fan, gushing about what a nice guy Dempsey was and how he was generous with his suggestions. Likewise, when he returned to his family home, he gave the same glowing review to other Tunneys in the house about his impressions of the new heavyweight champ.

It was a strange one-off meeting of friendliness between a superstar of the moment and a nobody of the moment in the same sport who were destined to be pitted against each other attempting to knock the other out. But that was still to come.

Dempsey's demeanor and kindness made a favorable impression on Tunney, but so did another aspect of Dempsey's bearing—a physical one. His fists, hands, seemed enormous to Tunney.

"They looked big to me," Tunney said, "terrible weapons to tell you the truth. He had been pickling his hands for a time and in places the skin had cracked into a hard, scaly, substance." He also acknowledged that he would have his work cut out trying to take the title away from Dempsey.[1]

Dempsey had reached the pinnacle of the profession. Tunney was paying his dues, working his way up. He was still learning his trade, gaining critical experience. Most of it came in New Jersey, a convenient location for club fights just that short ferry ride away from Greenwich Village, where Tunney was still based.

In 1920, Tunney fought as often as he could, starting with Whitey Allen on New Year's Day. Then, by either knockout or technical knockout, Tunney plowed through a string of opponents all over the New Jersey map, and occasionally elsewhere, taking out Bud Nelson, Jim Monahan, Al Roberts, Ed Kinley, KO Sullivan, Jack Clifford, Jeff Madden, Ole Anderson, Sergeant Ray Smith, Paul Sampson Koerner and Leo Houck twice, back-to-back.

When Tunney began fighting, especially early on, he was known as a defensive fighter who invested time studying his opponents after the bell rang and they circled the ring. He did his best never to offer an opening. The first hint that Tunney could adapt to opportunity came against Allen, whom he stalked aggressively from the start. It worked for him. A successful test, although Tunney was often still thought of as a cautious fighter.

His manager and promoters lined up the foes and Tunney knocked them all over like a tenpin bowler throwing strikes. During this period, Tunney weighed in at 175 pounds and regularly fought light-heavyweights. It didn't matter much. The goal was to gain ring time against professionals and this was the typical path followed by many future champions.

If Tunney ever wanted to do more than shake hands with Dempsey on a ferry, he had to fight through the lineup of hopefuls, wannabes, contenders and pretenders on the road to a place in the ring against the champ. It was an apprenticeship often served. Dempsey had spent his time on the road, in the dusty small towns, as well, trying to break through on his own journey.

This was not much of a lifestyle for an impatient man. The pay was not good and the trials and travels came frequently and were long. "I continued broke and in debt," Tunney said of this time of his life.[2] He had barely scrounged together the money needed to purchase his own boxing gear when discharged from the marines and this skein began.

Roche tried to dig up fights for Tunney and he took them, but he made little money. Once, he recalled, after giving Roche his 25 percent cut, Tunney's take-home was $150.75.

Tunney may have reeled off nine straight knockouts, but sometimes the men who harbored their own dreams landed their own big punches from the heart, even if they overall were not the same caliber of boxer he was. Tunney always recalled his Al Roberts bout as one of his toughest, despite his stopping the foe. "He closed one of my eyes and split my lip," Tunney said. "He staggered me with rights to the jaw again and again."[3]

Those are the types of fights that sometimes make champions, withstanding the best an opponent can dish out and still persevering and overcoming. One other attribute made Tunney as a fighter. No matter whom he was fighting, he hoped to learn something from the confrontation. Since he was young, Tunney had been a book learner and he always said he studied the best in his field when they competed and he hoped to pick up pointers from their actions when they were under duress in the ring. If he someday fought them, he might be able to use it against them. If he never fought them, he might be able to apply the lesson to some other situation of his own. This fight-a-month type of pace was like going to class regularly.

Those who become doctors must finish high school, college and medical school before they earn their own titles. It was like that for most boxing champions, especially in that era when there were only eight weight-class divisions and lines of hungry men who sought stardom, lines almost as long as there would be later in the decade when men waited to satiate real hunger in bread lines.

# 10

## Radio and All That Jazz

**W**HAT A TIME IT WAS. The declaration of peace seemed to loosen the corsets on the women and the strictures on moral sensibilities and set free the purse strings and outlook of Americans who wanted to have fun.

Prohibition, the Volstead Act, just didn't fit, except if viewed as something so out of character, so restrictive that the average person, never mind the average criminal, just didn't care about following that law. Otherwise, the '20s learned to roar in one way or another very quickly.

Radio was heard of, if not heard very much, but suddenly, it was a thing, and something that would broadcast the deeds of a few to the many, almost by magic, penetrating living rooms rather than requiring someone's presence live and in person at an event.

Thank you, Pittsburgh. On August 5, 1921, KDKA radio broadcast the first Major League Baseball game over the airwaves. Announcer Harold Aldrin sat in the stands at Forbes Field behind home plate to handle the play-by-play, telling homebound fans what they were missing at the ballpark. His microphone was a converted telephone. The game pitted the host Pirates against the visiting Philadelphia Phillies and Pittsburgh won the game, 8–5.

At a time when many large cities did not yet even have radio stations, KDKA broadcast at 500 watts, which meant not many people, even if they wanted to tune in on their new $60 sets, could hear Aldrin's voice.

Soon enough—very soon—boxing would invade this medium and supporters of Jack Dempsey and Gene Tunney would be able to listen to commentators describe how crisply they were throwing their fists.

To a certain degree, this advance in technology, and in Americans connecting with one another, was a wild development the people would not have imagined only a few years earlier. Now the new was bursting upon the scene in American life in so many ways it was difficult to take it all in. Some of these fresh things provided entertainment.

**Actress Louise Brooks, who had a bobbed haircut, was considered to be the epitome of the 1920s flapper.**

In 1915, to most people a flapper was probably a bird flying south for the winter. Less than a decade later, a flapper was a bird of a different sort, a young woman defying social conventions, dancing wildly, smoking in public, dressing more freely. Her hairstyle resembled nothing like what straitlaced ladies wore and she didn't give a darn what anyone thought about her behavior.

And even if it was against the law, the young lady might well have been imbibing drinks at a speakeasy in the company of friends and single men while perhaps even becoming a character in an F. Scott Fitzgerald short story or novel.

At least before Fitzgerald and wife Zelda fled to Paris with other American expatriates such as Ernest Hemingway, Ezra Pound, Henry Miller, Gertrude Stein and Alice B. Toklas, personages of the so-called "Lost Generation."

Fitzgerald penned *Tales of the Jazz Age*, *The Beautiful and the Damned* and *The Great Gatsby*. Hemingway, who had been wounded in World War I as an ambulance driver, was a journalist and short-story artist before making a major splash with the novel *The Sun Also Rises* in 1926.

One of the chroniclers of this period quoted Fitzgerald saying, "None of the Victorian mothers—and most of the mothers were Victorian—had any idea how casually their daughters were accustomed to be kissed."[1]

There were flappers and flippancy in America, though, while those disdainful purveyors of the written word scorned the home front. They put themselves above the fray, in a way, looking from outside in at the masses who so adored the Dempseys and the Tunneys, the grassroots livers who thrived on the combat they espoused on such an elemental level.

The "Jazz Age," it was called, as music with a new beat and rhythm percolated from the smoky clubs of Harlem into the mainstream singing and dancing clubs everywhere, the sounds giving the patrons itchy feet and making them twitch all over. They were new sounds and people liked them. They were blues sounds and they spoke to people of all kinds.

The irresistible music wound its way northward along the Mississippi River from New Orleans and jumped the railroad tracks from Chicago to New York and spread like a summer forest fire to the largest cities to Europe. Jazz was a good-news pandemic.

Jazz was the closeted sound of Black Americans bursting free for singing, dancing and listening, even if the freedom it espoused did not come so easily to the race it personified. People loved Louis Armstrong on stage but still didn't embrace him or other individuals who were geniuses of the genre, like Jelly Roll Morton, Bessie Smith, Fats Waller, Duke Ellington and Kid Ory's Original Creole Band, as human beings.

If you wanted to witness the best entertainment, it did not yet come from the radio, nor did it necessarily appear in clubs in Times Square. You had to make the trek to Harlem, to stop in at the Cotton Club, The Alhambra, Small's Paradise or the Savoy Ballroom.

Virtually concurrent with this explosion in so-called new music was the emergence of the Charleston, the wacky dance that was named after the city in South Carolina but went public in the Broadway stage show *Runnin' Wild*, which ran in 1923 and 1924. Some credit its origins to the African American dance Juba, with twists in steps added for the show. It was good to have flexible knees if one danced the Charleston.

The 1920s was labeled the Harlem Renaissance and it wasn't all about jazz, singing and dancing, but wide-ranging expressions in literature and art, fashion, politics and culture, as well, for Black Americans making their mark. There were writers such as Langston Hughes, and others.

The boost in all of these realms was an outgrowth of the Great Migration from the South. Black men seeking work and their families escaping the Jim Crow segregation laws of the Deep South by the millions relocated from the hot, humid, hateful region of the United States that did everything possible to keep them down, to the northern cities where at the least better job opportunities awaited.

Historian James Weldon Johnson hoped that culture "would bridge across the chasm between the races"[2] and said such cultural contributions of music and dance literature "helped shape and mold and make America."[3]

Black people might have said thanks a bunch for such an evaluation, but even as the Harlem Renaissance played out and the sounds of those jazz horns penetrated many a closed door, there was so much hate so deeply ingrained in so much of the country, one might wonder if the Civil War had ever been settled and if slavery had ever been abolished.

The clock was turned back in Indiana by the reemergence of what was thought to be the dormant Ku Klux Klan, the parading crusaders of loathing in their white sheets who campaigned against Blacks, Jews, Catholics and anyone else they chose.

Over a few-year period in the early 1920s, the Klan virtually took over the levers of government in the Hoosier state, from the top down, from law enforcement to church life. David "Old Man" Stephenson became a near-dictator running an Indiana fiefdom, perpetuating horrible crimes against women, as well as minorities, while enriching himself and spewing hatred nonstop.

It was probably the most shameful stretch of time in that state's history and Stephenson was halted in carrying out more nefarious schemes only when he was convicted of murder.

More than 200,000 Black men served in World War I, fighting for America. When they returned home to the United States, many wondered about their sacrifices since they faced a revival of discrimination.

Stephenson cared naught about them. Beginning in Evansville, he plotted a Klan coup that would enrich himself by getting a cut of any new member's dues and by rising to power within the Invisible Empire's hierarchy. Along the way he established himself as a sexual predator of young women and corrupted police departments as a way to enforce his edicts and protect his mob rules.

At one point, before the law caught up to Stephenson, the Klan's new troops reached as high as six million members.

"It came about that American citizens in Indiana were judged by their religion, condemned because of their race, illegally punished because of their opinions, hounded because of their personal conduct, and a state of terror was substituted for a state of law."[4]

Raising the specter of a charismatic, hate-spewing leader, the book *A Fever in the Heartland*, chronicling those few years in the first half of the 1920s in Indiana, asked the question, "But was it an aberration?"[5]

That Pittsburgh radio station carrying the Pirates game went on the air November 2, 1920, just months before as the first commercial station in the United States, founded by Westinghouse Electronic Corporation.

Radio had been used for point-to-point communication, but its mission that day was something new—to provide presidential election results. That was the election that put Republican Warren Harding in the White House after he defeated Democrat James Cox.

Between that newsy debut and the baseball game, KDKA experimented by broadcasting a local boxing match. The fight between Pittsburgh's Johnny Dundee and Johnny Ray was the first fight ever heard on the radio. Dundee was the featherweight champ and owned the nickname "Little Bar of Iron." The men fought a 10-round draw on April 11, 1921.

KDKA kept looking for new ways to flex its muscle. As it so happened, Aldrin broadcast a Davis Cup tennis match on the day after he experimented with the ballgame.

In the industry, fledgling as it was, there were some with vision who had a strong sense radio was going to be a big hit and felt it was important to get in on the ground floor using it to advantage and for profit.

David Sarnoff, a corporate mogul at RCA, who later founded NBC, read the tea leaves well. He believed in the widespread future of radio reaching masses of listeners and he played a role in what became the first big-league broadcast of a boxing match.

## 10. Radio and All That Jazz

The new heavyweight champion, Jack Dempsey, was prepping to take on French challenger Georges Carpentier and this became one of the first true mass entertainment productions extending beyond a stadium or arena boundaries.

# 11

# Life Gets Complicated Outside the Ring

Jack Dempsey was the heavyweight champion of the world, but it seemed his life was as tumultuous as ever. Doc Kearns gave him reasons why he didn't take home as much money from the gate as the fighter thought he should.

He also gave him some bad advice about his public image. Although Dempsey had boxed for the war effort, raising money for the United States, and was about to try to enlist just as World War I ended, a wildfire of criticism followed him, calling him a slacker, or draft dodger.

Even some of whom he thought as friends among the sportswriters gave him grief on that topic, notably Grantland Rice. Rice was a giant of his genre and someone Dempsey thought of as a guy on his side. Rice had taken a hiatus from the sports world to cover the real world, going overseas to write about the war, and that made an impact on him. That proximity to real fighting altered his outlook on boxing.

"It would be an insult to every doughboy that took his heavy pack through the mules' train to front-line trenches to go over the top to refer to Dempsey as a fighting man," Rice wrote.[1]

Dempsey was stung because he did not think of himself as someone who had ducked out on the army. Having achieved his longtime goal, Dempsey was distraught over being belittled.

"Forget the war-story stuff, champ," Kearns told Dempsey.[2] But he couldn't, being regularly insulted, and eventually being brought to trial as a draft dodger, the culmination of an investigation of his draft deferment.

Along the way, as Dempsey fought his way to the top of the rankings, he had been married. He fell for an older woman named Maxine, whom some labeled a prostitute. Although Dempsey loved her, she did not show much more than temporary infatuation with Dempsey.

Maxine was a major-league thorn in his giant fists. He sent her money, which she didn't appreciate. He sought to reconcile, which she didn't want to do. Then she testified against him in court, lying under oath. Dempsey was acquitted and ultimately, sometime later, Maxine died in a fire.

Men are often blinded by love, but it seemed Dempsey was more innocent than most, and more foolish perhaps. This same trait may have infected Dempsey's faith in Kearns. A young man who was somewhat lonely, Dempsey seemed to want so much to believe in those close to him. These were two instances where his naturally generous soul was abused of trust.

Dempsey was eventually married four times, but in between his legal hitchings, he was not adverse to meeting, dating and bedding attractive women. He spent time in Hollywood and there were many actresses in the movies who vied for his attention. He was a magnet for gossipers, almost as if the 1920s was introducing social media and the internet ahead of schedule. Anyone could say anything about Dempsey, it seemed, and mostly get away with it.

After the dust settled on Jess Willard's prone body and he admitted in post-fight reckoning that Dempsey was the better man who pounded the living daylights out of him, the former champ started belittling the new champ.

Despite evidence to the contrary in the way Willard and his people had watched Dempsey slip on the gloves, Willard began saying Dempsey had soaked them in plaster of Paris. This would have turned the gloves into clubs, enhanced weapons. Nat Fleischer, editor of *The Ring* magazine, was one who disavowed the possibility, saying he witnessed up close the gloves being placed on Dempsey's hands.

Decades later, Kearns, who by then had become a Dempsey enemy, wrote a book as he was dying. An excerpt appeared in *Sports Illustrated* in 1964 in which he claimed Doc had doctored the gloves to favor Dempsey. There was never really any proof to support Willard's or Kearns's stories, however. The tale came off more as an excuse from Willard and a conspiracy theory motivated by no known reason.

Life was almost always clearer for Dempsey when he was in the ring. The bell rang, his cornermen pointed him to the center of the canvas and he whaled on his opponent until he fell down. That was the object of the game, wasn't it? Dempsey played by those rules where his fists reigned, not words uttered by characters far removed from the roped square, verbally or in print. He sued *Sports Illustrated* and the magazine settled with him out of court.

For a mix of reasons, there had not been a steady stream of high-profile heavyweight title fights in recent years. Jack Johnson faced his pressures because of race and being on the lam. World War I deflected attention. Willard was busy touring with the circus. And the drumbeat of propaganda about Dempsey being a slacker who had ducked out on overseas fighting diminished his popularity in some corners.

Yet gradually, after Willard shut up, the country settled into peace and eyes turned again to the sporting landscape, Dempsey returned some normalcy to the grandest individual prize in sport.

When sports teams win a championship, their season ends, they get a trophy and they are toasted as titleholders until the next season rolls around. When a boxer wins a world crown, he is immediately besieged with questions about whom he will fight next. This is often a tricky circumstance. Sometimes there is an obvious No. 1 contender screaming for a chance and with all officials agreeing who should be next in line. Other times there are fighters waiting in line who are not automatic top candidates. Often, the champion and his manager want to be picky, choosing an opponent of some credibility but whom they believe has no chance to dethrone the big guy.

In a way this is Russian roulette. There are no sure things in the ring and such careful choices have gone awry, producing surprising results. Perhaps the most extreme example of that happening in the heavyweight ranks occurred in 1978. Champion Muhammad Ali gave Leon Spinks a shot at the title and the challenger, who was in just his eighth pro fight after winning an Olympic gold medal, pulled off the stunning upset. Ali didn't take Spinks seriously and didn't train seriously and he lost his title on a split decision.

Dempsey had to fight and there was no indication he didn't really want to fight. There was no wealth of standout opponents in the wings, except possibly Harry Wills, the Black man snubbed by all.

On September 6, 1920, Dempsey engaged in his first defense of the title he won from Willard. The foe was Billy Miske, a fighter from Minnesota known as "The Saint Paul Thunderbolt." Miske was a solid fighter who compiled a 74–13–16 record but was no superstar. He was a hardworking pro but not really to be feared in the ring by the likes of Dempsey.

Dempsey, in fact, liked Miske, whom he had twice previously battled to no-decisions on the scorecard, even though observers felt Dempsey won both bouts. "I fought the guy," Dempsey said. "I loved the guy. Hell of a guy, Billy Miske."[3]

What was really going on was Dempsey did Miske a favor by granting him the title shot. Miske was dying from a kidney ailment and needed money to help provide for his wife and kids. The men met in

## 11. Life Gets Complicated Outside the Ring

Benton Harbor, Michigan, and Dempsey stopped Miske at 1 minute, 13 seconds of the third round. Miske ended up passing away on New Year's Day 1924.

"When the ref counted him out, I helped Miske to his corner," Dempsey said in an autobiography years later. "I really felt bad for him, but I knew I had done him a good turn by giving him a chance and a share of the purse."[4]

After that Good Samaritan title defense, Dempsey squeezed in another bout before the end of 1920, taking on Bill Brennan, the old war horse, on December 14. Dempsey had defeated Brennan in 1918. Dempsey knocked him down five times in that contest, so there were not many people outside of Brennan's closest relatives who looked for him to lift the title. Still, Brennan had had wars with Harry Greb and gone up against Miske, too.

One thing different for Dempsey this time was fighting in Madison Square Garden in the heart of New York City. The New York state legislature had legalized professional boxing and the Garden was on its way to becoming the showpiece of the sport under the guidance of promoter Tex Rickard.

Brennan made a much better accounting of himself against Dempsey with such high stakes. Dempsey was left bleeding from the left ear and the mouth, but he finished off Brennan with a knockout in the 12th round.

In a strange confluence of circumstances, Miske died from his illness at just 29 years of age, and Brennan also died young, not so very long after his grand opportunity in the ring. Brennan was shot to death by gangsters in 1924 at age 30. He had bought a bar with his ring earnings, but one day during Prohibition he had an unexpected visit from some thugs who told him he was purchasing his beer from the wrong source. Brennan was popular and respected and an estimated 5,000 people attended his funeral.

Such was the violence—outside the ring—during Prohibition in some of America's big cities.

By now, Rickard was thinking bigger than making matches between the heavyweight champ and some of the been-around guys in the rankings. He wanted the next Dempsey fight to be a humdinger that would become the talk of the sport against a sexier opponent and one that would make a lot more money for everyone involved. Rickard was a promoter who saw the possibilities and understood how to build a sporting event into an EVENT.

# 12

# THE BABE SAVES BASEBALL

WHEN THE CHICAGO WHITE SOX sold baseball's soul, the cheating in the 1919 World Series was a gross betrayal of the sports fan and the American public. Their actions of taking bribes to lose on purpose to the Cincinnati Reds were deemed so grievous many believed irreparable harm might cripple the game.

More than 100 years later, the so-called "Black Sox Scandal" remains the most extreme scandal in American team sport—though there have been others that sought to contend, such as point-shaving in college basketball.

Baseball was brought to a tipping point and it was fortunate a sweeping breath of fresh air collided with the stink of the fumes from this blow at just the right moment.

As a team sport during the late 1800s and the early part of the 20th century, baseball had no competition. The later major sports leagues dominating the North American landscape were either not yet established or in fledgling stages. Baseball was king.

Baseball was mostly the same yet different from the modern game of the 2020s, but at least it was recognizable. Games were lower scoring. Starting pitchers stayed on the mound for many more innings. Few managers regularly called for relief pitchers. Fielders' gloves were smaller and less reliable. Bats were bigger. However, the distance from the pitcher's mound to home plate was the same 60 feet, 6 inches from 1893 on. The distance between the bases was the same 90 feet. Scheduled games called for teams to play nine innings.

The best baseball players were celebrity heroes, Ty Cobb, Tris Speaker, George Sisler, Babe Ruth, "Shoeless" Joe Jackson, Walter Johnson, Eddie Cicotte and Grover Cleveland Alexander among them.

One of the finest teams in the sport approaching 1920 was the Chicago White Sox, with stars including Red Faber and Eddie Collins, who were winners of the 1917 World Series. The White Sox then won the pennant in 1919 and prepared to face the Reds.

## 12. The Babe Saves Baseball

Even before the World Series began, and while it was being played, rumors circulated that the fix was in. Some sportswriters, notably Hugh Fullerton and Ring Lardner, were suspicious. In the movie *Eight Men Out*, based on the book of the same name by Eliot Asinof, there is a scene where sportswriters talk about keeping track of plays they considered to be of suspect authenticity and then comparing notes. That really happened. There is another scene where the Ring Lardner character is walking through the team's train singing, "I'm forever blowing ballgames" to the tune of "I'm forever blowing bubbles." That also really happened.

Slugger Babe Ruth burst on the national scene just when Major League Baseball needed him most as the sport tried to recover from the Black Sox Scandal of the 1919 World Series.

To this day, many details of this scandal remain murky. The players were felt to be susceptible to bribery because they believed themselves underpaid. More than one source, and perhaps three, sought to put the fix in, though gangster-gambler Arnold Rothstein is credited as the man who truly pulled it off and made many thousands of dollars from his bets.

Such clues that the Series was fixed were delivered by Cicotte—who until that point might have been on a career path to the not-yet-created Baseball Hall of Fame. His signal the deal was on was plunking the first batter in his first game.

The players' defense crumbled and confessions made, but during trial it was said their confessions vanished. Disgusted and worried their sport was going to hell, the owners took drastic steps to rebuild credibility. They hired an all-powerful commissioner to replace a governing board, bringing in federal judge Kenesaw Mountain Landis and giving him a job for life, which lasted until 1944.

Landis's rulings did not have to be supported by the same standard of evidence as they did in the legal system. Despite the White Sox's acquittal, Landis banished all eight indicted players from baseball forever after court proceedings were over.

In what was probably Landis's most famous speech, he said, "Regardless of the verdict of juries, no player who throws a ball game, no player who undertakes or promises to throw a ball game, no player who sits in confidence with a bunch of crooked ballplayers and gamblers, where the ways and means of throwing a game are discussed and does not promptly tell his club about it, will ever play professional baseball."[1]

Third baseman Buck Weaver insisted for the rest of his life that he had done nothing wrong. Periodically, over the years, efforts were made to reinstate Shoeless Joe because of his greatness and his overall performance in the Series. Mostly the argument on his behalf was that his ignorance dragged him into the scam. When banned players tried to organize exhibition games, Landis doubled down, insisting he would banish other players who competed against them if they participated. Landis had as much power in his fists as Jack Dempsey and was willing to use them for a knockout.

The White Sox did not win another pennant for 40 years, from 1919 until 1959. The Sox did not win another World Series between 1917 and 2005.

If Landis was the muscle that showed it would not be business as usual in baseball behind the scenes, baseball desperately needed a savior to focus the public's attention back on the field. The sport did not quite yet realize it already had such a character in the fold.

George Herman Ruth gained the nickname "Babe" while residing in a Baltimore orphanage. By the time he was 19, Ruth was a rookie with the Boston Red Sox. By the next year, he was a budding star. As the Red Sox picked off World Series crowns in 1915, 1916 and 1918, southpaw Ruth emerged as one of the sharpest pitchers in the American League.

However, by the end of that stretch, it was obvious that as wonderful a hurler as Ruth was, he was an even better hitter. Home runs were a rare commodity during the dead-ball era, but in 1918, Ruth smacked 11 to lead the AL. The next season he slugged 29 homers to lead the circuit again. In those days, Ruth, who stood six-foot-two, weighed a comparatively slim and muscled 185 pounds. Later, when he developed a potbelly from too much wild living, he registered around 215 pounds.

Neither baseball, nor America, had ever seen such a personality. Ruth not only towered over his competition in results but also provided good copy for sportswriters, mingled with children who adored him and changed the entire offensive tenor of the sport with his war club of a bat. More than once, he predicted he would hit a home run and did so. Ruth was a force of nature who was rarely reined in by teammates

## 12. The Babe Saves Baseball

or managers. The little boy from the orphanage had been set free to indulge in all the fun things in life he had previously been denied while growing up.

At that point, the most famous athlete in the United States was likely Jim Thorpe, with the new heavyweight champion Jack Dempsey coming up on the outside. Ruth's fame would not only eclipse theirs among everyday Americans, especially when his grinning face regularly began showing up in black-and-white newsreels, during the 154-game baseball season, stretching from spring to fall. He was in people's faces almost every day, not retired like Thorpe, not boxing once in a while like Dempsey.

Ruth was already a star with Boston. He became a megastar in New York. New York itself was in the process of becoming a city that turned people into stars in the movie world (still no talkies until the end of the decade), but during the Roaring Twenties, New York published 20 daily newspapers. They all wanted something fresh about Ruth every day.

One of the shrewdest moves Yankees owner Jacob Rupert made as his team was being edged out of the Polo Grounds was build a new, gigantic ballpark. The massive, three-tiered stadium became known as "The House That Ruth Built," and that was no exaggeration. Opening day, April 18, 1923, lured more than 74,000 spectators. The fans could not get enough of Ruth, on the streets, in nightclubs after hours, his chasing of women and, above all, tales of his bashing home runs.

"None of the new gods," it was said of the fresh sporting faces of the 1920s, "compared to Ruth. None of them so captured the public imagination. None of them—no other professional athlete anywhere—transformed their sport the way that Ruth did his, merely by switching positions."[2]

Most students of Ruth know the story of a former Yankee teammate saying he did not really room with Ruth in a hotel on the road, but with his suitcase, as a way of expressing how The Babe was never home, but the author of a recent book noted that two different teammates made the same comment over the years.

Ruth and Jack Dempsey knew one another but were not pals who generally hung out together. Dempsey did not party the way Ruth did. He took much greater care of his body. If any sporting figure approached Ruth in stature at all during the 1920s, it was Dempsey after he won the heavyweight crown and cut through all of the ancillary aggravations that threatened to derail him.

If Ruth slept, it was a secret. He prowled the cities he visited, meeting on his own, or through intermediaries, legions of women. He wanted to own the most up-to-date car, but if he cracked it up, so what?

He drank to excess, even during Prohibition, as if that was a law written for others. He ate big meals and he ate many hot dogs.

Ruth was the living, breathing example of a lifestyle that ignored good judgment, that didn't require solid exercise training and was on the go-go-go all of the time instead of scheduling some restraint.

After 22 years in the big leagues, Ruth had 714 regular-season home runs on his résumé; owned a .342 batting average, a remarkable .474 on-base percentage and an astounding .690 slugging percentage; led the American League in walks 11 times because pitchers were scared of him; and led the AL in home runs 12 times. He knocked in 2,214 runs and scored 2,174 runs.

Ruth will forever be associated with the long ball. When he hit 29 home runs in 1919, that was a record. When he hit 54, that was a record. When he hit 59, that was a record. And when he hit 60 in 1927, that was a record, too, one that stood until 1961.

Ruth had his own theories about hitting, and not surprisingly, they were not based in science so much as in feel. "Baby is going to hit one today," he sometimes said before or during a game. "They'll tell you the science of line shots is what counts. But that's all baloney. What counts is socking that ball and giving it a ride,"[3] Sometimes, Ruth made fun of himself at the plate as if he was a comedian, staring at his trusty bat in shock if he swung and missed.

This home run explosion showing the world how the game could be enlivened followed Major League Baseball's introducing the lively ball. But it was Ruth who demonstrated what a slugger was really about. In the beginning, Ruth outhomered entire teams over the course of whole seasons. It was Ruth who lifted the excitement level of the game and weaponized the home run. Lou Gehrig, Jimmie Foxx and Mel Ott followed while few other players adapted.

Ruth, who once pontificated on the difference between greatness and legend, is treated as a legend by baseball, history and the Baseball Hall of Fame. Appropriately, he is one of the few individuals who are members of the Hall who have a large exhibit devoted only to him.

"Babe Ruth is not just a legend now, he was a legend in his own time," said Hall of Fame senior curator Tom Shieber. "That's rare. And that's a big reason why we've got an exhibit dedicated to only him."[4]

Babe Ruth would deck himself out in a fancy bowler hat and pop a big cigar in his mouth to celebrate that observation and demonstrate his agreement. And the Black Sox should thank him for repairing their fix.

# 13

## Parlez Vous Knockout?

AFTER HIS FIRST TWO HEAVYWEIGHT title defenses, it was time for a big fight. Jack Dempsey thought so. So did Doc Kearns. So did Tex Rickard. Who was the right guy to stand in the ring opposite Dempsey? Who could sell tickets? Who had personality and credentials?

Styles make fights in the ring, but matches must be made in the public's mind, as well. People may have a strong rooting interest for one participant, but they must have doubts that the bout won't be a simple walkover, or they might pass on investing ticket money.

No one understood this better than Rickard. He aspired to put on great promotions that would break records. He wanted the fight to pass the street test, where people who bumped into one another would be drawn into talking about the upcoming battle and who might defeat whom. These days promoters talk about creating buzz. In the early 1920s, the phrase was "ballyhoo," the popular synonym for hype at the time.

It might be said Dempsey really didn't care whom he fought. After years of scraping by, of carrying cardboard suitcases, of hitching rides beneath rail cars, of not being able to afford respectable hotels, he wanted to be rewarded for his blood and sweat.

He was growing a little bit skeptical of Kearns's explanations of where all the money was going, being spent on building his name and not lining the fighter's pockets at a rate he felt he deserved. Rickard, who met Kearns in Alaska and considered him to be somewhat of a shady character, sometimes warned Dempsey about trusting Kearns too much.

Yet Kearns had made good on most of his promises, lifting Dempsey from obscurity to the heavyweight championship. Dempsey was wary about not getting his fair share, but he was not ready to break with Kearns. It seemed that after besting Billy Miske and Bill Brennan, they were on the cusp of making big bucks. Kearns wanted to promote a Dempsey title fight overseas. Rickard was a step ahead in terms of being able to bring parties together for newsreel rights, radio rights and a bigger live crowd than had ever attended a prize fight before. To date, in 1921, the largest crowd on-site for a bout was 20,000.

In all of these instances, the creative matchmaker was thinking bigger, with big-league paydays for the fighters, and, of course, him. There was a clamor to give Harry Wills a shot at the title, but Rickard did not want to go down the path of giving a Black man the opportunity. All he could envision was controversy of the type lodged in his brain from the Jack Johnson experiences—and he wondered how many tickets would sell.

The opponent who emerged from the contenders to face Dempsey was Georges Carpentier, a French war hero, who was the light-heavyweight champion. This was an odd choice to some degree. Carpentier had little to no profile in the United States—his following was across the Atlantic. His credentials were compiled in a lower weight class, so he didn't on the face of it seem to be a threat. But salesmen sell and Rickard was good at that.

Carpentier was born in 1894 and had his first pro fight in 1908 while staying active until 1926. Carpentier was a sergeant aviator for his home country during World War I and was wounded in combat. When discharged, he took up rugby for a time but returned to boxing.

Nicknamed "The Orchid Man," Carpentier was regarded as a smooth boxer rather than a powerful puncher and his best weight class really was the 175-pound light-heavyweight division. In October of 1920, Carpentier won the world championship in that division by defeating Battling Levinsky in New Jersey. Due to his triumphs in the ring, Carpentier was also called "Le Grand Georges," the Great Georges, by his fans.

The Dempsey–Carpentier fight was set for July 2, 1921. The location was established in New Jersey, minutes from New York City, on marshy land called Boyle's Thirty Acres. By some definitions, despite proximity to Manhattan, this was the middle of nowhere. Just as he had done in Toledo for the Dempsey–Jess Willard bout, Rickard hired a construction crew to build an arena for the fight from scratch. The promoter said it cost $250,000 to erect the stadium.

Once the opponents and site were established for Dempsey's third defense, Rickard went into overdrive on the ballyhoo. Whether the sportswriters' predisposition to say certain things created the lead-up or not, Dempsey, the American, became the villain of the set-to, discussion again returning to the fact he did not fight during World War I and Carpentier did.

Although the phrase has been applied to numerous matches (in more than one century) since, the bout was billed as "The Fight of the Century." If that gave the buying public more incentive to make sure to be on the site, fine. The suspense kept building. Originally, Rickard intended to cap seating at 50,000. Things were going so well in advance, he went for a capacity of 70,000 and then didn't stop building until he hit 80,000 seats. After fight day, the attendance was given out as 80,183.

There had never been a live turnout anywhere close to what ticket sales produced and this fight became known as the first million-dollar gate. The dollars exceeded that number by far, totaling $1,789,238. Occasionally, after that, Dempsey was called "The Million-Dollar Man" and, indeed, eventually, a book written about him had that title.

No doubt thinking ahead, Rickard invited women to see the fight, the type of event that previously was thought to be too low-class for them. This emphasis seemed a natural outgrowth of women gaining the right to vote and their taking it upon themselves to dress more freely and smoke in public as shackles were loosened in society.

Over his long career, Carpentier, who was either 5-foot-11½ or six feet tall, won 89 fights, lost 15 times and had six draws and one no-decision. Carpentier, who later became an actor, aided his popularity in the U.S. by being remarkably handsome. Women loved him and he dressed the part of an upper-crust man, wearing silk shirts and specially tailored suits.

However, Carpentier's training camp was off-limits to sportswriters. He and his entourage refused to let the writers watch workouts and there was some supposition it was because he was actually so light they would view his skinniness and write based on size alone he had no chance against Dempsey. Ironically, when Dempsey was younger and malnourished, he was subject to that very type of once-over scrutiny by promoters who felt he was too small to be a heavyweight.

While Carpentier set up a training camp in Manhasset, New York, Dempsey established his own operation in Long Hill, New Jersey. Dempsey did not shy away from sportswriters and his preparations were open to visitors. As was his long-standing habit, Dempsey beat his sparring partners to a pulp. There may have been prestige in being a sparring partner to the champ, but there was no glory in it after he bloodied the other men's faces and left them with bruised ribs. The same aggressiveness Dempsey displayed in his bouts when the clock began ticking was on display in practice. Most of the time Dempsey just couldn't help himself and he battered many a man who aided him in training.

One good reason why Carpentier did not wish to banter with the press is that his English was limited. However, of all things, the two combatants met for a round of golf some weeks ahead of the bout.

At that time, Carpentier, who was a naturally friendly man, said to Dempsey, "I hope we will still be friends after the fight."[1] If Carpentier had watched what Dempsey did to sparring partners he knew, he may have adjourned back to France right then.

Sportswriting star Grantland Rice said the only way Carpentier could have become a legitimate heavyweight was by adding "two sandbags of ballast" to the scale.[2]

What Rice did admire was the magnificent creativity of Rickard in building up a fight into more than it probably should have been and making people want to buy tickets to see it. Rickard, Rice said in his biography decades later, "sensed more and better gate-building tricks in one minute than today's promoters can dream up in a year." Rickard, he noted, "had the kind of promotional touch that would have them storming the gates today instead of taking in the fight through a camera."[3]

If the sportswriters were skeptical Carpentier was enough of the real deal to be a threat to Dempsey, those 80,000 ticket buyers certainly felt they were paying for a good show. Ringside seats sold for $50, pricey for the time, and the cheap seats of $5 were situated practically in another area code. It was advisable to bring binoculars.

By the time binocs were focused, of course, Dempsey was tearing holes in Carpentier. Dempsey had weighed in at 188 pounds, small for a heavyweight today, but 20 pounds more than Carpentier, who must have lost weight by staying away from rich French food during his U.S. stay. The fight was scheduled for 12 rounds. Carpentier did not last the distance. Dempsey was too big, too strong and overpowered the visitor from France.

As if he suddenly realized what he had arranged, shortly before the fight started, Rickard spoke to Dempsey and said, "Jack, don't kill him, Jack. If you kill him, you'll kill boxing. Promise me, you don't kill him, Jack." Many years later, Dempsey reflected on the comment, saying, "You know, it wasn't as if I had a gun."[4]

Dempsey was the aggressor from the opening bell, and Carpentier boxed and moved but stayed on his feet.

However, as proof there is always danger lurking in the ring, in the second round Carpentier landed a strong blow to Dempsey's jaw and it shook the champ. It was not the challenger but the champ who was briefly in danger of going down. Dempsey stayed upright, cleared his head and started to take over the proceedings in the third round.

Three minutes can be an eternity when measuring a single round with one man pressuring another. Dempsey was all over Carpentier in the third round, but he did not knock him down. He did gain the upper hand, and come the fourth round, Dempsey seemed to have learned all he needed to know to polish off Carpentier.

This wearing-down effect took over, as often happens in longer championship fights that end up not lasting as long as scheduled. Dempsey's fists—both of them—caught up to Carpentier's face less than a minute into the round. The left-right combination belted Carpentier to the canvas. As referee Harry Ertle counted, reaching nine, Carpentier struggled to his feet. The challenger beat the count to 10. However, it did him little good. As soon as Ertle told the men "Fight!" Dempsey clobbered Carpentier with both hands all over again and put him on the floor again. This time Carpentier was officially knocked out at one minute, 16 seconds of the three-minute round.

The fight was a sporting success as an event, as a moneymaker and as a milestone, being the first million-dollar gate for boxing. On that day, more fans watched Jack Dempsey pummel Georges Carpentier than watched Babe Ruth beat up on baseballs.

Ruth and Dempsey, who met that year, 1921, and retained an appreciation of one another's skills, were perhaps the two most vivid sporting personifications of the Roaring Twenties. That day, the New York Yankees, still two years from opening their new Yankee Stadium, were on display at the Polo Grounds. The Yanks were involved in a double-header against the Red Sox, one the completion of a previously carried-over game and the other an additional encounter. Ruth bashed a home run in each game. Attendance was reported as 36,000 in New York.

If Ruth could not be present for the fight later that evening, perhaps he listened on the radio. The Dempsey–Carpentier bout was the first widely broadcast boxing match, far eclipsing that little neighborhood attempt in Pittsburgh a few months earlier.

Typical of the ballyhoo, Rickard announced that everyone, coast to coast, would be able to listen to the fight. That would have been remarkable since the technology extended the broadcast only as far away as Ohio. However, it could be heard over a 125,000-square-mile area, quite the increase in territory over that Pittsburgh local fight transmission.

The sportswriters heard from both combatants up close and personal when Dempsey decked Carpentier for good. Dempsey expressed a certain affection for the challenger, saying, "I'm sorry that I had to knock out such a good man." Carpentier, who had mostly kept whatever English-language skills under wraps in the lead-up to the bout, spoke English to Dempsey. "Jack," he called to Dempsey from his corner, bringing the champ closer. "Well done, champion. I congratulate you."[5]

Jack Dempsey had solidified his grasp on the heavyweight crown with his third defense since besting Jess Willard. At the time, no one had reason to think he would not defend the belt again for two years—and then in one of the strangest settings for a major fight of all time.

# 14

## WHERE CAN A GUY GET A DRINK? EVERYWHERE

**B**ACKED BY TEAMS OF HENCHMEN, and such tools as machine guns, pistols and baseball bats, Al Capone was the heavyweight champion of Chicago in the 1920s, the king of Prohibition violations, the primo gangster who ruled the streets.

If they had not been so pathetic, the results wrought by the men and women who strong-armed the approval of Prohibition, supposedly banning easy access to liquor, would have been evaluated mostly as hilarious, bizarre and depressing.

Chicago gangster Al Capone made millions of dollars from illegal booze running during Prohibition and intimidated his competition and the populace.

The do-gooders of Prohibition accidentally invented a crooked industry out of thin air, fell so far short of their goals as to be laughable and gave rise to contemptible, murderous thugs when the innocent only wanted to stop at the corner tavern to down a cold one on the way home from work.

Where there was money to be made, by smuggling whiskey from Canada, by offshore shipping of rum through Florida, those with an evil bent rose up to fill the vacuum. They thrived on ripping off the businessman and the public, and if it took muscle to enforce their policies, they didn't mind bashing some heads or firing bullets into chests.

Prohibition and the Roaring Twenties created Al Capone, one of the most notorious and enduringly famous criminals in American history. Capone, of Italian heritage, was born in Brooklyn, New York, in 1899 and he worked at becoming Public Enemy No. 1, as he was labeled, after a brutal, harsh climb to power in Chicago.

The short version about Al Capone was that he wanted to be the overseer of all illicit money deals in Chicago, especially those revolving around booze, and he didn't care whom he killed to attain the goal. Imported from New York to aid Johnny Torrio's hold on the illegal alcohol market, Capone was an enforcer. It might be said he was chief of security for the bootlegging arm of the business. He was supposed to keep Torrio out of harm's way. But when the kingpin was nearly killed, Torrio decided retirement was his next life chapter and Capone succeeded him and was running the show by 1925.

Capone made it known in the proper circles—law enforcement, politics, the underworld—that he was now the Big Boss, as he liked to be called, but publicly he pretended to be a legitimate businessman. Even as Capone crushed skulls of opponents by swinging baseball bats, a scene basically accurately portrayed in the movies, he conducted press conferences professing his innocence and tried to promote his good name by donating to charities. Rarely are philanthropists anointed with such nicknames as "Scarface," however.

Given that it was a manly sport, it was no surprise Capone was a boxing fan. He liked to work out with boxing drills and sparring, sometimes in a ring at a home in Florida. There is an enduring photograph of Capone with early 1930s heavyweight champion James J. Braddock and a medicine ball. Jack Dempsey tried to keep his distance from Capone, but he knew him and when the Big Boss beckoned, it was wise to at least converse. On a couple of occasions, Capone hinted at injecting himself into Dempsey's career, or fight plans, out of fondness or interest, but there was no proof he ever actually got too involved. At least not beyond an offer in 1919 for Dempsey to box at one of Capone's clubs. That did not happen and that was before Capone came to true power in Chicago.

Barney Ross, who won titles in three divisions, including lightweight, at one time during his hardscrabble early days worked for Capone. In the beginning, Ross wished to make enough money from the ring to buy his family a home and there was some talk before Ross became prominent that Capone bought a number of tickets to help the gate for a bout and give Ross a larger purse.

To whatever degree Capone was a sports fan—and he did attend

Chicago Major League Baseball teams' games—his strongest allegiance and what he was the biggest fan of was running booze. While Babe Ruth was renowned for wielding a big club, one noted for being a 54-ounce hickory bat, but more often a bat in the 42-to-45-ounce range, to slam home runs, it was unlikely Capone waved any stick that large to smash heads.

Whether with his own vicious swings, or his gangster employees firing bullets, Capone had a lot to protect from other bad guys who wanted to infringe on the territory. One account of the 1920s suggested Capone and the Chicago Outfit supervised some $60 million worth of booze, most of it in beer.[1] Many have gone to war for much less. Clearly, the era was mislabeled as Prohibition. It should have been called Permission.

The most outlandish aspect of gangland control of the booze market, besides the creativity in importing the alcohol from Canada and offshore southern islands, was the total corruption of the Chicago and, subsequently, suburban Cicero's police departments and political offices. Capone bought immunity with bribes and campaign contributions and de facto controlled the political and police chief machines on down.

Dissecting Capone's true mindset was probably a waste of time, but in some ways, he probably thought of himself as a businessman supplying a market need. The public was thirsty and he was going to quench that thirst. Just because it was illegal to be in the booze business, so what?

"I make my money by supplying a public demand," Capone said in a rather obvious confession of his illegal work, suggesting that if the average Joe did not want to drink beer, he would not have customers.[2]

It was not as if Capone was seeking to cover up his lawbreaking. But it didn't make much difference, either, since the Chicago police were not in the habit of arresting suppliers or drinkers who were in violation of the Volstead Act unless they did something extreme. Go to the speakeasy, give them the password, go inside and stay there and drink as much as you want, just be quiet about it. Follow etiquette, not the law.

Capone operated on his own set of laws, or rules, and nobody stood up to him about importing and disseminating booze. It was basically hands-off. It was not so different in other places—Detroit, New York, other major cities—but Capone was the capo, the most high-profile dictator of the booze world in Chicago, and what he said went in so many ways.

One of the most remarkable aspects of Capone's booze-running operation of the 1920s was its blatant openness. Over and over again,

Capone would masquerade as just a salesman giving the customer what he wanted. He was brazen and made jokes about bootlegging. Unless an innocent pedestrian was run over by a runaway automobile, or stepped into the middle of a gun battle, the average person might never really notice Capone was not engaged in genteel commerce. Just ask him.

"Public service is my motto," Capone said, as if he polled customers on his company's commitment to first-rate business practices, and, oh by the way, let us know if your order was late. "When I sell liquor, it's bootlegging. When my patrons serve it on a silver tray on Lake Shore Drive, it's hospitality. Ninety percent of the people in Cook County drink and gamble and my offense has been to furnish them with those amusements."[3]

In Capone's mind, or at least in his words, he was just helping to make the good times roll, supplementing the Charleston dancer's vices, helping to define the Jazz Age. Capone was very much a man of his time, even really a man of the moment since his time in the spotlight was fairly short for all of the notoriety he gained.

Surprisingly, perhaps, given the extreme racist nature of the era, Capone seemed to harbor no, or little, prejudice against Black people. He loved the jazz music that predominated and the gangsters that knew him understood his preference. On the occasion of his 27th birthday, some of those imaginative workers kidnapped Fats Waller at the point of their guns, hustled him to Capone's place and required him to play for Scarface.

This party lasted for more than three and a half days, and when it concluded, "Waller was sent home, his pockets stuffed with thousands of dollars lavished on him by a delighted Capone."[4] Waller was luckier than most people who had been taken for a ride by Capone thugs.

Capone loved the nightlife in Chicago, where many of the finest jazz men played, and he routinely lived it up in the clubs, reportedly passing out $50 or $100 tips to those who worked there, from waitresses and musicians to hat-check girls. He had an image to live up to and it wouldn't do to be seen or characterized as a cheapskate.

If Capone made himself tolerated by force, there were still solid-citizen Americans who didn't drink, who supported law enforcement and who even let out a little cheer if someone in the bootlegging world got busted. Not every lawman was on the take.

During the Roaring Twenties, two inconspicuous fellows named Isadore Einstein and Moe Smith, guys who would blend with the crowd, emerged as crimefighters extraordinaire in New York City. In the beginning, when the Volstead Act was introduced, mostly at the behest of rural Americans, the government felt there would be violators to make an example of with arrests and jail sentences. Since social drinking had gone undercover, newly hired government Prohibition Unit agents also went undercover.

The assignment for Izzy and Moe was to infiltrate speakeasies and get the goods on the purveyors of booze. Their first task was to gain entrance to the private clubs. To be admitted past the front door, a drinker had to know someone, or, as has been portrayed in many movies, know a secret password.

In one of his greatest scams, Izzy knocked on the door of a speakeasy in Brooklyn. A peephole opened with the gatekeeper quizzing him on who-goes-there. Izzy gave his real name and when asked who sent him, as in a known reference, he said, "My boss sent me. I'm a Prohibition agent. I just got appointed."[5] The door-blocker laughed, said that was the best approach he had heard and let Izzy in. Izzy kept up the ruse. He even showed off his badge to the crowd, with people exclaiming how much it looked like the real thing.

Izzy repeatedly pulled off that scam, perhaps 20 times, using a variation of an appeal to give an agent a drink. Those on the other end of his con thought he was a comedian. He was an average-looking dude in plain clothes who often carried a fishing rod, a bottle of milk or a jar of pickles with him as average-guy props.

As they got to be better known, and more readily identifiable, Izzy and Moe began donning disguises, sometimes with fake beards, oversize coats and floppy hats. They once nailed 16 bartenders in one hour. Their skits became more elaborate. Once, Izzy stood outside a speakeasy door shivering in short sleeves. When Moe shouted to give this man a drink, they did, and the duo made the arrest.

Ultimately, the expert agents became so popular, their exploits described in newspapers frequently, it became difficult to stay anonymous. Saloons began attaching their photos to the walls behind the bar. But for a time, they were heroes of sorts, if for entertainment value only.

Izzy and Moe were stars in New York, but there were no agents like them roaming the streets of Al Capone's Chicago.

It was probably just as well that the acerbic, sarcastic journalist H.L. Mencken was based in Baltimore for decades rather than in Chicago when Capone was king because the gangster might well have become annoyed enough to have him bumped off.

Outside of the political arena, it would be difficult to find anyone who so loudly ridiculed Prohibition's goals than Mencken, who would have been happy to see an early repeal and the disintegration of the bootleggers' domain in the 1920s. He possessed a bluntness with the pen, as published in the *Baltimore Sun* and a variety of other mediums such as his *American Mercury* magazine, that left little room for subtlety in the eye of the reader.

Mencken repeated his attacks on Prohibition for years, sometimes overall, sometimes looking inward to his home city of Baltimore. He concluded that it took less than five years for all of the arguments in favor of Prohibition to be proved incorrect, that there was more drunkenness than before, more crime than before, more insanity than earlier and the cost of running the government had risen.

Sometimes he just flat out wrote that drinking seemed to be a good thing. "Baltimore is now knee-deep in good beer," he said. "I begin to believe in prayer." Another time he slyly contradicted a comment made by a clergyman that a stranger could just march into any bar in Baltimore and be served promptly. Not true, Mencken said. "You would have to be introduced by a judge, a policeman, or some other reputable person."[6]

There are eras and epochs in history, in sports, by the calendar that people are in the midst of and think will last forever, but they always end, as empires always end, always disintegrate. Leaders change, laws change, sports teams' lineups change. Circumstances in individuals' lives change.

Certainly, no one in the 1920s would have found it easy to envision the heavyweight championship not being tightly grasped in Jack Dempsey's hands, the newly minted Prohibition law not lasting for many years or Al Capone's grip on the flow of booze being ripped from his fingers very quickly.

All of those taken-for-granted aspects of American life seemed likely to endure for a long time, with no changes in the offing. If there were any lessons of history, even recent ones, with the conflagration of World War I erupting in 1914, to the realignment of world powers by 1918, from baseball players playing for one run at a time, to baseball fans admiring a smiling, overpowering king of the diamond who might knock in four runs at a time, all Americans had to do was blink and they might comprehend a swirling, soon-to-arrive future.

# 15

## Tunney Goes to School

Some married couples do not spend as much time in clinches as Gene Tunney and Harry Greb did.

Remembered best for his links to the two wars with Jack Dempsey, in the years following his discharge from the marines, Tunney still had to build a résumé as someone who might be thought of as a potential heavyweight contender. At that point, the only place such a thought had life was in Tunney's imagination.

After his regular appearances in New Jersey juiced up Tunney's record, he began showing his face and fists in different locales, from Madison Square Garden in New York City, to Brooklyn, to Philadelphia, to Grand Rapids, Michigan, to Pittsburgh.

"The Fighting Marine" became better known, gained a bit of a following beyond Greenwich Village and worked on his style and punching power, gaining critical experience. Tunney would tell people one day he was going to beat Jack Dempsey for the heavyweight title, but most likely the majority of the people that heard such a boast thought, "Yeah, yeah."

For one thing, during those first years after his military service, Tunney wasn't even a heavyweight but really a light-heavyweight with its 175-pound weight cap.

At this point in his life, Tunney was quite single-minded. He had his eyes on the bigger prize, fought frequently, sometimes more often than once a month, and was sympatico with managers Billy Roche and then Frank "Doc" Bagley. (Every other boxing person seemed to be called Doc and none of them went to medical school.) As was the custom among clever managers with the wherewithal, they believed in bribing sportswriters to compose nice stories about Tunney and the fighter cooperated in going down that path.

Tunney spent considerable time in Red Bank, New Jersey, his favorite training camp site, and never let himself get out of shape. He was handsome with wavy hair and women were attracted to Tunney, but he seemed to have no major love interest. It was said if Tunney took advantage of nightlife, he did so mostly on the QT, when he was at home, not training, and despite having an alcoholic drink named after him, he was not publicly known as a hard drinker at all.

At one point during his trek through the lineup of men seeking to derail him, Tunney ended up with injured thumbs on both hands. He hardly would have been able to lift a glass if so inclined.

Tunney had been in one bout lasting one round after a six-month layoff from the thumb problems when he appeared on the undercard of the Dempsey–Georges Carpentier Fight of the Century in New Jersey.

He was overweight and not at his sharpest, and while they were not gathered there to watch him, Tunney was on display to the vast array of judgmental sportswriters present for the main event. Not to mention 80,000 other interested parties. Tunney won by technical knockout in the seventh round over Soldier Jones, but the unfortunate form he showed in victory didn't please even him.

"It was a sorry exhibition that I gave that afternoon," Tunney said. "It was particularly disappointing to me because of the number of people who saw it. I was so slow I could not get out of my own way, much less out of the way of the wild swings that Jones was pitching at me. Had I not possessed a rather tough chin, I am convinced that my career would have ignominiously ended that day."[1]

Clearly unhappy with his showing over the tough Canadian born in Quebec, Tunney was exaggerating what a defeat would have meant to his long-term prospects. It would not have been the end of the world but just a simple loss, and he would have gone on from there.

No doubt sportswriters who listened to him opine on the defeat, however, would have been surprised by Tunney's use of the $5 word "ignominiously." The sports scribes did not ever hear the players in the fight game speak in such a manner.

The fighters were stereotyped as "dese" and "dose" guys and the sportswriters perpetuated that image because it was what they were used to hearing and felt that was how the public perceived the purveyors of the violence seen in the ring.

Tunney, as they would gradually come to learn, was different from most. He was not a college graduate and certainly had not matriculated at one of the finest four-year institutions, but he was a devoted reader and had been for most of his life. He learned from books and he devoured books. Sometimes that meant he learned big words.

More so than any other boxer the journalism gods of New York ever encountered, and more so than almost all of the athletes they wrote about, Tunney defied the image that they were all a bunch of dumb jocks. Not only did Tunney read more Shakespeare than the sports pen men, but he could also quote it. They often found that hard to believe, and as time passed and Tunney spent more time with the same writers and flaunted his vocabulary with the flair of the Bard, it was they who behaved ignominiously at times.

In whatever manner Tunney believed he had shown in the ring, by then promoter Tex Rickard sensed the then–24-year-old had the goods and could produce a long-term payoff if he kept winning. Rickard, as all promoters do, needed to keep scouting for fresh talent.

Tunney won three more bouts and then was matched against Jack Burke at Madison Square Garden, The House That Tex Rickard Built. Tunney slashed his way to a win, stopping Burke on cuts. Again, Tunney picked off a couple of more victories and positioned himself for a more meaningful fight on January 13, 1922.

Battling Levinsky, who was born Barney Lebrowitz (some say Lebowitz) in Philadelphia in 1891, would fight anyone anytime anywhere. A very busy man, he officially had 196 wins, 55 losses and 38 draws, and those totals don't include the many fights he competed in under the name Barney Williams beforehand. Levinsky performed most notably as a light-heavyweight and held the championship from 1916 to 1920. Eventually, he was voted into a mix of halls of fame.

Levinsky's reign ended with a loss to Georges Carpentier, though in between he lost a nontitle fight to Dempsey. Although Levinsky was aging and past his prime, he was regarded as a serious test for Tunney when they faced one another in Madison Square Garden with the American light-heavyweight crown at stake.

"Dumb" Dan Moran, who was not so dumb and induced Williams into changing his name to Levinsky, said, "How Levinsky loved to fight. He once fought five times in one week."[2]

When Tunney and Levinsky met at the 175-weight limit, Levinsky goofed up and topped the scale at 176½ to Tunney's 172. Tunney could have won by forfeit but refused the gift.

It was a sold-out Garden and Tunney gave the patrons a show, outboxing Levinsky from the start while mixing harder blows in periodically. A left hook was a big contributor. As the rounds passed, Levinsky bled from cuts over his left eye, his nose and from his lips. Tunney could not finish Levinsky, but he wore him down and won the decision.

Years later, Tunney said that when the 12th and final round began, Levinsky said to him, "Please let me stay, Gene." By that Levinsky wanted the glory of ending the bout on his feet and realized he might not be able to do so if Tunney had gone for the knockout.[3]

Levinsky, however, may well have been playing a psychological trick on Tunney since in midround Levinsky belted Tunney with a right to the chin that carried a kick. Tunney almost viewed that as a deal-breaker, or betrayal of a confidence.

"Then, lo and behold, the Battler lets me have it right on the jaw with a right-hand punch. I felt so foolish, and actually laughed, realizing I had been had by a great old pro. But I declined to respond in kind and let him finish the fight."[4]

Tunney filled his time after that with a few more bouts, including a fight where he knocked down Jack Clifford six times in a dominating demonstration. Then Tunney stopped Jack Burke for a second time.

What came next for Tunney was like taking a step up from English 101 at a nearby state college to signing up for a graduate course in physics. In a match that was prelude to the next level in his career, Tunney put his American light-heavyweight title on the line against Harry Greb.

Greb, one of the most intriguing and greatest all-around fighters of all time, was not a large man but would take on any opponent of any size. Boxing experts who cannot reasonably make what-if comparisons between the biggest boxers and the smallest like to talk of who may be the "best pound-for-pound fighter." Many believe Greb, who was a champion at middleweight and light-heavyweight, to be among those.

An illustration of Greb's guts can be found in the title of a biography of the Pittsburgh native nicknamed "The Pittsburgh Windmill" and "The Smoke City Wildcat." The book was named *The Fearless Harry Greb*.

# 16

## Dempsey, Kearns and Shelby, Montana

One of the strangest episodes of Jack Dempsey's boxing career took place in Shelby, Montana, when he defended his heavyweight crown there against Tommy Gibbons on July 4, 1923.

There was no more unlikely a site for a heavyweight boxing match, a place where the ripple effects of staging the huge sporting event led to dreams of glory colliding violently with the crunch of reality and to bankruptcy of the small town just south of the Canadian border.

A killing of sorts was made in the ring by Dempsey and for the bank accounts of Dempsey and his manager, Doc Kearns, as the bizarre promotion went awry. And yet a century after the widespread bitterness that engulfed the operation, the sleepy town has celebrated its odd brush with greatness and history.

For Dempsey, Gibbons was just another notch on his belt, with the details arranging the bout in a peculiar location and guaranteeing a good payday left to his negotiator, Kearns. Kearns maximized the payoff and Dempsey ensured the results and it was darned certain neither ever passed through Shelby again.

Yet the financial hurt that ensued could also be said to be mainly self-inflicted by local leaders whose eyes were as wide as saucers over what they thought they would reap by the scheme to put the community on the map. For a few months only, Shelby did garner outsize attention, and then it receded to being simply a dot on the map—a small one.

Dempsey needed an opponent. It had been two years since he defended the heavyweight title with the flashy, highly publicized defeat of Georges Carpentier. Promoter Tex Rickard basked in the phrasing of that fight's designation as the first million-dollar gate. However, there was a shortage of legitimate contenders to step up and take their chances with Dempsey as a follow-up fight. Also, Rickard had other problems at the time. He was charged with luring underaged girls to his

Shortly before they began battling for the heavyweight title, Jack Dempsey (left) and challenger Tommy Gibbons met in the ring in Shelby, Montana, on a scorching-hot day (Library of Congress).

New York office for sex, faced criminal charges and was tied up in court. Although Rickard was acquitted, these troubles left him short on time to focus on any type of major boxing promotion.

The way Kearns told the story of the beginnings of the Shelby approach, he was occupied with a babe in a Chicago hotel room when his phone rang. A stranger from Montana, indicating he represented Shelby, was calling to offer him a $300,000 deal to place a Dempsey defense versus Gibbons out West.

Kearns paused his sex life long enough to spell out the terms of any meeting up front. He would talk if $100,000 in advance money accompanied the chat. Loy J. Molumby, the Montana commander of the American Legion, showed up. "I'm here to negotiate," Molumby proclaimed. "I ain't here to play tennis," Kearns replied.[1]

Shelby, which was an oil town and had delusions of becoming a major-league oil boom town, the "Tulsa of the West," was ill-equipped to handle a great influx of spectators. But Rickard had proved it was possible to construct a new, temporary arena out of thin air to host a big crowd.

There were somewhere between 500 and 1,000 people living in Shelby at the time and businesses were scarce, especially hotel rooms, lining its unpaved streets. It was not a Toledo, nor a New Jersey locale a stone's throw from New York. But there was first-rate railroad access, which is how the spectators would arrive to watch the fight. Molumby said, "Oil has brought us some money. Now a Dempsey fight will put us on the map."[2]

These are the types of schemes that often get hatched in bars when those sitting around talking as closing time approaches have had more than their share of liquid refreshment. Frequently, such ideas go no farther than the front door. Once in a while, though, even after people sober up, the plans are pursued. It might be said in retrospect this one should have died aborning. But it did not, beginning with Molumby as the emissary to embarrassment.

This played into Kearns's hands in several ways. He felt he was working with rubes he could outmaneuver. Rickard was not involved in the promotion, so Kearns could show off a little bit, proving his promotional mettle. And Gibbons was the kind of opponent who seemed suitable for Dempsey, with some credibility but probably posing no danger. Oh yeah, and the money was good.

Gibbons was a respected veteran who was 32 years old at the time of the Dempsey fight. He was from Saint Paul, Minnesota, and was a durable boxer who was tough to knock out. More often, if you were going to top Gibbons, it was going to be on a points decision.

A solid guy and a solid opponent, but with Kearns in charge, it was designed for Gibbons to get the short end all around. He was guaranteed no money except for expenses, yet as training camps were set up, Gibbons became the popular favorite in Shelby. He brought his wife and

## 16. Dempsey, Kearns and Shelby, Montana

Champions Park is a small outdoor park with no admission in Shelby, Montana, where Jack Dempsey defended his heavyweight title in a July 4, 1923, bout against Tommy Gibbons and virtually bankrupted the town (photograph by Lew Freedman).

children with him and acted very much like an everyday guy in mingling with the local people.

Dempsey, on the other hand, leaving details to Kearns, was pretty much sequestered. He came off as aloof, which he wasn't, and as segments of the negotiations finalizing the bout were reworked, Kearns played the bad guy. He had demanded advance payments and if things bogged down, he regularly threatened to call the whole thing off. He made Dempsey unpopular.

The remote site, with limited lodging, discouraged many people from arriving too early and the reports from Shelby were erratic and provoked worries the bout would never happen at all. By the way Kearns handled himself, he jeopardized his own promotion.

Problems arose with the Shelby adherents after delivery of the first $100,000 Kearns demanded. Dempsey set up a workout camp in larger Great Falls some 85 miles away, but when the due date arrived for the second $100,000 payment, the Shelby fight committee could not come through. Apparently, the bankers and money men were not as gung-ho as some of those idea men.

Kearns went ballistic. "You've got to pay Dempsey every red cent or you won't see him at all," Kearns said. "Don't take us for fools. I warn you."[3]

Once Kearns began threatening to halt the fight, citizens from Shelby became exceptionally irate. At one point, a group of about 20 traveled to where Kearns was in Butte and essentially implied if the fight did not come off as planned, the mob would do bad things to Kearns and Dempsey, such as tar and feather them. Dempsey came up with the solution. He suggested the final $100,000 part of the guarantee hanging out there be paid out of the gate receipts. This took the iffiness out of the deal.

Meanwhile, after a two-year layoff, Dempsey didn't look particularly sharp during his sparring at his training camp, basically resembling a fighter who hadn't fought in that long. Gibbons was a boxer who might well give Dempsey trouble from a stylistic standpoint, even if he was not likely to unleash a bomb to knock Dempsey out. That meant Dempsey should be prepared for the fight to go the distance, a long 15 rounds.

Even the day of the fight was a fiasco. The temporary arena was constructed, but because of the remote site of the bout and concern about whether it would actually happen or not, practically no one came, first-rate train service or not.

Thinking of how Dempsey drew 80,000 fans to the Georges Carpentier bout, Kearns wanted to be able to house as many people as possible willing to make the trek to Montana. Like Rickard, he set about building his own arena in the shape of an octagon that could hold slightly more than 40,000 fans. He did not know how many might descend on the little community but was sorely disappointed by the turnout on fight day.

Paid attendance was 7,202, though it was estimated another 4,000 people beat the system and sneaked into the vast seating grandstand. As if anyone needed more aggravation, the temperature was in the high 90s that day, closing in on 100 degrees.

Gibbons was an able fighter who got himself ready for this opportunity. He didn't fear Dempsey and he felt he had the style that might out-finesse the heavy puncher. It did not turn out that way. Dempsey may have been rusty, and all of the planning circumstances on Kearns's end may have been a mess, but the champ retained his focus. He was able to put pressure on Gibbons mostly throughout, was not threatened and retained the championship on a decision.

## 16. Dempsey, Kearns and Shelby, Montana

**Metallic silhouette figures act as a town reminder that in 1923, at the behest of the city fathers of Shelby, Montana, Jack Dempsey agreed to defend his heavyweight title against Tommy Gibbons (photograph by Lew Freedman).**

"Gibbons turned out to be a fine defensive fighter," said Dempsey, who described the contest as going "15 long, grueling rounds. He was a perfectionist, not a slugger. For 15 tough rounds, I couldn't corner him to score a knockout. Even though I was awarded the decision in the end, I felt that this fight hadn't done my reputation or my popularity any good."[4]

That assessment was correct. Reading the atmosphere at the end of the fight, Kearns worried the crowd would turn on him, prevent him from gathering the gate receipts and do harm to him or Dempsey due to its pique. After the decision was read, Kearns made swift arrangements for Dempsey to get out of town and scurry back to Great Falls. Kearns did believe there were some people mad enough at them they might be in danger. The boomer planners were not getting what they wanted from the fight, whether it was the crowds for business or the spotlight on the map.

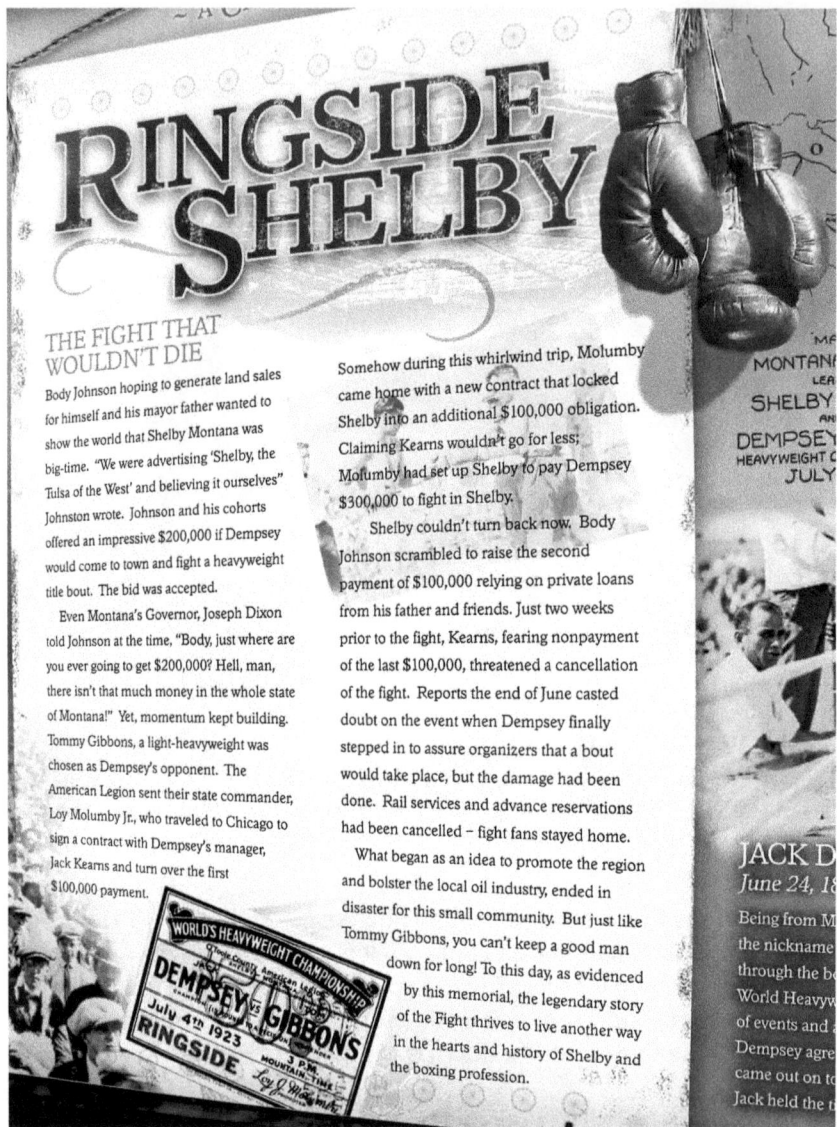

An explanatory sign adorns Champions Park in Shelby, Montana, telling the story of how the small community hosted a heavyweight championship boxing match on the site in 1923 (photograph by Lew Freedman).

Not even to save his skin, however, was Doc Kearns going to flee Shelby without the cash from the ticket sales. He quietly maneuvered to obtain the money, stuffed the cash down his pants and made a run for it—a successful one. Shelby, which had tried to pull off a big score,

## 16. Dempsey, Kearns and Shelby, Montana

Another silhouette figure that portrays the Jack Dempsey–Tommy Gibbons fight of 1923 in Shelby, Montana, a match Dempsey won by decision (photograph by Lew Freedman).

ended up being ruined; the town and four banks were bankrupted. "After the fight, Doc was portrayed as the villain responsible for Shelby's going bankrupt," Dempsey said.[5]

There actually was one more source of major income that Dempsey and Kearns shared in, but also Gibbons. In those days, film rights were sought for such big fights, and that topped $50,000.

Gibbons pretty much understood he might get screwed on a payday from the bout but knew his expenses would be covered and he would get a cut of those movie rights, so he felt it valuable to get the chance against Dempsey. Being chosen for the opportunity was no easy task and it might not come his way again.

"You've gotta eat," Gibbons said. "I have a big family and I have to support them. I fought Dempsey on a percentage basis and he got just about every penny that made its way through the gate. Sure, I took a chance—and lost. What little money I had was deposited in the bank in Shelby, which went bust. What a mess. I did, however, get a vaudeville contract. I had to compete with trained seals to get enough money to feed the wife and kids."[6]

Shelby never did strike it rich through oil. Shelby never did gain major fame through any other big event, either. There has really never been another event that matched Dempsey–Gibbons in terms of prolonged national attention in Shelby. As of the 2020 United States census, Shelby's population was 3,169.

For a long time, residents were bitter about how they believed Doc

Kearns fleeced them, even though their own businessmen and political officials initiated the plan and overshot their aspirations. There was considerable financial hurt.

Sports and boxing historians remember Shelby as the place where Jack Dempsey bankrupted the town. However, decades later, the same kind of boosterism that got Shelby into the fix in the first place began to prevail.

Shelby officials introduced ideas to help capitalize on the cost and failure of 1923. These days—rather remarkably some might say—Shelby commemorates the Dempsey–Gibbons fight in an outdoor, free-access museum called Champions Park.

Displayed are interpretive signs and life-size cutout silhouettes of the fighters and other historical figures made of iron. There is a replica of the ring in the center. Just across the street is the Oyo Hotel, participating in similar fashion with framed black-and-white photographs on its lobby's walls of the fighters and the occasion spotlighted in history.

As the 100th anniversary of Dempsey–Gibbons approached, what did the town fathers of Shelby, Montana, do to commemorate it? Conduct a boxing card. Really. And they ballyhooed all the attention of that heavyweight title fight of long ago. They turned July 4, 2023, into a bigger deal than July 4, 1923.

Shelby threw a Dempsey–Gibbons II party that included a breakfast, car show, firemen's barbecue, dedication at Champions Park, a street dance and a fireworks show. It was reported that nearly 100 descendants of Tommy Gibbons attended the events, some of them traveling from Ireland. Boxing matches were held at the Marias Fairgrounds. They could have played a baseball game, but despite any lingering hurt feelings about the original mishmash, Shelby stuck to boxing for its sporting event choice. There was no mention of any Doc Kearns relatives turning up.

One of Gibbons's grandsons, an optometrist from California, who wrote a book about Shelby and the original title match, was in attendance. Gerard Gibbons said, "Shelby is kind of like the last stand of the Wild West to pull off this audacious dream, to hold a world championship fight in the middle of nowhere."[7]

As part of this centennial celebration, a 10-match boxing card of amateur fights was scheduled in Shelby. The main event featured Tristan Gregori of Great Falls against Ryan Gibbons, Jr., yes, of the same Gibbons family, still hailing from Saint Paul, Minnesota. Tommy Gibbons was his great-great-great-uncle. That Gibbons's brother, named Michael, also fought during the centennial.

These fights were not held in the octagon built for the Dempsey–

## 16. Dempsey, Kearns and Shelby, Montana

As part of a billboard-type display in a small, grassy area in Shelby, Montana, the heavyweight title fight between champ Jack Dempsey and challenger Tommy Gibbons is commemorated by a black-and-white sketch of sorts (photograph by Lew Freedman).

Gibbons fight, which is now the site of Champions Park, but in another temporary structure thrown up for the occasion. Shades of yesteryear on the construction front.

Tickets at ringside for the modern fights sold for $50. Kearns actually priced ringside seats for the title bout at the same amount, and on down to $20. He didn't count on the freebies by the people who rushed the gate.

Unable to envision the future, when sports collectors now abound and items emblematic of sporting events take on extra value with the passage of time due to their historical significance or because of simple nostalgia, no one around a century ago could predict a ticket to Dempsey–Gibbons would simultaneously be available for purchase on something called eBay.

At a time when the centennial was being celebrated, as a present to oneself, a collector could have then bought such an unused ticket for $495.

# 17

# Baseball, God and Moving Pictures

**B**ILLY SUNDAY DID NOT RIG his last name to conform to his religiosity. He was born William Ashley Sunday in 1862 into poverty, and eventually, after his father died and his grandparents couldn't truly raise him, Sunday's mother abandoned him to the Soldiers' Orphans Home in Glenwood, Iowa.

He was 10 years old at the time and subsequently moved on to the Iowa Soldiers' Orphans Home in Davenport, Iowa. By 14, he was working on his own. Although Sunday never graduated from a formal high school, in two ways, totally different from one another, employing totally different skills, Sunday became nationally famous.

One of Sunday's gifts was his athleticism. When it came to sports, he excelled, and against the odds—such odds were high for anyone seeking this type of success—he became a big-league baseball player. Sunday was not a huge man, standing 5-foot-10 and weighing 160 pounds, but he was a good enough outfielder while batting left-handed and throwing right-handed to spend eight years in the National League with the Chicago White Stockings, the Pittsburgh Pirates and the Philadelphia Phillies.

Sunday was fortunate to have a high-profile mentor in Adrian "Cap" Anson, perhaps the top player of the 19th century, whose own hometown was in Iowa. Anson discovered Sunday during a trip back to his roots. Sunday was playing professionally by the time he was 20 years old.

Once he got a chance at the majors, Sunday compiled a lifetime .248 batting average, exhibiting almost no power. In eight seasons, Sunday swatted just 12 home runs and didn't bash many doubles or triples, either. Sunday's chief talent was the efficient way he ran the bases. His fast feet made him a more valuable commodity than his average might indicate. In all, Sunday stole 246 bases during his career with a high of 84 thefts in 1890 and 71 in 1888.

## 17. Baseball, God and Moving Pictures

Besides the daring he showed on the basepaths, Sunday was fleet in covering the outfield with his glove. His was regarded as an ebullient personality, making him popular among teammates. That outgoing nature would serve him well in the coming years once he retired from baseball.

Sunday's last full season was 1890 and by then he had found God and become an exceptionally religious man who began preaching. Soon enough, Sunday acquired the nickname "The Baseball Evangelist."

Then, even in the early days of Major League Baseball, being a ballplayer carried a certain amount of stature in the community and certainly name recognition. No one would have guessed in 1890 that far from being at the peak of his fame, Billy Sunday would be embarking on a new life chapter that by the late 1910s and the 1920s would bring him far more notoriety and recognition.

Sunday was not quite a teetotaler and the Chicago club had strict rules against drinking and partying, which he adhered to as required. Not all of his teammates did, however, and Anson, and the rest of team management, blamed poor field performance on reckless off-field behavior. After the 1884 season, Anson and his cohorts in leadership imposed an even tougher regimen requiring abstaining from booze altogether. This was accompanied by a threat that if a player violated the rules, he would be kicked off the team.

As someone who at most was a sipper, not a drinker, Sunday was fine with these tough regulations. Those who thought the evangelist Sunday never touched a drop of liquor in his life would be mistaken, however. "I never drank much," Sunday said. "I was never drunk but four times in my life. I never drank whiskey or beer. I never liked either. I drank wine." Sunday said when he went out on the town with his teammates and they visited saloons, his order differed considerably from theirs—he drank "lemonade or sarsaparilla."[1]

He already pretty much had the habits of a nondrinker. In 1903, Sunday became an ordained minister in the Presbyterian Church. Whether his talent as a speaker and revival event organizer was aided by name recognition as a former baseball player is not certain, but as the Prohibition movement gained steam during and immediately after the World War I years, Sunday emerged as one of the leading voices preaching in favor of the United States going dry.

Sunday viewed himself as a certain kind of preacher, one who could appeal to men because of his athletic background but who was a loud speaker backing temperance while also seeking salvation through Jesus Christ.

He still loved baseball, though, and thought it was good sport.

While traveling widely spreading the temperance message, Sunday made periodic forays back onto the diamonds. He umpired when asked and at 53 he competed in an old-timers game.

A revival in New York took him back to the Polo Grounds, where he used to play ball, and he spoke about the wonderful reception he received there from the religious fraternity, just as he had as a ballplayer. "I notice you're the same warm-hearted, enthusiastic bunch you used to be when you sat in the grandstand and bleachers when I played at the old Polo Grounds," Sunday said. "It didn't matter if a fellow was on the other side or not. If he made a good play, he got the glad hand rather than the marble heart."[2]

Sunday counted the numbers of souls he saved in the tens of thousands, presumably new commitments to Jesus Christ and new believers in the philosophy that drinking was an evil habit. There were many who could claim credit, or who celebrated when Prohibition was approved in 1919 requiring Americans to holster their shot glasses. Sunday was one of those in the forefront of the movement who could take credit, or be blamed, as many others felt.

Sunday, who married and had four children and never stopped preaching against the ill effects of booze in the 1920s and beyond, remained a preacher for the rest of his life. He passed away in early November of 1935, soon after attending a World Series game between the Chicago Cubs and Detroit Tigers. Sunday still had baseball in his blood, though surely not alcohol.

To illustrate the craziness of the times, Sunday managed to lobby as vociferously as anyone to promote Prohibition, speak on the road constantly as the Volstead Act was failing during the 1920s and outlive Prohibition's repeal.

Somehow, pretty much proving the description itself false, every decade had a sporting event of the century, a crime of the century, a movie of the century and a trial of the century. The events are of grave and great moment when they occur, balloon into massive newspaper headlines, monopolize radio and television coverage and, in the 2020s, of course, generate internet attention.

Most of the time, people just live, go through their daily lives, doing their regular thing, without being distracted by the monumental stuff that gains that something-of-the century designation. In the early part of the 1920s, the Jack Dempsey–Georges Carpentier bout was called the Fight of the Century. Prohibition became the Law of the Century, one might say, since there had never been anything like it before and there hasn't been since.

It might be said that the arrest, prosecution and eventual execution of Nicola Sacco and Bartolomeo Vanzetti, Italian immigrants and anarchists, was the Crime of the Century. The crime of murder they were accused of, the political climate surrounding them and their appeals were suspicious, and the wonder whether a miscarriage of justice was carried out has kept their story alive for a century.

Arrested for a 1920 Massachusetts armed robbery, the men, who really seemed little alike in their political commitments, were tried in 1921 and executed in 1927. The righteousness of their conviction and punishment lingered for decades and with the exception of a very few other crimes of violence of the Roaring Twenties, this case is still readily recalled.

There really was a Trial of the Century, too, the "Scopes Monkey Trial." This case, in Tennessee, pitted religious fervor against science, public education against the Bible. Given the polarization in the United States in the 2020s, it is not so difficult to imagine a rerun taking place in modern times.

The *State of Tennessee vs. John Thomas Scopes* involved no violence but considerable talking and speechifying—and turned into a highly regarded movie, as well. Located in Dayton, Tennessee, the trial from July 1–25, 1925, conducted in scorching weather in an un-air-conditioned building, riveted the nation.

The case revolved around a Tennessee law that proclaimed it illegal to teach evolution in the public schools. Opponents of the extreme position cajoled Scopes into becoming the defendant in a test case, even though the teacher wasn't even sure he had broken the law. The American Civil Liberties Union felt the so-called Butler Act was unconstitutional and ultimately Clarence Darrow, the most famous attorney in the country, was hired to defend Scopes and make the case. Initially, Darrow turned down the work because he felt the scene would be a circus. He reconsidered upon realizing the scene would probably be a circus whether he was involved or not.

Radio was in its infancy, television didn't exist yet and the internet wasn't even in the imagination, so the medium that was counted on all over the nation to find out what was going on was the daily newspaper. Reporters from large papers descended on little Dayton, one of the most notable being H.L. Mencken of the *Baltimore Sun.*

Mencken, who so eloquently sliced Prohibition to bits with his sharp-edged prose, served a similar function with his observations making fun of those who dismissed the advances in science study as inappropriate. Those who put their faith in religion and the Bible for every guidance were offended to hear humans might have descended from monkeys, as evolutionary Charles Darwin suggested.

Of all the scribes, assuredly, Mencken was among the better-equipped to recognize a circus when he saw it and had the ability to convey the vivid images.

"There was a friar wearing a sandwich sign announcing that he was the Bible champion of the world," Mencken wrote. "There was a Seventh Day Adventist arguing that Clarence Darrow was the beast with seven heads and 10 horns described in Revelation XIII, and that the end of the world was at hand. There was an ancient who maintained that no Catholic could be a Christian. There was the eloquent Dr. T.T. Martin of Blue Mountain, Mississippi, come to town with a truck-load of torches and hymn-books to put Darwin in his place. There was William Jennings Bryan followed everywhere by a gaping crowd. Dayton was having a roaring time."[3]

The verbal battles in the courtroom were extraordinary, as they should have been given the stakes. In the end, Scopes was convicted but fined just $100, and his conviction was overturned on a technicality. Bryan, the multi-time candidate for the U.S. presidency, who at times during the overheated (in more ways than one) trial seemed on the verge of imploding, died only days after the case concluded. That certainly seemed to symbolize the changing of an era.

Much later, a play called *Inherit the Wind* made its mark on Broadway, debuting in 1955. In 1960, a highly regarded black-and-white movie called *Inherit the Wind*, with the sting of hindsight and the immediacy of stage presence, was released about the trial. Spencer Tracy played Clarence Darrow. Gene Kelly played Mencken. Dick York played Scopes. And Fredric March played Bryan.

After that, the story was remade additional times for television. There was something timeless in the tale. At times, those who directed or produced wished to revisit the way religion and science sometimes clashed, and at least once the story was intended to be a metaphor about American hysteria during the McCarthy era.

It is rare that a movie of such power conveys the story of a time period and event that is enduring. *Inherit the Wind* was basically all about words, not so much about pictures. When the trial was taking place in real life, the movie world was still in its infancy. The Roaring Twenties was basically still rooted in the era of the silent movie.

The movies were coming on, though, and the best-known actors and actresses who appeared on neighborhood screens were becoming as famous as Babe Ruth, a Jack Dempsey, a Gene Tunney or other individuals the country was just beginning to recognize.

Charlie Chaplin made the United States laugh, along with Buster Keaton. Rudolph Valentino made women swoon. Mary Pickford was

America's sweetheart and everyone wanted to know why Greta Garbo wanted to be alone. Men wanted to date Gloria Swanson and Clara Bow. Douglas Fairbanks and John Barrymore stirred souls. And Lon Chaney made everyone scream with horror.

The public never heard some major stars speak and others transitioned into talkies seamlessly. Ironically, if you were a star in one realm, promoters wanted to put you on stage in vaudeville, in the theater or in movies.

Rough, tough Jack Dempsey, the powerful slugger who ruled the ring, had a high-pitched voice that did not play well in the movies. It didn't hold him back much. Soon enough, Dempsey, previous claimant to sharing the label of the Fight of the Century, would team with Gene Tunney as a main star of a newly anointed Fight of the Century.

# 18

# MEETING HARRY GREB

**H**ISTORY IN A BROAD-BRUSH VIEWING of the Roaring Twenties tells us that Gene Tunney's greatest boxing rival was Jack Dempsey. Dissection of history, with intense scrutiny, in more of a vacuum, might tell us differently.

Truthfully, Tunney's greatest rival in the ring was Harry Greb. To Tunney, Greb was the mosquito that just wouldn't go away, the nemesis that spoiled his unblemished record, the opponent who always seemed to have the best chance of figuring out Tunney's defense.

Boxing aficionados know the name Harry Greb. They are aware of his accomplishments and skills. And it is to Tunney's credit that when challenged again and again on his climb to the top, he was able to best Greb when he had to do so.

The average sports fan of the 2020s has little or no knowledge of Harry Greb, but it is guaranteed that Gene Tunney never forgot him. Harry's crime was that he was too small to be taken seriously as a heavyweight contender at a time—which has been most of the time, actually—when heavyweights were all that mattered to the boxing public.

Oh, fans may have loved watching Greb dance and move and pummel away, but unlike the heavyweight champ, which at this time of the 1920s was Jack Dempsey, he didn't fit the bill as the behemoth with the big punch. Greb was much-admired, but unlike Dempsey, who wore the mantle of being the toughest man in the world by virtue of owning the heavyweight crown, Greb was not going to scare a big truck driver or laborer who used his muscle on his day job.

Greb stood just five-foot-eight. He weighed as much as he had to weigh to fit into a convenient boxing division as a welterweight, middleweight, light-heavyweight or even a heavyweight, which was fundamentally ridiculous, although he owned a heavyweight heart.

Starting in 1913, Greb took on all comers at any weight class and usually he beat them. He was scared of none of them and his lopsided

## 18. Meeting Harry Greb

**Harry Greb's greatest success came in lighter weights, but he did not shy away from battling heavyweights and he delivered Gene Tunney's only loss of his career.**

nose, the recipient of overhand rights and left-hand jabs from men of all sizes, bespoke of his toughness. It was a nose that had been around.

Greb was anchored in Pittsburgh, but he got around, too. His nicknames reminded those meeting him where he was from. He was called "The Pittsburgh Windmill" because of his wild punching ability, or "The Smoke City Wildcat," harkening to the city's then-industrial base and Greb's attitude toward opponents in the ring.

If anyone wished to study Greb's training habits, they would be at a loss. He practically never took time off to heal from his paying fights, so who needed to train in between? In 1917, Greb fought for real 37 times, the most on record of any boxer, but typical of a man who on the record fought about 300 times.

Eliminating no-decisions, it is likely Greb's lifetime record was 261 wins, 16 losses and 19 draws. At different times, Greb owned the world title belt in the middleweight division and in the light-heavyweight division. That windmill reference was due to Greb's swarming style when he might bury a foe with punch after punch coming from the left or right side—make that the left and right sides.

*The Ring* magazine and individual boxing historians have lavished praise on Greb over the decades in terms of his overall stature in the fight game. Reviewing boxers of all generations and fighters from all weight classes, Greb routinely comes out in the top five all time as pronounced by just about everybody.

Since Greb was never really a heavyweight, Tunney did not ever have to face him, yet Greb was so omnipresent and his reputation so formidable, and Tunny presumably had a weight advantage, so it would have looked bad if he ducked him. Instead, it felt bad whenever they collided.

Tunney, who mostly had Dempsey on the brain, faced Greb for the first time on May 23, 1922, in Madison Square Garden. At stake was Tunney's American light-heavyweight crown. Greb came in weighing 162 pounds to Tunney's 175 and the bout was scheduled for 15 rounds. Greb had defeated Tommy Gibbons to earn the chance at the regional crown and at Tunney and really had his eyes on a world title fight against Georges Carpentier, who then possessed that 175-pound crown.

It was Dempsey, of all people, who had the clearest image in his mind of what Greb could do to a man, and when he was interviewed before the fight, he said, "Funniest hitter in the world. He makes you think you're in a glove factory and shelves of them are tumbling down on you. He can slap you to death, I tell you."[1]

Dempsey knew what he was talking about because he had sparred with Greb. Thinking the smaller man would present a no-sweat challenge, Dempsey was taken aback by Greb's elusiveness and abilities. Dempsey knew he would never have to take on Greb for real, and he was glad of it.

At this point in his career, Tunney was unbeaten. An hour after meeting Greb up close, that was no longer true. Greb demolished Tunney, slicing him to bits. While the fight went the distance, the decision was not close, with Tunney being granted only a few rounds on the points. He was cut in the nose, the mouth and above both eyes. Some at ringside claimed Tunney lost two quarts of blood, although any way of

## 18. Meeting Harry Greb

measuring that would be suspect. The first blood was drawn, however, in the first round.

Practically overwhelmed from the start, Tunney did land some solid body punches in the fifth round, but Greb regained his command the next round. Greb, as was his wont, rarely let up and although Tunney was not knocked out, he was lucky to be standing when the final bell rang. Even before the decision was made official, Tunney congratulated Greb, telling him he won.

Tunney then told the world how Greb beat him. "He was never in one spot for more than a half a second," Tunney said. "All my punches were aimed and timed properly, but they always wound up hitting empty air. My arms were plastered with leather and although I jabbed, hooked and crossed, it was like fighting an octopus."[2]

Tunney bled all over the canvas, and Greb's gloves were regularly wiped clean by referee Kid McPartland. Cries of "Stop the fight!" rang out from Garden fans appalled by how Tunney looked. Grantland Rice reflected on what he witnessed with vivid commentary, saying, "Greb handled Tunney like a butcher hammering a Swiss steak."[3]

Whatever the volume of blood sucked out of Tunney by Greb's fists, he was weak enough from the beating that he had to be helped to his dressing room after the bout. Abe Attell, the one-time bantamweight champion rehabilitating his image after his loose involvement in the Black Sox Scandal World Series fix, was a friend of Tunney's manager, Doc Bagley, and showed his face in the locker room while acting cheerier than Tunney felt he should be. "Kid, you're the gamest fighter I ever saw," Attell said. "I lost $2,500 on you, but to hell with it."[4] Apparently Attell saw the makings of a future champion in Tunney's guts standing in the way he had.

When the fight ended, promoter Tex Rickard, a seize-the-moment type of guy, sent a communication to France trying to make the match for the light-heavy title with Carpentier for a $150,000 guarantee. Greb and Rickard were turned down.

It took two hours for Tunney to regain enough strength to be aided out of the Garden. He had intended to head to nearby Greenwich Village to the family home, but one look in the mirror informed him that was a poor plan. His parents would freak out if they saw him all cut up, so Tunney went to a hotel.

Regardless of mathematically how much blood Tunney actually lost, he definitely had his confidence shook. Overnight he went from undefeated to wondering about his future. It was not as much of a shock to the rest of the world—Greb had been favored 3–1 in some betting quarters—as it was to Tunney that he lost. The sheen of invincibility was lost and especially for such a cerebral fighter, Tunney had to take time and analyze what happened, why he lost, why Greb had been able to dominate.

Perhaps the most remarkable element in this bout was the status of Greb's fading vision. He had gradually been losing sight in his right eye. During an era when physicians' reviews of boxer's health under the auspices of state-backed commissioners was sketchier, a fighter could hide an ailment and still box. If boxing was his livelihood, he didn't want it taken away. Greb, very much an independent soul anyway, hardly told anyone he was losing his vision, which would have gotten him sidelined.

It did not become known until later that by the time Greb met Tunney, he was basically blind in one eye, making his achievement even more astounding, if not foolhardy for his own well-being. But that was Greb, cocky to the extreme, and basically able to back up that outlook. He had never even seen Tunney fight before and yet that didn't worry him at all. On this fight night he proved he was by far the superior man with his fists.

Yet the strangest part of the immediate aftermath of the bout was how the two protagonists came to think of what transpired.

Afterwards, Greb was with friends at a speakeasy, though it was said he drank only ginger ale while he was dancing until dawn. But when his pals commented about how easily he handled Tunney, he contradicted them. It may have appeared easy, he said, but, "it wasn't an easy fight. It was my hardest. I was so arm-weary and leg-tired from trying to knock Gene out, I was in almost as bad shape as he was."[5]

Tunney, who received numerous stitches and was too embarrassed to go home and show his face, told anyone who would listen in his little group—and they all thought he was crazy, from Doc Bagley on down—that in the middle of the fight, even though he knew it was too late that night, he figured out he could beat Greb a second time around.

There he was, bleeding all over the floor, and in his head, he was explaining to himself that hey, next time, Harry Greb, you better watch out. It made no sense to his friends, especially since there was no fundamental reason, besides Tunney's pride, that he had to face Greb again at all.

Of the 13,000-plus fans in Madison Square Garden, plus those sports-writing experts and Tunney's entourage, not one of them would have envisioned a Tunney–Greb II turning out differently. Nor would any of them, looking ahead, have believed the two combatants would engage in four more such battles over the coming years.

# 19

## HORSES AND OTHER HEROES

**I**T IS SOMETIMES TIMING, sometimes an unusual spark, but there is no way to truly predict the way lightning strikes to make what could otherwise be an overlooked figure in history a superstar of the moment that lasts forever.

Man o' War was basically the first Thoroughbred racehorse worshipped by the masses—and that was without even winning the Kentucky Derby, the greatest horse race on the planet.

The horse that accomplished this feat ended up competing with humans for the title of the greatest athlete, and much later, long after the animal retired from racing and passed away, received recognition as one of the greatest Thoroughbred racehorses of all time.

To be sure, by the end of the 1900s, there was serious competition from many quarters, not the least being Secretariat, Affirmed (who engaged in the greatest two-horse duel with Alydar throughout all three Triple Crown races), Seabiscuit, Citation and Seattle Slew.

One difference between a beloved horse with fleet feet and a baseball player, a boxer or another human star is that the horse needs someone to make decisions for him and to speak for him. The flip side of that was a certain purity attached to the horse, whose only job was to run when called upon, run like the wind and win with the run.

The chestnut Man o' War won 20 out of 21 races in a two-year racing career during 1919 and 1920. His size and coloration helped endear the horse to Thoroughbred fans and he gained the nickname "Big Red." He also had a white star and stripe on his head, making the horse's appearance stand out distinctively from afar—easier to cheer for, it might be said.

The only question about Man o' War from reviewing history in hindsight is what Big Red might have done in the Kentucky Derby at Churchill Downs. The horse's owner, Samuel Riddle, did not believe in racing horses the 1¼ distance early in their careers as three-year-olds, so he held Man o' War out of that most prestigious of races. Still, soon

Man o' War, one of the greatest and most popular Thoroughbred race horses of all time, was the dominant four-legged sports star of the Roaring Twenties.

enough, Man o' War was entered in the Preakness Stakes in Baltimore and the Belmont Stakes in New York and won both of those events.

During an era when payoffs were much lower than they are in the 2020s, Man o' War's prize money from the track was a smidgeon under $250,000. The horse won nine out of 10 starts in 1919, the only loss coming at Saratoga Race Course, beaten by a neck by a horse that seers might have bet on because its name was Upset.

Man o' War won eight stakes races in 1919, including the Belmont Futurity, a highly rated event for two-year-olds, and besides the Preakness and Belmont in 1920, the horse won the Jockey Gold Cup and the Travers Stakes. The original intent was for Man o' War to continue racing in 1921, but when it became apparent that officials were going to force the horse to carry much more weight as a four-year-old, Riddle changed his mind and turned Man o' War out to stud.

There was something about Man o' War in full stride that inspired people. He was poetry in motion and muscle on the fly, a beautiful animal captivating the human eye, a horse in full flower of speed that made people fall in love with him.

"There never lived a horse that was more horse than he was that afternoon," said Ray Dickerson, the assistant starter for the 1920

Travers. "He was so beautiful that it almost made you cry, and so full of fire he made you thank your God that you could come close to him. No horse ever lived who could have beaten him that afternoon."[1]

Trainer Louis Feustal felt lucky to guide such a horse. "He had speed, stamina, courage and heart, and he broke most of the existing records of his day," Feustal said. "I was his trainer, and I can truthfully say there has never been another horse like him. He was the kind of horse from which dreams are made."[2]

Appropriately enough, owner Samuel Riddle had a favorite story to tell about his favorite horse. It went like this: "Upon seeing him in action, a railbird asked a groom 'Who's he by?' meaning the horse's genealogy." The reply was, "He's by himself, and there ain't nobody gonna get near him."[3] The funniest part of the tale was the follow-up. When Man o' War retired to stud to produce more race horses, Riddle named the first progeny "By Hisself."

Man o' War won the Belmont by 20 lengths, but had already won the Lawrence Realization, a now-defunct race that was an important one a century ago, by an astounding 100 lengths. That race attracted just one other entry, Hoodwink, on September 4, 1920. Man o' War set the clocking record for 1 5/8th miles in that event, a record that was tied 40 years later by Kelso.

Man o' War lived for 30 years, until 1947, and a life-size statue of the horse adorns the grounds at Kentucky Horse Park in Lexington, Kentucky.

Human athletes could only dream of the adoration heaped upon Man o' War, but it was beginning to happen for them as the Roaring Twenties took hold.

Babe Ruth had it happen for him, with his own little nudge, creating a persona, a fantastical character for the public to consume, mostly from his actions on the baseball diamond, though in contrast to Man o' War, he could aid and abet his own legend by speaking outside the playing field.

Ruth was appreciated as a superb southpaw pitcher but then came the home runs. It was his weaponization of the game as the king of clout that created the Ruth who is remembered as the greatest slugger of all time.

No matter that he wore silk shirts and changed them several times a day; carried thousands of dollars in his pockets for impulse buys; reportedly ate, drank and was merry every waking minute when he wasn't playing baseball; was the idol of American youth and apparently every woman he came into contact with, too—it was the home runs that guided the story.

People don't even remember that Ruth led the American League in home runs twice while playing for the Boston Red Sox. Being sold to the New York Yankees, where he switched to the field full-time and gave up pitching, is what led Ruth to make his mark. Baseball insiders commented, "I wonder how many home runs he would hit if he played every day," and Ruth did, too.

Before you knew it, Ruth was playing every day and seemingly hitting a home run every other day. No one had seen the explosion of such power. The true ascent of Ruth into stardom can be dated to the 1920 season when he slugged 54 home runs.

Jaws dropped, eyes blinked wide. No one had seen anything like that before. Besides also driving in 135 runs and batting .376, mighty fine numbers in themselves, it was the home runs that dazzled. When Ruth smacked his 29 in 1919, that was a Major League Baseball single-season record. By hitting 54 the next season, Ruth's production boggled minds.

Entire teams during their 154-game schedules did not hit as many home runs as Ruth did individually. As the decade changed to the 1920s, before everyone realized what a lively ball in manufacture might mean in terms of offensive production compared with the now-dead dead-ball era, fans and other players still thought of a home run as a rare occurrence.

Ha. Not for Ruth. Not for the Sultan of Swat, one of the slugger's many nicknames, such as the Bambino and more.

In 1920, when Ruth hit his 54 home runs, the team with the next closest total was the Saint Louis Browns with 50. The leaguewide average for the American League was 46. In the National League, the Philadelphia Phillies did hit 64 homers to exceed Ruth's total, the only team in that circuit, which averaged 33 home runs per club. No wonder the rest of baseball was astonished by Ruth's killer home run stroke. It was as if Ruth was zooming around at 60 mph while everyone else was puttering along at 25 mph.

Ruth's was such an unfathomable performance that no one believed they would see the likes of that again. Of course, they were wrong. The very next year, in 1921, Ruth embellished his own record by hitting 59 home runs. He was swinging for the sky while others were trying to hit ground balls up the middle for singles.

The occasional injury or illness caused Ruth to miss some games, so he did not bash 50-some home runs every season. However, in 1927, when the Yankees assembled "Murderers' Row," whom some consider the finest team of all, Ruth broke his own record with 60 home runs, a record that lasted until 1961. Somewhat overlooked was that in 1928

## 19. Horses and Other Heroes

Ruth accumulated more than 50 home runs in a season for a fourth time when he clubbed 54.

By then, eight years into the decade, as Ruth had become the most dominating force in baseball and one of the most famous Americans in the country, the home run was here to stay and other players were adapting and learning how to become power hitters.

Yet none of those superstars, not even Lou Gehrig, Jimmie Foxx, Hack Wilson and the others who finished in the top 10 in seasonal home runs, often challenged Ruth for the annual home run title. Often, he still doubled their totals. Beyond that, none of the other greats of the game at the time attained his fame in the 1920s. The Roaring Twenties roared around him as he posed for every picture requested, signed every autograph sought and winked at every young fan and pretty woman he came across.

Babe Ruth had turned hitting home runs into an art form, completely transforming baseball, which had been teetering from distrust created by the fixers of the 1919 World Series. He swiftly morphed from man to legend.

"You know, I saw it all happen from beginning to end," said Harry Hooper, who was a Red Sox star when Ruth broke in. "But sometimes I still can't believe what I saw: This 19-year-old kid, crude, poorly educated, only lightly brushed by the social veneer we call civilization, gradually turned into the idol of American youth and the symbol of baseball the world over—a man loved with an intensity of feeling that has perhaps never been equaled before or since. I saw a man transformed from a human being into something pretty close to a god."[4]

Swimming, except in the modern era during the Summer Olympics, has never been much of a spectator sport, but once in a while a transcendent figure rises up. Mark Spitz and Michael Phelps won so many medals and set records people who couldn't even dog-paddle took notice.

Yet years before their heyday, one stroke-master of the Roaring Twenties became a household name. When it came to water, Johnny Weissmuller was the master of the waves. Over the course of the 1924 and 1928 Olympics, Weissmuller won five gold medals in swim events and repeatedly set world records. Then, also for kicks, it seemed, he was part of a bronze-medal-winning water polo team.

Americans never tired of admiring Weissmuller's muscular chest. After his competitive days ended, he became the movies' Tarzan, making 12 of those films over a 16-year period ending in 1948. He also starred in 16 movies playing a character called Jungle Jim and followed that eight-year stint up by acting in a television show based on the same

Jungle Jim figure. He was vastly popular, even if he didn't speak on film much more than Man o' War did at the track.

If citizens knew of one swimmer, it was Weissmuller, who won 52 national championships and set 67 world records in the pool. And that was without Jane's assistance. Weissmuller caused a sensation in one early Tarzan movie by appearing wearing what was said to be only a fig leaf. Those films featuring a wild man of the jungle didn't require much dialogue, but anyone who ever heard Weissmuller's Tarzan yell never forgot it.

If Man o' War helped kick off the decade, and the 1920s truly belonged to Babe Ruth and pretty much Jack Dempsey and Gene Tunney as they worked toward their own denouements, overall it was a good decade for sports idols of several kinds.

While there is not a specific claim that truly explains the origin of golf, there are adherents who refer to the sport being created in Scotland during the Middle Ages, with the game in particular being referred to from 1297 on. Fast-forward to the Royal and Ancient Golf Club of Saint Andrews, and the spread of the game recognized today through the British Empire and the United States burgeoned in the second half of the 1800s.

One of the heydays of expansion of the sport took place in the 1920s. In 1910 there were 267 golf courses counted in the United States, and shortly after the end of the Roaring Twenties there were 1,100.

Those who enjoy putting can thank Walter Hagen and Bobby Jones for their ascension on the world stage to boosting the popularity of the game during that era.

Hagen, born in Rochester, New York, in 1892, in 1922 became the first American to win the British Open and also won the U.S. Open twice and 11 majors. He came to be known as "the father of professional golf," not an honorific he would shy away from since he began contributing money to his family budget from working as a caddie for 10 cents a round before becoming a teenager. When he was not carrying others' bags, and hoping for nickel tips, he played the game himself and developed his skills.

During that time period, the be-all of the sport did not rest with professionals but more so with amateurs who looked at their calling as a higher form of competition. There were many rules in place at different golf clubs that made it tougher on visiting professionals, and as he worked to raise the stature of professional golf, Hagen faced them all and had to fend off decisions that put him at a disadvantage while competing.

Sometimes he was not allowed to use clubhouse locker room

**Although he refused to turn professional, Bobby Jones uplifted attention on golf and designed the course at Augusta where the Masters is played.**

facilities to change and prepare and he was known to rent a car for his portable locker room. At one British Open, Hagen was not allowed to enter the club through the front door. His effort and success in various tournaments led to rules changes at some of the snootier clubs.

Hagen was a superb player and he flashed a sense of style wherever he traveled, including wearing dashing clothing. He became a key product endorser for Wilson Sporting Goods' golf line, was the first player to win $1 million and, by staying on the go at the same time he honed his own skills, spread the word about the game of golf in hundreds of exhibitions.

Hagen won 58 tournaments, 45 of them Professional Golf Association events, including several PGA Opens and the Western Open when it was virtually a major. In later decades, such publications as *Sports Illustrated* and *Golf Magazine* rated him as one of the top eight players of all time.

In the 1920s, besides being the top professional golfer, Hagen was the front man for everlasting change that helped the common man breach the country clubs that would have shut them out.

There was tremendous irony in the 1920s competition between Hagen and Robert Tyre Jones, Jr. One was the ultimate pro and the other the ultimate amateur. As influential as Jones was in the history of golf in the United States and during the 1920s, he clung tenaciously to his amateur status as a player, at least between 1923 and 1930 before he played professionally in order to participate in the Masters annually over a several-year period.

As a player, Jones won the U.S. Open four times, the U.S. Amateur six times and the British Amateur once. While a golfer, Jones attended college, graduated from law school and became a lawyer, his primary occupation.

Jones, later famed as an equipment endorser for Spalding, still in competition with Hagen, was from Georgia and helped build the Augusta National Golf Club and founded the Masters golf tournament in the 1930s.

Unlike the other heroes of the 1920s sporting firmament, Jones remained an amateur in his sport for the duration, never accepting a paycheck for playing. While he became famous for his accomplishments, he did his best to duck the limelight. Jones could be one of the boys on the course, lose his temper over mistakes, but mostly was regarded as a decent sort who avoided scandal and retained his amateur purity as a player despite numerous opportunities and urgings for him to go pro.

Strangely, Jones was not in any way against professional golf. He enjoyed the company of the pros and even liked playing against them. He just didn't want to be one of them.

"I love to play against the pros, match or medal," Jones said. "I found there was the spur of competition, and masters of the game who were all set to drub me—and usually did. When I manage to beat them, I am inordinately proud."[5]

Whatever dichotomy lived within Jones's mind, the same man who chose not to play pro was paid as a company man to sell golf equipment, make films about the game and help design the most famous course in America.

When he did play, amateur or not by designation, Jones could be a fierce competitor who hungered to win. During the U.S. Open of 1923, at Inwood Country Club in Inwood, New York, Jones, then 21, had a big lead and then watched over the last holes as it seemed to be slipping away.

Everyone told him he had the crown in the bag, but with a contender, Bobby Cruickshank, still on the course, Jones refused to accept the good wishes. Sure enough, his own bogeys and a rally from Cruickshank left them in a tie, calling for an 18-hole playoff.

The next day, on they went, up and down, good luck and bad shifting, good shots and poor ones occurring, until finally they were deadlocked again on 18. His foe went first and made a double bogey, leaving Jones with a chance to clinch things right there.

Jones was not conservative. Still perhaps angry at himself for blowing a big lead, he wanted to prove something. His longtime caddie, Luke Ross, glanced at the self-belief written on Jones's face and his quick decision to go for the win. "Honestly, I think he'd have knocked Jack Dempsey out with a punch if he had been in the way of this championship," Ross said.[6]

Jones struck the shot perfectly, and he and the crowd watched with anticipation and fluttering hearts as the ball flew, landed by the hole, bounced off the flag and stopped rolling six feet from the cup. Jones putted his way in and won his first major championship by two strokes; fans carried him off the course on their shoulders.

That is how legends are made.

# 20

# A Champ at His Leisure

In the 1920s, being heavyweight champion of the boxing world conveyed a status on a man that is difficult to imagine a hundred years later. The belt as a prize was the biggest individual honor in sport, and with the mythology of the man wearing it being the toughest man in the universe added in, it created immense celebrityhood.

Dempsey, with his very dark, black hair, firm physique and easy manner when interacting with strangers, was a handsome man who appealed to women. When he and Doc Kearns embarked on a cruise to Europe in 1922, visiting England, France, Belgium and Germany aboard the *Aquitania*, the trip was chronicled by Damon Runyon, the scribe who like Dempsey was from the West and had also struck it big in New York.

Travel by steamship was an invitation to publicity, far from the anonymity that would be offered to later celebs winging their way thousands of miles in a few hours by jet plane. The boats took their time crossing the Atlantic and the passengers reveled in their journeys being accessorized by public figures.

In a peculiarity of the era, though perhaps of the same type of coverage a film crew might have brought to the scene somewhat later, newspapers detailed the comings and goings of the ocean liners and announced who was aboard in their pages.

Such personages as Dempsey were meat for the grinder of those simple reports. It was a thing to do for folks to go down to the docks and wave bon voyage. Rather strangely, though, it could have been a calculated move by the fighter or his manager, Luis Angel Firpo, the Argentinian heavyweight who was angling to move up the rankings, showed up in the mob and managed to maneuver his way up close to Dempsey. In a sign of hubris, respect, publicity seeking or just what, it wasn't clear, Firpo planted a Euro kiss on each of Dempsey's cheeks as a send-off. "I had no idea who the hell he was," Dempsey said.[1]

Whether it was for Dempsey's benefit, or just part of the scene, a bevy of showgirls were part of the send-off festivities, also, and Dempsey didn't have any idea where they came from, either. Newspapermen urged him to kiss willing women who were actresses and dancers, then blew up the exaggerated relationship in faux gossipy stories.

Aboard ship, Dempsey, who was single and very eligible at the time following his unfortunate marriage to Maxine, became the object of some young ladies' attention, which he appreciated when he wasn't preoccupied with seasickness, something he feared.

Before the liner, carrying about 1,500 people, departed, Dempsey actually shouted (in what became something of a movie cliché later), "Give my regards to Broadway!"[2]

Even if Dempsey had no impending fight, he did not simply laze about during the journey. He ran five miles on the ship's decks in the early morning and did some basic workouts. He also sparred at times with one of his regulars, Joe Benjamin, on the journey.

The Dempsey who as a youth and young man had skirted poverty, if not been engulfed by it at times, mentally compared his stateroom with the boxcars he had ridden, then, once in England soaked up every sight as an enthralled tourist.

While on vacation, Dempsey virtually advertised for a European contender to step up and face him in the ring, combining on a first-person story dispatched by Runyon. Kearns said a couple of opponent offers had been floated, but they were not to be taken seriously.

In France, Dempsey visited the Louvre and even got a personal tour of Paris from his old rival Georges Carpentier. Dempsey crossed paths with some of those American expatriate writers, notably Ernest Hemingway. Although there is a vagueness about their encounter, they apparently did not hit it off. It almost sounded as if Hemingway, 23 at the time and someone who fancied himself somewhat advanced with his fists, wanted to have a go at Dempsey. That did not happen, but years later in a reference to the author, Dempsey said, "I would have really had to hurt him."[3]

In Berlin, Dempsey and Kearns witnessed a boxing show featuring all German females who worked in a café. Rather than being at all titillated by the event, Dempsey found it distasteful and did not enjoy the scene. He diplomatically commented that he supposed he preferred boxing himself rather than watching others fight.

After this voyage that Dempsey so much enjoyed, he was still not much closer to finding a foe for another title fight. There was talk of a rematch with Jess Willard, but no hunger for it. There was discussion about fighting Carpentier again, but no groundswell for that. Some boxing experts thought Dempsey should give a title shot to Harry Greb, but naysayers pointed out Greb was really just a middleweight. There was lobbying for Dempsey to take on Harry Wills, but there was no will from promoter Tex Rickard to make the match with the Black fighter. He worried greatly about a public unrest in protest as was evident during Jack Johnson's reign and he didn't want to be the man facilitating that.

As a humorous aside, with no sporting news to write about Dempsey and his title, the papers ramped up their fake coverage about his love life. Becoming increasingly sophisticated in how he handled the press, when speculation about whom Dempsey was dating and romancing broke into print and he got sick of it, he invented a response. He told writers that he was going to get married to someone they had not heard of before.

Setting their pens all aflutter, Dempsey declared the love of his life to be a Helen Rockwell, a 19-year-old student at the University of Colorado. The writers bit on this tidy tidbit and their newspapers blasted out headlines telling the world Jack Dempsey was succumbing to matrimony.

However, when Dempsey saw how the newspapers reacted, he burst out laughing among friends, who also quizzed him about the mysterious Helen. "Helen Rockwell doesn't exist," Dempsey told them. He made her up to fool the writers.[4]

No Helen Rockwell stepped out of the woodwork to place her arms around the heavyweight champ, and that was the end of that. Dempsey's next big date was in California, where he traveled to visit his mother at the house he had purchased for her there.

Around this time, in 1922, Nat Fleischer, who became a legend in the boxing world, established *The Ring* magazine, the Bible of boxing that became a must-read across the sport.

Early on, Fleischer advocated for Dempsey to at last fight Harry Wills, the six-foot-two, 220-pound boxer who had anxiously been kept on ice because he was Black. Fleischer said Wills was a very different type of person from Jack Johnson (as if that should have mattered). Still, it was important for some that the two men be differentiated.

Other newspapermen began chiming in, as well, backing Fleischer's point of view. Mostly, they were all trying to kick-start some activity in the heavyweight division, Wills if for the lack of anyone else.

Eventually, Kearns and Dempsey agreed to make a match with Wills. There were holes in the deal, such as where the fight was to take place. It never happened and this was as close as Wills came to obtaining his chance at the crown.

# 21

# THE CRAZIEST FIGHT OF ALL TIME

THE THING ABOUT THE HEAVYWEIGHT title is that once you win it, you've got to defend it sooner or later. It is not a crown bestowed on you for life like being named king. No one doubted Jack Dempsey earned his way to the title, but that didn't give him the right to paralyze the title indefinitely.

Other boxers, the public, even Dempsey himself really, were all getting edgy and anxious. The heavyweight champion was not retired, he was in limbo. There were few, if any, suitable fighters in the ranks who deserved a shot at the title. But one of these days, Dempsey was going to have to line up someone in a risk-the-crown match.

Time was passing. Years were passing. Dempsey became heavyweight champ with his destruction of Jess Willard in July of 1919. Then he polished off Billy Miske in 1920. In 1921, he overpowered Georges Carpentier. At least for the third defense, promoter Tex Rickard promoted the heck out of the conflict, got fight fans excited, turned the match into a memorable occasion.

Then Dempsey did not fight for two years. If the promotion of the Tommy Gibbons fight in July of 1923 was actually a fiasco for Shelby, Montana, it was a legitimate fight and Gibbons went the distance.

Now those calendar pages were beginning to turn again. At this moment, it wasn't so much that the gap was significant compared with the recent one, but that there seemed nothing on the horizon, no opponent standing out, no location, no date for a next title bout.

And then, finally, there was. Luis Angel Firpo made himself relevant. Born in 1894, Firpo, who had thick, sometimes wild hair and a large physique, was from Argentina and emerged as the first Latin American to challenge for the heavyweight crown. Firpo stood more than six-two and in some photos presented smoldering good looks that would have made Hollywood scouts happy to put him in film. Like all

**When Jack Dempsey faced Luis Angel Firpo in a heavyweight showdown, their first round became one of the most memorable in boxing history. Firpo knocked Dempsey out of the ring, but Dempsey knocked Firpo down seven times. Artist George Bellows painted the scene.**

boxers, in and out of the ring, in and out of training, Firpo's weight fluctuated. He was loosely described as a 200-pounder, but by the time he met Dempsey in the ring, he weighed in at 216.

Firpo came to the United States bearing a fabulous nickname that must go down in boxing annals as one of the best ever. He was called "The Wild Bull of the Pampas." It didn't matter if hardly anyone had a clue what the Pampas were—it sounded great. The reference was to local plains grassland where Firpo was from, but it didn't really matter since none of his American fans were going there or had been there. The musicality of the moniker just added to his mystique. He wasn't just another Bill from the Bronx.

During the early stages of his career, which is natural, Firpo fought close to home in Argentina, sometimes in Buenos Aires. Interestingly, his backers lured Gunboat Smith to Argentina for two bouts, back-to-back, about five weeks apart in the spring of 1921. Smith was rated as one of the better heavyweights of the moment and had taken on

Dempsey. Smith lost to Dempsey and faced 12 Hall of Famers in a career in which he won 52 bouts, and what he offered with a victory was credibility and confidence to Firpo.

Fighting in Argentina, it was not easy for Firpo to gauge his true talent and judge whether he was a real somebody in the division or just an isolated home-grown product. In early 1922, Firpo made the journey to the United States to test himself and build his reputation.

His American debut occurred on March 20, in Newark, New Jersey, and he knocked out Tom Maxted in seven rounds. Good start, but the win did not yet prove much. From there, Firpo began adding to his résumé, stopping Joe McCann in New Jersey and Jack Herman in Ebbets Field, home of the Brooklyn Dodgers, and beat Jim Tracey back in Buenos Aires.

Then Firpo got serious. In a scheduled 15-rounder at Madison Square Garden, he stopped Bill Brennan in 10 rounds. At Yankee Stadium, Firpo knocked out Jack McAuliffe II in the third round of a slated 15-rounder. Boxing fans were starting to recognize that Firpo had thunder in his fists and might be someone important to watch, and maybe sooner than they had thought.

After that, appealing to his Hispanic supporters, Firpo kept his knockout stretch going when he took out Herman for a second time, in two rounds, in Havana, Cuba. Then he KO'd Jim Hibbard in another second-round finish in Mexico City. Whatever Firpo's first language, it was clear he could speak loudly with his fists.

It still was not obvious if Firpo had the right stuff to meet Dempsey for the title. Enter Tex Rickard. After Dempsey removed the crown from his head, leaving him a bloody mess, Jess Willard said he felt there was no reason to talk about a rematch.

Willard receded into the background and everyone believed he was retired and was going to stay retired. Instead, even though he was now past 40 years old, he mounted a comeback. Willard discovered he missed being heavyweight champ. And it wasn't as if the field was thick with worthwhile candidates. He probably figured one really good victory would put him in line for another crack at Dempsey.

When Willard returned to Kansas after losing to Dempsey, he addressed a crowd of hometown well-wishers. "Boys," he said, "I am out of the fight game and now a plain business man."[1] Actually, he was more farmer than businessman as the role is thought of today. There have been many, many such retirements by prominent fighters who later changed their minds about giving it one last go in the ring. They forget how hard training is and how much punishment the body takes.

Although much time had passed, and despite Willard's declaration, he wasn't 100 percent all in on the retirement thing after a year or so. He met with Rickard to talk about a rematch with Dempsey, and when Dempsey was asked about it, he was amenable to giving him one. Willard wasn't making as much money in Kansas as he thought he would, so his mind was not closed to fighting again. Nothing came of that Dempsey rematch idea, though.

Willard attended a match at Madison Square Garden, and when he was introduced to the crowd, he drew a nice cheer. That buoyed his spirits. Willard was trying to be more of an oilman than a farmer, but now he had the itch to get back into the ring, with Dempsey or not.

There was considerable talk of a rematch with Dempsey, but Dempsey was also facing some pressure to fight Harry Wills. Time dragged on and Willard kept scheduling exhibition matches as part of a vaudeville tour. He may have fooled himself into believing he had more left in the tank than he did.

Finally, Willard scheduled another real fight. On May 12, 1923, nearly four years after his divestiture of the title, Willard scored a technical knockout over Floyd Johnson at Yankee Stadium. Floyd Johnson was not to be confused with Jack Johnson, but it was a legit win.

After that, Willard signed to meet Firpo at Boyle's Thirty Acres in Jersey City. Willard, it should be remembered, was six-foot-six and weighed in at around 240 in his farmer's overalls. Rickard billed the fight as an elimination bout with the winner to face Dempsey. If Firpo was for real, this was his chance to show it.

Rickard, being the salesman that he was, hyped the match well. Besides labeling the contest "The Battle of the Giants," since they were the two largest dudes in the mix, Rickard talked up Firpo's ability. "Why, he's the nearest thing to [former champ Jim] Jeffries I ever looked at," Rickard said.[2] Whatever value that had in ticket buyers' minds, it is difficult to fathom for sure, but Rickard's role was to pump up the volume.

New York would have been the first choice of venue, but as part of what seemed to be New York's ever-changing regulations, the state decreed it would license no one to fight in the state who was older than 38. Willard claimed to be 36, but in reality, he was turning 41. One reason New York placed that age limit in these arbitrary rules was to take aim at Jack Johnson. Johnson had served time in prison and was out and looking for work. He was also 45 years old. Being Black was still being held against him.

Willard did fine-tune his body, lose weight, add muscle and get in solid shape to meet Firpo. Both men had the incentive hanging in front of them of a promise of a title bout. At one point, Jack Johnson was paid $250 to act as a sparring partner for Firpo. Even at his so-called advanced age, Johnson retained enough speed and skills to dance around the ring and make Firpo miss with his biggest shots. Johnson may well still have been as legitimate an opponent as anyone else.

Rickard proved once more that given half a chance to sell a decent match in Willard–Firpo, he could unleash his skills as a premier salesman. Tickets were in great demand for the New Jersey fight, and approximately 100,000 people shelled out to watch two sluggers— a huge crowd, though seats were priced low, from $15 down to $1.

Firpo came out attacking, trying to get the quick knockout. Willard held him off. There was much back-and-forth in a generally even battle for some time. Firpo took charge in the seventh round. Then, in the eighth round, Firpo connected with a big blow, put Willard on the canvas and he was counted out.

That was the last time Willard fought for pay. So, it was Firpo who prevailed, Firpo who survived and Firpo who gained the title opportunity against Dempsey.

There was a lot of dithering in the Dempsey camp. Doc Kearns wanted to promote rather than rely on Rickard. He also didn't want Dempsey to fight more than once a year so that each gate would be sufficiently hyped, and he didn't think there were many worthy contenders out there anyway to satisfy. Dempsey wanted to fight more often. He liked his job and he was good at it. For a time, Kearns shopped a Dempsey–Wills fight around the Midwest but had no takers. The political times, especially with the rise of the Ku Klux Klan in Indiana and nearby states, were stacked against the bout.

Interestingly, around this time, Kearns also compared Dempsey's power to Babe Ruth's. Just as no one really knew when Ruth would clobber a pitch, no one knew when Dempsey would penetrate a challenger's defenses and land a big blow on his chin. In both cases, Kearns said, fans responded to the sports heroes' creation of "an air of anticipation."[3] Sooner or later, Ruth and Dempsey were going to lower the boom.

Drawing 100,000 fans for a nontitle fight between Willard and Firpo was quite the accomplishment. It showed there was a hunger in the public for good matches and maybe even particularly so if heavyweights were involved. Firpo took Willard out of the picture for good, and if he was not quite a well-known quantity yet, he was at least a fresh face. He was also a big man for the times.

Firpo had appeared as an unknown from Argentina, but by knocking out all comers in the United States, he had established himself. He had been seen. He also had been analyzed. It was conceded the man had a big punch. Questions arose about the slickness of the rest of his offensive package and his defense. Could he move well enough to stay out of trouble if an opponent was pelting him with dangerous blows? Some critics claimed he was a clumsy boxer who lacked those talents.

"Firpo had a terrific right-hand blow, that could stun a bull, but most observers believed it could be avoided easily," Dempsey said. "I took descriptions of Firpo's clumsiness with many grains of salt."[4]

Rickard, when it came to promotion, knew what he was doing. Firpo's eliminating Willard as a viable contender boosted the public fascination with Firpo. Rickard said, "The public's goin' to be so anxious they'll be willing to put a mortgage on the old homestead just to buy a ticket."[5] Hyperbole? Certainly. A strain of truth gauging the mood? Yes.

Still, no one who bought in for the Dempsey–Firpo fight anticipated what they got.

The intrigue was sufficient to draw 86,000 fans to the Polo Grounds in New York for the September 14, 1923, bout that lives on in legend. Since Dempsey weighed in at 192 pounds, Firpo outweighed him by 24 pounds. That was not a factor in Dempsey's mind because he had overcome an even larger weight disparity against Willard. Firpo had taller hair, but even without it, he was still an inch and a half taller than Dempsey.

One of the most famous boxing paintings of all time, if not the most famous, came out of the Dempsey–Firpo fight, a virtuoso artistic effort by George Bellows (1882–1925). It depicts, in its drama and savagery, one of the most astonishing moments in heavyweight boxing history. What a war it was. What a fight it was. What extraordinary action was contained in the first three-minute round alone.

After the bell clanged starting the fight, Dempsey was the one who acted like a wild bull, charging straight for Firpo to demonstrate what real power was like. In his over-anxiousness, Dempsey slipped and basically put himself down. Nonetheless, his big blows were penetrating Firpo's attempts to deflect rather easily. Pow! Down went Firpo. Boom! Down went Firpo again. Wham! Another Dempsey swing decked Firpo. It didn't take long, but Dempsey had knocked down Firpo four times in about half a round, making everyone wonder what all of the fuss had been about.

Dempsey, in white trunks as Firpo wore black, was too swift for the challenger and kept pounding him with short, hard rights, repeatedly dropping him. The number of knockdowns reached seven, though Firpo was up either without a count or a very quick one most of the time. The exception was the sixth knockdown when Firpo went down flat, rolled over on his back and did not appear to be capable of rising in time to beat a 10-count from referee Johnny Gallagher.

However, Firpo made it back to his feet and then, firing wild punches in rage or desperation, got Dempsey against the ropes. The Argentinian unloaded a short, hard right that caught Dempsey on the jaw and Firpo aided his cause with a little shove, and stunningly, the champ fell through the strands of ropes out of the ring altogether.

Dempsey plummeted directly into the laps of his good friends the sportswriters, startling them. Dempsey quickly clawed and climbed his way back into the ring, with perhaps a boost of some of those men, but did so quickly, making it to the end of the round.

The combination of Firpo being belted to the canvas so frequently and Dempsey being knocked out of the ring made for perhaps the most surreal, historic and astonishing single round in boxing annals.

The pace was a little bit slower in the second round—it had to be—and Firpo seemed firmer on his feet until a combination from Dempsey knocked down the challenger for an eighth time.

Going toe-to-toe, the men continued, each throwing heavy leather. Only Dempsey's was heavier and the ninth time he knocked down Firpo, the challenger again rolled onto his back and seemed unlikely to get to his feet. This time Gallagher counted out Firpo to end the bout in the second round. As soon as the match was declared over, with Firpo still on his knees, Dempsey rushed over from his own corner and helped his opponent to his feet and to his own corner in a gesture of caring and sportsmanship rarely seen in a ring.

Dempsey finished Firpo after nine knockdowns, some of them accomplished immediately after others since at that time fighters did not have to retreat to a neutral corner before the ref began a count.

The rules did state in a case where a boxer is knocked from the ring he must reenter it under his own locomotion or be declared the loser. Gallagher had reached a nine-count on Dempsey during his exit from the ring. Although several sportswriters, partially because they wished to remove Dempsey's sweaty body from their own, claimed they helped Dempsey back up, it remained vague what truly transpired when Dempsey went flying.

Many years later, when he was penning an autobiography, Dempsey summed up the Firpo fight by noting it lasted just three minutes and 57 seconds, "but those minutes were damned tough ones. Every blow Firpo landed staggered me. He seemed to live up to his nickname as he kept charging and pawing. Nevertheless, I managed to floor him seven times in the first round. But he wouldn't stay down—the lust to kill was burning in his eyes, and nothing was going to stop him."[6]

In this version of those crazy seconds out of the ring, Dempsey said that sportswriter Hype Igoe, one of the most prominent New York writers of the time, "was nearly demolished by my fall. I don't remember climbing back into the ring, but I remember seeing about 20 Firpos standing in front of me."[7]

That all illustrated just how hard Firpo hit Dempsey, and Dempsey said he also remembered mumbling to Doc Kearns asking what round he had been knocked out in. Over the following years, Dempsey gained much amusement from hearing, one by one from several of those seated at ringside, about how their typewriter broke his fall and how they each helped send him back into the ring as if he was a fish caught and released.

In the end, it was a stiff challenge and Dempsey survived it. The phrase "He lived to fight another day" comes to mind on this one as the heavyweight champ's scrape was a close call but permitted him to keep the crown.

Except for the artwork, and the legend of the amazing first round, Firpo faded from the scene, moving back to Argentina, investing his payoffs wisely and eventually growing his land holdings to 205,000 acres.

Dempsey was about to invest in matrimony again—and divest himself of manager Jack "Doc" Kearns.

In 1957, more than three decades after they met in the ring, Firpo threw a huge party at one of his ranches and Dempsey was not only invited in an expression of the bond that linked the men, but he also made the trip south for the festivities.

## 22

## The Serum Run

**S**TOP A PEDESTRIAN ON THE STREET in Denver, Phoenix, Chicago, Orlando or Nashville these days and mention the Serum Run and a blank look will come upon the faces of 99 percent of those quizzed.

"The Serum Run" is how it is quite simply called in the state of Alaska, but a century after a most dramatic event that was front-page news across the country and has been commemorated in various manners since, it is not only old news but more so forgotten news across most of the land.

Alaska itself had practically faded from American consciousness in the nearly three decades since the Klondike Gold Rush of the 1890s by 1925. This throwback event of drama and heroism stoked fresh thought about the Last Frontier when dog teams and mushers answered a plea and rushed lifesaving medicine to the old Gold Rush town of Nome to help keep its children alive in the face of a diphtheria epidemic.

This was a situation where the populace, millions of Americans spread across the country, were riveted to whatever news source they could devour as they coped with the suspense of learning whether men and dogs battling extreme storms and mushing against the clock could reach Nome in time to deliver the all-important remedy.

Citizens in New York, Chicago and everywhere else might have been mostly focused on beating the system of Prohibition to down the alcoholic drinks of their choice,; young women were inhaling their first cigarette smoke and with their partners were boogeying to the Charleston; Babe Ruth was smoking home runs with clockwork; and Jack Dempsey and Gene Tunney were on a collision course to try to smite one another.

Arguably, though, most Americans were distracted and enthralled by the "Great Race of Mercy," as the carrying of the serum was also called, from any of those other comparatively frivolous pursuits.

Alaska was far away, mostly inaccessible and still mysterious to most other Americans once the Gold Rush died down and stopped wooing adventure seekers chasing riches. It was "up there," somewhere close to Canada, and it was always cold and wintry. Alaskans prided themselves on being self-sufficient anyway.

This was a half century before the Iditarod Trail Sled Dog Race, the so-called "Last Great Race on Earth," got started, and the only thing those other Americans "Outside," inhabiting other states, knew about dog mushing was what they might have seen in old black-and-white pictures, had reported back to them from Grandpa's visit to the Far North after returning from the Gold Rush and any book on investigating lands of ice and snow or trying to climb 20,310-foot Mount McKinley, since renamed Denali.

Although there had been a number of high-profile competitive races of 400 miles or so called the All-Alaska Sweepstakes between 1908 and 1917, which went out of business at the start of the United States' entry into World War I, the sweepstakes had little publicity outside the territory. In its own way, Alaska and its wintry environs were as alien to most Americans as Africa. The Siberian huskies and malemutes used as work dogs seemed as alien as putting a team of lions to work hauling goods.

No one anticipated the type of emergency that mobilized the populace and in a magnificent confluence of circumstances turned hardy mushers and their determined, savvy dogs into national heroes.

Even in the 2020s, there is no road to Nome for someone with a modern truck to drive. Nome can be reached by jet plane or ship. Or, as is proved each March with the running of the Iditarod between Anchorage and that Bering Sea community, by dog team.

Obviously, dog teams operate over snow, breaking their own trails or trotting over cleared ones. Nome and its surrounding area suffer from harsh winters, feet of snow, howling winds and frigid temperatures, all of which remain features of the Iditarod race at irregular intervals.

In that way, Nome can very much be an isolated place. It comes with the region and anyone who lives there understands that is one characteristic of the place. In 1925, before air travel was much developed, Nome was supplied by visiting large steamships, but by November, when the Bering Sea froze, the community became icebound.

Nome was incorporated as a city in 1901, and during Gold Rush days some estimated the population hit 20,000. After gold petered out for individuals tying to stake their own claims, the population thinned, as well, to about 2,600 in 1910. In recent decades, only about 3,500 people have lived there.

## 22. The Serum Run

In the mid–1920s, there was just one doctor in the community, Dr. Curtis Welch, and four nurses to help him minister to the sick. In December of 1924, Welch realized his supply of diphtheria medicine had passed its expiration date and he placed an order for more. However, the ice of the Bering Sea closed in and the medicine did not arrive. That meant no antitoxin could be delivered until spring when the port became free of ice again.

In January of 1925, within weeks of Welch's discovery, he began receiving child patients that he thought were suffering from sore throats, or perhaps tonsillitis. At first, there was little sign of contagion spreading to other family members, so initially Welch felt things were under control.

That outlook did not last. First one child, then a second one, showed signs of diphtheria. Welch tried to use the expired medicine as an antidote, but both children died. The children of the community, perhaps especially those of the Native population, had only a few years earlier suffered so much during the influenza outbreak. Welch informed mayor George Maynard of his fears of a deadly epidemic and the town council convened.

Aviation was in its infancy and there were no planes flying to Nome. Many of the early machines could not take off, land easily or restart if temperatures reached minus-50 or the like, a genuine threat. These days, with modern jets, it is a flight of only a couple of hours from the big city of Anchorage to Nome, but in 1925 it was no sure thing that a plane seeking to deliver diphtheria serum would even get through. Besides, the only three planes in the vicinity had been taken apart for the winter season.

Then came a proposal to try to bring the medicine to Nome via dog team from Nenana, a rail stop 675 miles from Nome. One sled team would depart Nenana and would be met in Nulato, the halfway point, by a second team coming from Nome. A musher would receive the medicine and turn around and dog-team-it to Nome. Welch worried that under extraordinarily cold conditions the serum would be good for only six days.

Meanwhile, as 1.1 million units were being scrounged up on the West Coast to be sent to Seattle, some 300,000 units in storage in Anchorage were uncovered. These units were the vanguard of what was shipped to Nenana in glass vials to be used in order to hold the disease in check until reinforcement medicine could make its way north.

At that time, the leading dog musher in the world was Norwegian transplant Leonhard Seppala, who had won three All-Alaska Sweepstakes championships and was regarded as an expert trainer of Siberian huskies. Seppala was assigned the task of mushing from Nome to Nulato, relying on his main leader, Togo.

The route from Nenana was an established mail trail. That was how the mail got through to Nome in winter. It was a challenging job, and the mushers who performed that task were regarded with admiration and appreciation.

The race against time—and for life—included 20 mushers and about 150 dogs. The serum arrived by train in Nenana on the night of January 27, 1925, and was handed to mailman-musher "Wild" Bill Shannon at 9:00 p.m. as the temperature did plunge to minus-50.

As newspapermen passed the word to their hometowns of the progress of the dogs and the 20-pound package of serum, more and more radio stations spread information, too, exciting the American population. Shannon mushed 52 miles in all. He suffered facial frostbite and three of his nine dogs were severely injured in the cold, badly enough that they subsequently died.

Over the last days of January, the mushers and dogs advanced, generally in increments of 30 or 40 miles. Seppala, meanwhile, then 48 years old, mushed 170 miles from Nome as far as Shaktoolik (these days a checkpoint in the Iditarod race) to receive the serum while using his 20 best dogs. At times he faced a strong wind, but with mainly Togo showing the way, Seppala mushed another 91 miles to Golovin to hand off the serum to Charlie Olson. Seppala's 261 miles covered was by far the most of any musher.

Newspapers around the country were producing banner headlines about the rush to Nome for riveted readers. On the front page, the *Cleveland Plain Dealer* reported, "Nome Takes Hope as Dogs Draw Near." The *Seattle Post-Intelligencer* headline read, "Dogs Winning Race with Death to Nome."

Yet that was an optimistic headline. Dr. Welch kept reporting to mayor Maynard as other youngsters checked in for treatment. Maynard sent telegrams to figures in Fairbanks and Washington, D.C., that stated, "The situation is bad. The number of diphtheria cases increasing hourly."[1]

As mushers and dogs labored, politicians in Nome and around the state tried to increase pressure on other governmental entities to authorize a plane to fly some units of serum from Juneau to Fairbanks and then on to Nome. That idea was never carried out.

Olson mushed 25 miles and gave the package to Gunnar Kaasen. Kaasen, 42, ended up carrying the serum the rest of the way to Nome, 53 miles, on February 1. He drove 13 of Seppala's backup dogs, including a previously unheralded leader named Balto.

## 22. The Serum Run

Balto was the lead dog when the serum reached Nome and as a result was heralded as the king of the trail, even though that was hardly the truth. Didn't matter. With a story of this magnitude, with the entire nation listening and watching, it was easy to label Balto the No. 1 hero dog. "Damned fine dog!" Kaasen was heard to praise Balto when they reached Nome.[2]

The serum delivered by dog team was sufficient to hold back diphtheria so it did not become an epidemic in Nome. Plus, more medicine was rushed in by other traditional means of transportation. Lives were spared and the disease quelled. Disaster was averted.

The nation rejoiced. Seppala was miffed that Togo did not receive the credit due him, particularly before the aging dog's death in 1929, and despite Seppala's position as the owner of Balto and Togo. To commemorate the Serum Run, a statue of Balto was erected in Central Park in New York. When Seppala moved to Maine, he brought Togo with him and the sled dog gained his own renown—and was immortalized there with a statue.

More than anyone else, Seppala, the dog trainer, understood Togo's value. This was the leader who deserved more credit than any other dog on Seppala's 261 miles of the Serum Run, the one that guided him and the other dogs across treacherous Norton Sound as they transported the lifesaving medication.

Seppala expressed anger when newspaper stories attributed things Togo accomplished to Balto. "In Alaska, our dogs mean considerably more to us than those 'Outside' can appreciate," he said, "and a slight to them is as serious a matter to their drivers as if a human being's achievements were overlooked."[3]

Kaasen took Balto on tour to an adoring public. Seppala took Togo on tour and then raced dogs in New England and developed a breeding program out of Maine. Balto and other dogs from the team lived out their lives at the Cleveland Zoo. After Togo died, the body was shipped back to Alaska and it was ultimately put on display at the Iditarod Trail Sled Dog headquarters in the city of Wasilla.

There have been books written about the Serum Run and movies have been made about both Balto and Togo.

Seppala, who also participated in the sled-dog exhibition sport at the 1932 Winter Olympics in Lake Placid, New York, died at age 89 in 1967. The last surviving musher from the Serum Run was Edgar Nollner of Galena, Alaska, who died at 94 in 1999.

The Iditarod race annually presents a humanitarian award to a musher at the conclusion of the race. It is permanently named after Leonhard Seppala.

For a few days in 1925, against the backdrop of a weird, energetic and unusual decade, Americans paused to focus on a dramatic emergency thousands of miles away as men and dogs banded together to save youngsters and halt the transmission of a deadly disease.

# 23

# THIS GUY GREB WON'T GO AWAY

MOST PHOTOGRAPHS OF THE movie-star-handsome Gene Tunney show him with beautifully coiffed hair, firmly in place. None of those pictures, however, were snapped right after Tunney climbed out of a boxing ring following one of his hand-to-hand combat wars with Harry Greb.

The smaller but devastating Greb did more than muss up Tunney's hair when they fought. Their first fight, which many believed would be the only one after Greb took Tunney apart and won a brutal decision, mussed up Tunney's hair, face and entire body.

As someone working his way up the rankings to gain consideration for a shot at the heavyweight crown, the then–175-pound Tunney had little to gain and little reason to fight the 162-pound Greb a second time, never mind several more times.

Except that he wanted to fight Greb again. Call it redemption in his own mind, but Tunney was super-motivated to meet the Pittsburgh Windmill in a rematch whether it made business sense or not. Tunney had astonished his friends later on the night of the first Greb bout by saying he wished to battle Greg again and he was certain he would win.

That pronouncement was just talk, his friends felt, since Tunney had shown zero indication in the ring on April 10, 1922, that he knew how to handle Greb. They thought, based on the bloody evidence from the beating he took, that Tunney was nuts, even delusional.

None of them suspected, including, no doubt Tunney and Greb themselves, their rivalry would become one of the most memorable in the history of the fight game, and nor could they have predicted the results.

The second meeting between Tunney and Greb took place on February 23, 1923, at Madison Square Garden in New York. Greb never thought he would lose to anyone. He searched out bookies and bet on himself to win. Tunney's confidence was supreme given that he had been whipped so thoroughly the first time around.

One difference for Tunney in preparation was the addition of former world champ Benny Leonard to his team to offer strategic advice against Greb. He suggested going to the body to slow down the Pittsburgh Windmill. Diminution of Greb's concentration was not something that was specifically cited in the Tunney camp, but Greb's young wife, Mildred, just 22, was in failing health and bedridden and he worried terribly about her and spent all of his free time with her.

Once again, the American light-heavyweight title was at stake. The weight spread in the second bout was not so dramatic, either, Greb at 166 pounds, Tunney at 174. Tunney landed good hooks to the stomach that scored points and kept Greb off him.

For all of Tunney's improvement over the 15-rounder, although unofficial, in a poll of 23 newspapermen at ringside, 15 of them said Greb won the decision, four gave the nod to Tunney and four thought they saw a draw. However, the official result going on his record was a decision victory for Tunney. To those sportswriters' eyes, Tunney–Greb II was more of the same as Tunney–Greb I, though not quite as extreme.

Tunney performed better, but Greb never retreated and seemed to take control in the middle rounds before Tunney rallied. "They told me in my corner I was losing and that if I wanted to win, I would have to capture the remaining rounds or knock him out," Tunney said.[1]

There was a lot of booing among the nearly 15,000 spectators in the arena when the winner was announced by split decision.

Nat Fleischer of *The Ring* may have been more clear-eyed. He called the scene the way he saw it: "It was a spectacular affair that had 15,000 persons—a packed house—at a high pitch of excitement from start to finish. The marine carried off the unanimous decision of Judges Charles E. Miles, Charles Meighan, former sports editor of the New York Morning Telegraph, and referee Patsy Haley after one of the stormiest ring encounters seen in the Garden since boxing was revived in New York.

"Pandemonium reigned when the decision was announced by Joe Humphreys and for a time, the police were kept busy quelling riots in various parts of the arena. The Pittsburgher's friends felt that he had been jobbed, but those who watched the bout closely, saw no basis for complaint.

"Sharp as was the division of opinion among the boxing fans as to who won, there was just as sharp a difference of opinion among the newspapermen. Some agreed with the official verdict; others felt that the least Greb should have gotten was a draw, and still others believed that Greb had won. Yet the officials voted unanimously in Gene's favor and that was sufficient to gain for him the title he had lost almost a year previously to the same 'Pittsburgh Windmill.'"[2]

When the results were read to the crowd, Greb jumped up and down in his corner in frustration. Then he let loose with his feelings. "I was jobbed," Greb said. "It was all fixed for the title to be handed back to Tunney."[3] Given the division of opinion on the result, it was apparent this was a close one.

A few weeks later, Greb's wife passed away. The underlying disease was tuberculosis, but she may have had pneumonia at the end, too.

Given the controversy, and perhaps to settle things in his own mind with the score between the men now being one–one, Tunney, who had his own doubts about the legitimacy of the most recent decision, agreed to fight Greb a third time, on December 10, 1923.

"I was given the decision at the end of 15 rounds," Tunney said of the second meeting. "Realizing there was some justice in Greb's claim of a bad decision, I offered him a return engagement."[4]

Never one to rest much or stay idle, and perhaps also fending off the grief over the loss of his wife, by then Greb had fought twice more. He knocked out Len Rowlands in June and then, on August 31, lifted the middleweight crown off Johnny Wilson's head with a knockout.

For most fighters, especially those competing today, that would have been enough. They would focus on protecting the 160-pound class. Not Greb. He felt he owed Tunney and he had that chip on his shoulder of something to prove, to himself and to the world.

While Greb was coping with the death of his wife, Tunney took himself on a working, or working-out, vacation in the Maine woods. He spent time hunting and fishing, but he also ran and walked and seemed to enjoy chopping wood.

Above all, Tunney was conscious of needing the mobility to keep going for 15 rounds if a foe pressed him. He was known for his boxing ability and he recognized the importance of backpedaling. In the original *Rocky* movie there is a famous line delivered by actor Burgess Meredith, Sylvester Stallone's trainer: "Women weaken legs." Whether Tunney believed that or not, he did believe it was critical to build leg muscle. "My legs were the mainspring of my operation," Tunney said. "I never lost sight of it."[5]

In addition to heeding Leonard's idea of going to the body more, Tunney was ready to apply what he believed he had learned in the first fight when he was getting batted around like a pinata. He had spied that Greb dropped his shoulder when he threw a right hook. In theory, that should provide openings. Also, Tunney's current manager, Billy Gibson, requested that the New York State Athletic Commission emphasize its rules against headbutting. Gibson felt Greb got away with a lot in the ring and he wanted the officials primed to penalize him if he pulled that stuff on Tunney again.

Anyone who had seen Greb fight knew he was no choirboy. Greb was going to try to get away with anything he could get away with in between his rapid-fire punches.

The commissioners did not seem pleased to be lectured. On the day of the fight, the chairman, William Muldoon, had a crafted reply in the *New York Times*. "So far as I know, there is nothing foul in Greb's boxing style," Muldoon said. "If there were, he would have been disqualified long ago."[6] Of course, the intent of Gibson and Tunney's camp was to make the public aware of their feelings, making a case in court, for the referee and judges.

Despite his learning curve, despite studying tactics, Tunney still couldn't easily get the best of Greb in Tunney–Greb III. Tunney fought better, but Greb fought well. Greb got away with holding Tunney with one hand and hitting him with the other. Tunney's cornermen complained. Then Greb opened a cut over Tunney's right eye leading up to the 10th round.

One of Greb's best rounds was the 11th. He belted Tunney with a big blow that caused the larger man to pitch forward a bit and grasp him in a clinch. The Windmill's arms were whirling and landing good shots to Tunney's head. Tunney's energy seemed to be sapping. Was Greb going to take him down late?

Beginning with the 12th round, however, the Tunney camp's prefight messages seemed to reach referee Patsy Haley's mind and he began admonishing Greb for trying to headbutt in the clinches. "Don't do that," Haley said. "Don't do that."[7] Those types of warnings can lead to the deduction of a round point from a fighter's score.

Tunney kept up his relentless body assault in these later rounds, but in the 14th, he scored big with a right to the jaw that rocked Greb. When the final bell clanged, both men were still standing, worn down, but upright. Once more, a Tunney–Greb mini-war was ruled a split decision, in favor of Tunney.

And once more there was loud controversy other the result. Many of the enthusiastic fight fans believed Greb won and they took out frustration on Haley, the ref being the decider between the two judges. Angry pro–Greb backers sought to assault Haley as he left the ring and soon after the bout there was a threat to his life. One thing Greb could do was inflame the passions of his fans. The sportswriters, too, seemed to back Greb as the winner of Greb–Tunney III, though only some referred to the results as being as egregious as Greb–Tunney II. At the least, many of them felt the call should have been a draw.

Again, Tunney appeared worse off physically, bloodied somewhat, though not nearly as violently and obviously as in the first showdown. The mentality of analysis seemed to have the overall score being one win and one loss for each boxer, plus one draw. It might well have been a logical time for the fighters to call it quits on their battles since they did have other things to worry about in life. One would think even if they liked one another and were not trying to knock each other's brains out periodically, they would be sick of spending so much time in each other's presence.

But no. Tunney–Greb was good theater. Greb–Tunney was good entertainment. A Tunney–Greb IV would be a matchmaker's dream, filling another arena, feeding the desires of a fight public willing to spring for tickets.

It really wasn't completely clear just how much the boxing fan hungered to watch Greb–Tunney IV because spectators needed to borrow some Leonhard Seppala dogs to reach the fight site. The fight took place at the Olympic Arena in Cleveland, Ohio, on September 17, 1924, after being postponed by bad weather three times. Attendance was estimated at between 9,000 and 10,000, those owning the best galoshes apparently. The weights were 166 for Greb and 175 pounds for Tunney, but it was predetermined newspapers would make the decision on the winner.

While it should not have been much of a surprise, the fourth edition of the mix-up between the two fighters was fairly similar to the others. Greb swarmed Tunney in his usual style, throwing punches from every direction with both hands. Tunney went for the body and alternated to the head while playing defense when he could stay out of the way.

At Madison Square Garden, Greb felt his Pittsburgh fans were outnumbered. But Cleveland was just 135 miles from Pittsburgh, so it may have felt more like a home-field advantage to him. As always, Greb was on the offensive, pursuing, pursuing, trying to outland Tunney by whatever margin his fists could produce. Tunney played the body.

Greb's best round may have been the ninth when he stayed busy throughout the three minutes. Tunney went to the canvas briefly in the 10th round, but it was a slip, not from a punch.

The prevailing view, in a fight that was not as bloody as some of the others, was that both men gave a good account of themselves, both scored well and evenly. It was called a draw. That pretty much meant after four battles nothing was still really settled between Tunney and Greb.

For a while after that, the boxers went their own ways. Greb fought as often as he usually did. Tunney, still with his eyes on the dormant

Jack Dempsey and a heavyweight title bout, was still working to build his résumé sufficiently to be viewed as a contender for that belt.

It is unlikely Tunney and Greb exchanged Christmas cards, or birthday wishes, but in idle moments they likely thought of one another and each likely believed he was the better man. Finally, talks began to get together once again for Tunney–Greb V. The match was scheduled for March 17, 1925.

Greb became entangled with two unconventional sparring partners. A widower, who thus had no shame attached to dating, Greb spent an evening in February in the company of two women. They were driving around when halted and robbed by five men, who stole $95 and a ring. Greb promptly reported the incident to the police but when the authorities visited the scene of the crime, they found a large amount of blood decorating the spot. It was hinted that Greb beat up his attackers.

The case resulted in Tunney–Greb V being postponed until March 27 in Saint Paul, Minnesota. Both men weighed more, though there was still a good-sized disparity between them when they stepped on the scales. Greb's weight was 167½, while Tunney, truly growing into a heavyweight, weighed in at 181 pounds.

Whether age, ring wear from so many bouts, his punching out of those five criminal fighters or the improvement of Tunney over the course of their boxing relationship accounted for it, this time it was the Gene Tunney Show.

It took five tries, but Tunney was the convincing, overwhelming victor in Minnesota, so thorough in his attack that Greb, who hardly ever took a step backward, found himself boxing defensively for much of the match. Greb started strongly, as he always did, but then his swift, smoking punches slowed and his assault died off. It was said later Tunney's body attack had injured Greb's ribs and that robbed the steam from his punches.

There was no debate about the result of this fight when it ended, no talk of how it should have been a draw. Tunney was the clear winner. After this, there would be no more Gene Tunney–Harry Greb conflicts. Greb said he had enough of Tunney at this point.

"He broke two of my ribs," Greb said. "He's getting too big and too strong for me now. Let somebody else fight him for a change. He'll beat Dempsey, for sure, maybe knock him out."[8]

Indeed, Tunney's dream was to face Dempsey and he went after him.

Greb was close to retirement and when he did leave the ring, he stopped pretending that he had vision in his right eye and had an operation to insert a glass eye. That worked out as well as possible for him.

Then, Greb checked himself into an Atlantic City, New Jersey, clinic to have a repair job done on his flattened nose and on some damage to his respiratory tract, which had occurred in an auto accident. However, Greb developed complications from the surgeries and he passed away in doctor's care on October 22, 1926.

Harry Greb was just 32 years old when he died, only about a month after Gene Tunney and Jack Dempsey clashed for the first time in the ring.

# 24

# Tennis, Anyone?

Tennis may have had some historic origins in remote corners of France in the 1200s, but that was without rackets. If one in a million Americans in 1920 knew that, it would be a lot.

The game began looking more like itself starting in 16th-century England, and by 1900 there was such a thing called the Davis Cup that was contested. Still, for quite some time in the United States, pretty much the only sport the average sports fan identified with swinging an implement made out of wood was baseball.

Like so many other things, Americans with free time on their hands first seemed to gain awareness of tennis as a spectator sport during the Roaring Twenties. And, as so often happened with a singular figure in the forefront of that public awareness, it took a somewhat larger-than-life individual to put it more in the forefront of consciousness.

In this case, it was a talented Bill Tilden, a.k.a. "Big Bill," who introduced Americans to high-level tennis. Back when sweaters were the rage in tennis, Tilden was the man who garnered the attention on the American scene—and exploded into international tennis, too.

Tilden was born in 1893 in Philadelphia. His height in adulthood was given as very specifically six feet 1½ inches (to the half inch), which did not really make him big, especially by modern athletic standards, but he was big enough to connect with a booming serve.

Tilden came from wealth in the suburban Main Line area of Germantown on the outskirts of Philadelphia, and his name first popped up in the sport in 1911. It took a few more years before he exploded into public consciousness, but when Tilden began winning, he won everything. He most likely would have made a big bang earlier except for a little thing that got in the way called World War I, starting in 1914.

A powerful player, Tilden had a large ego that he liked stroked and he enjoyed showing off his dominance on the court, even though he did not set out to crush opponents unless he had a grudge against them.

## 24. Tennis, Anyone?

**Suzanne Lenglen (left), the French tennis star known as "The Goddess," and American Helen Wills met just once, but the two women raised the profile of women in sport.**

Observers said he was more like a stage actor playing to a live audience in his tennis performances. No wonder he was popular. He put on a good show and he won.

There was a stretch from the beginning of the 1920s through much of the decade when Tilden did not lose a match for six years, and only then when he incurred an injury. Oh, he did play to the masses, who admired the way he had lifted what was generally seen as a country club sport out from behind tall walls of privilege. Fans liked that he was an athlete proud to show off his stuff in much the way Babe Ruth did in baseball.

Biographers of Tilden, always mentioned as one of the primary figures of the so-called "Golden Age of Sport" in the 1920s, found him an intriguing character to analyze. A large man with great sex appeal, they felt he was either asexual, or perhaps gay, though he kept that side of himself submerged. He postured for crowds but didn't necessarily enjoy mingling with them. "I can stand crowds, only when I am working in front of them," Tilden once said. "But then I love them."[1]

Why not? They did cheer him. Between 1920 and 1925, Tilden was ranked as the top amateur in the world. In 1931, 1932 and 1933, different experts ranked him as the top professional in the world. Tilden won 14 titles, 10 of them Grand Slam tournaments. When Tilden won Wimbledon in 1920, he became the first American man to do so. He thrived on representing the United States in Davis Cup matches.

Tilden never weighed more than 175 pounds, keeping trim throughout his life, and he was not only strong on the court but he also moved quickly, with excellent footwork, the type of nimbleness that would aid a running back or a boxer.

Tilden was a private man in his private life, but when he was in public, he could be flamboyant. He acted in movies and in stage plays and wanted to be recognized on the street. He took a shine to being recognized in France and Germany, where he also spent time.

Although it was not as if he had been a front man for Prohibition campaigning, Tilden abstained from alcohol. He guzzled coffee and ice water, and while in France he drank mineral water by the gallon. Given that there is an alcoholic drink named after fighter Gene Tunney many years after his death, there might well have been such a concoction in Tilden's honor, if he actually drank. Instead, it was so well-known that Tilden did not drink booze and that he heavily imbibed the local mineral water, during a 1928 visit to Paris people began ordering a glass of cold water by saying, "I'll have a Tilden."[2]

Tilden's father and his older brother were drinkers, and Tilden seemed to blame their alcoholic consumption for their deaths, although that may not have been technically accurate. His antipathy toward liquor was well-known, though. "Alcohol is a poison that affects the eye, the mind, and the wind," Tilden said.[3]

Tilden not only excelled on the court the way no other American did for years, but he also taught tennis to legions of young players, wrote books about the sport and, through his own force of will, slapped the public across the face hard enough to make them at the least notice the sport.

Over the decades, writers and other experts have anointed Tilden the first truly great American tennis player and said his stature was such he remains a player still considered one of the all-time best. Allison Danzig, decades-long *New York Times* tennis beat writer, said Tilden was the best player he ever saw. Don Budge, another great, ranked Tilden in his top five. Jack Kramer, more of a contemporary, put Tilden on his top-six list. Bud Collins, the longtime *Boston Globe* tennis writer and network television commentator, said he researched Tilden's amateur career spanning 1912 to 1930 and found an overall record of 907–62, or a winning percentage of 93.6.

It may have been that Tilden was unique because he worked at being unique. He thought of tennis less as sport than art and he came by that attitude through a famed opera singer of the time, Mary Garden, who was a friend. "You're a tennis artist and artists always know better than anyone else when they're right. If you believe in a certain way to play, you play that way no matter what anyone tells you."[4]

In life, Bill Tilden comfortably accepted any acclaim that came his way because he felt he deserved it. Although he died in 1953, even now Tilden would probably believe he was the finest tennis player of all time.

In the closing days of 1949, The Associated Press announced the results of a poll reviewing the top athletes of the first half of the 20th century. Babe Ruth led baseball. Bobby Jones led golf. Jack Dempsey led boxing. Jim Thorpe was the overall winner as best athlete of the time period. Bill Tilden was ranked tops in tennis, by a margin much larger than any of the other individual sport leaders.

The flip side of Bill Tilden in tennis in the Roaring Twenties was Suzanne Lenglen and then Helen Willis, women of the sport. It took decades, generations, actually, for women to gain equality in the tennis world in terms of equal pay. But those two stood out as stars of the '20s and their names shone as if they were Hollywood actresses as much as sports figures.

Lenglen, the French woman whom the press referred to as "The Goddess," came first. At a time when women were barely given any opportunity to compete in high-level sport, Lenglen emerged to become the first No. 1–ranked female in tennis. She was rated the best from 1921 to 1926 and won nine Grand Slam singles titles, eight Grand Slam doubles tournaments and 83 tournaments in all. Lenglen won Olympic gold in singles in 1920 and bronze in doubles.

Overall, Lenglen compiled an astounding record, going 332–7 in singles, 254–6 in doubles and 381–18 in mixed doubles.

Victories at Wimbledon and then capturing singles, doubles and mixed doubles crowns in 1925 and 1926, the first two years the French Open was conducted, made her a superstar. Lenglen, the start of whose career was delayed by World War I, was such a sensation particularly because she gave her home country something to cheer about after those years of war hardship.

As an individual, Lenglen was flamboyant and outgoing and loved showing up for her matches in flashy clothing that was sometimes critiqued as not being suitable for a woman in public. As a little girl, she was a swimmer and a cyclist, but her father, Charles, began teaching her tennis when she was 11. At one point, Lenglen, who is regarded as the first woman in sport to become internationally known, recorded a 179-match tennis winning streak.

Men wanted to date her. Men wanted to marry her. The only thing that bugged the French public about Lenglen was when she decided she wanted to make some money off her tennis and her name.

In certain sports, amateurism still reigned. Jim Thorpe had been disgraced with his Olympic medals stripped because he made a few bucks playing semipro baseball. Lenglen had conquered all amateur worlds, even ground the competition into dust, again and again.

There was a great backlash when Lenglen announced her intention to play tennis professionally. In years of play, she had probably made only $5,000 and now it was time to capitalize. The vehicle to do so appeared in the form of C.C. Pyle, one of the first great sports promoters.

Sportswriter Damon Runyon, Jack Dempsey's old friend from Colorado, watched the Lenglen phenomenon closely and sought out Pyle and told him she would be the greatest show business hit in the United States. When someone said he was wrong because people hated Lenglen, that made her appeal to Pyle even more. Charles "Cash and Carry" Pyle was a man ahead of his time, a promoter (outside of Tex Rickard in boxing, perhaps) whom no one had seen the likes of until that era. He understood there would be people willing to buy tickets to see Lenglen play tennis, to win or maybe even just to see her lose. "The fact that people hated her was enough for me," Pyle said. "People will pay to see anybody they hate."[5]

Pyle rated alongside Rickard and P.T. Barnum as a skilled purveyor of ballyhoo. He sent an emissary to France to woo Lenglen. Friends approached light-heavyweight Georges Carpentier, who was friendly with Lenglen's family, to persuade her to make an American tour. The courting did not go well at first. Sportswriters in the United States printed rumors Lenglen was going to be guaranteed $200,000 at a time she and the promoters had not even spoken, and her father was an enraged intermediary, saying it was all a sham.

An offer was finally made that would have paid Lenglen $200,000 for her to appear in movies and play tennis while retaining her amateur standing. The world would love to see her as such a performer, on stage and screen, with books she wrote marketed, the creative Pyle told her. Pyle and his helper knew, though, that there would be no show business interest unless Lenglen played high-profile tennis.

In Pyle's mind, he saw Leglen coming to America and touring the land professionally and, presumably, triumphantly, where she could rake in big dollars for herself and for him. The sentiment at the time was against professionalism and even though Lenglen had won everything available to her as an amateur, she was still skittish about going pro.

"Her great fear," Pyle said he took from their negotiations, "was lest she would forfeit friends and social position." She did not, he said, want to give up "social prestige."[6] Pyle bluntly told Lenglen she could make so much money by doing this American tour she could be set for life and he emphasized that having money rarely hurt anyone's social position.

Pyle was a persuasive guy and he and Lenglen signed a contract that had her beginning a U.S. tour at Madison Square Garden and playing tennis across the country, in Canada and even in Havana, Cuba. Then she would obtain a movie role and glean endorsement opportunities, including one for perfume. True to her splashy nature, Lenglen liked dress-up, sometimes receiving visitors in negligees while carrying a lapdog.

As much of a pioneer Lenglen had already been as a female athlete and tennis champion, she could reach new heights of visibility and popularity from this Pyle arrangement. It was understood Lenglen would play tennis against Mola Mallory, with whom she already had a rivalry, and other professionals.

The pro-amateurism crowd provoked a huge outcry among tennis officials and in newspapers ripping Lenglen for her choice. But she stuck to her plan and seemed to embrace it even more enthusiastically the more grief she took. Lenglen began saying things that offended purists.

"Some people think I am tied up hand and foot by becoming a professional," she said. "To me, it is an escape from bondage and slavery. No one can order me about any longer to play tournaments for the benefit of the club owners. Now I am going to make some money, to have some fun, and see the world. I have been working for others for 14 years and now I am going to work for myself."[7]

As Lenglen was resetting her career, setting out to make money playing tennis after all of her amateur triumphs, a likely rival had been emerging in the United States. A Californian of great skill named Helen Wills, who had been born in 1905, was regarded as being as pretty as a Hollywood starlet and just maybe as good at tennis as Lenglen.

Her father, Clarence, was a doctor and her mother, Catherine, trained in college to be a teacher but taught only her daughter. Mother and daughter were best friends. Mom somewhat quietly shepherded Wills's tennis career, beginning when the child was eight years old, even acting as her practice partner. Tennis became a popular activity in California before it spread across the rest of the country, probably because of the nearly year-round sunshine.

If the sporting press believed Wills was a coming threat to Lenglen's dominance, the notion was correct. Once Wills matured and began playing big-time tennis, she collected 31 Grand Slam titles across all disciplines, 19 of them in singles, including eight Wimbledon crowns.

Lifetime, Wills was 398–35 in singles. She was so good she transcended sport, transcended the tennis public and became an international celebrity. Wills introduced flowing skirts as a player and a white visor to block the sun.

In 1926, Wills, full of confidence and curiosity and with a desire to go one-on-one with Lenglen, at last faced her in a tournament in Cannes, France. Wills was 20, Lenglen 26. The meeting was touted as "The Match of the Century."

Lenglen prevailed, 6–3, 8–6, coming from behind in both sets for the victory. Wills was slated to compete in the French Open and Wimbledon but was felled by an emergency appendectomy.

Enter Pyle, and his offer of riches to Lenglen. She turned pro in September that year. Wills remained an amateur, and the two women never played singles against one another again. It was the rivalry that never was, a far cry from Martina Navratilova versus Chris Evert, except in the imagination.

Lenglen went off with Pyle and made a pile of money. It was not quite clear exactly how much, but she said it was plenty. Wills remained an amateur until her retirement in 1938, at one point stringing together a 180-match winning streak.

Lenglen was always a diva and often made excuses citing illnesses when she lost a match. Then, in the late 1930s, whatever ailed her became more serious. There were suggestions she had leukemia, or pernicious anemia. Lenglen passed away on July 4, 1938, when she was only 39 years old. It was probable that Lenglen loved every minute she spent in the limelight.

By contrast, Wills, who resisted much of the attention she gained from her achievements, tried to shun it. She lived to be 92, dying on New Year's Day 1998.

The two women, so different in temperament, like other preeminent sporting stars of the 1920s in tennis, helped to define the era of their primes. They, like Tilden, raised the profile of the sport of their passion and essentially became the two most famous female athletes of the time period.

## 25

## Doing Everything but Fighting

Gene Tunney and Harry Greb got tired of dating and finally broke up for good. Jack Dempsey was so happy to be the heavyweight champion, he tried to keep the crown forever without defending it.

From the time Dempsey laid a whipping on Jess Willard to capture the title during the summer of 1919, the man who had been a longtime, aggressive pursuer of a chance to contend for boxing's biggest prize had been comparatively lackadaisical.

In 1920, Dempsey topped Billy Miske and Bill Brennan, acceptable foes. In 1921, he bested Georges Carpentier in a highly publicized intercontinental match that put the "world" in world heavyweight championship. Then he went on vacation for a year before the muddled-up defense against Tommy Gibbons in Montana.

Two months later, Dempsey engaged in an epic defense against Luis Angel Firpo, a fight remembered forever. But then he seemed to go into hibernation, less focused on taking care of business with his fists than leading the high life.

Dempsey always said he enjoyed fighting, but he came under scrutiny, faced cajoling and took some ribbing and outright criticism for not fighting. After mid–September of 1923 and the rugged bout against Firpo, Dempsey was a celebrity in name and appearance, but he was invisible from the ring.

Several factors contributed. After the war with Firpo, Dempsey may have believed he deserved a break, a chance to bask in the limelight. Also, there were few leading worthy contenders, compounded when it came to matchmaking to the off-again, on-again, off-again discussions about whether he might face Harry Wills. Wills being Black killed any such promotion.

Two affairs of the heart also intervened and conspired to keep Dempsey on the sidelines. They were interrelated issues.

Jack "Doc" Kearns had handled Dempsey's career with astuteness and as his manager did guide him from an unknown to the heavyweight title. He hitched his own wagon to Dempsey as a plough horse and together the men went through some tough financial times before the good times struck.

However, after several years of working together and relying on one another, Dempsey was more mature, much less of a beginner rube than he had been when they joined forces. Whether they were his own suspicions, or whispers from Kearns's enemies (and he made his share of them), Dempsey began to wonder why he wasn't collecting more cash from the purses he earned.

A typical arrangement would have a full-fledged manager receiving no more than 33 percent of the take. Frequently, Kearns banked more than that for himself. Also, Kearns fancied himself a manager who could promote. He watched Tex Rickard in action, pulling off huge shows attracting many thousands of people, and felt he could do likewise. Why did they need Rickard at all?

Ordinarily, when Rickard organized a promotion featuring Dempsey, once the ticket receipts were counted, Kearns collected the booty and then gave Dempsey his cut. This time, after the Firpo fight, Dempsey went directly to Rickard to get paid and walked away holding the $500,000 payout.

When Kearns found this out, he was angry and confronted Dempsey. The way Dempsey remembered that session, Kearns said, "What the hell did you do with our money, Jack?" Dempsey told Kearns he had placed $200,000 in an annuity. When he was vague about the terms of interest, Kearns said he could have gotten much more. Dempsey's retort was that at least the principal was not going to disappear, a hint Dempsey was sensitive about how his money had been handled by Kearns. This incident was one that would linger in bad feeling.[1]

To capitalize on Dempsey's continued reign as heavyweight champ, Kearns managed him right into exhibition bouts, shows and various public appearances. Dempsey was everywhere except the ring, even at the White House.

Following Warren Harding's untimely and somewhat mysterious death in 1923, he was succeeded as president by his vice president, Calvin Coolidge, who previously had been governor of Massachusetts. Coolidge, whose nickname was "Silent Cal," would have been the anti-presidential candidate a century later, the antithesis of being long-winded.

If Abraham Lincoln was quoted from his Gettysburg Address speech for decades, Coolidge was remembered as a man of few words, which he may or may not even have uttered.

## 25. Doing Everything but Fighting

One version of Coolidge being nonverbal is attributed to a woman who sat next to him at a dinner party when he was vice president. This woman said she had been challenged by someone who knew the seating arrangement with a bet that she could not pull more than two words from Coolidge during the course of the night. When she told him this, Coolidge supposedly replied, "You lose." Sensing this reflected poorly on her husband, Grace, the first lady, was said to have retold the anecdote from the perspective of demonstrating what a good sense of humor Coolidge had.[2]

In another version of the story, speaking at an Associated Press membership meeting in New York, the president of that organization, Frank Noyes, offered the "you lose" story in an introduction of Coolidge. Then Coolidge promptly refuted its accuracy in his speech, saying it never happened. The Noyes speech occurred on April 22, 1924, yet the story has persisted in American political lore for a century, anyway, perhaps because it is so funny no one wants to admit it is not true.

On the other hand, Grace Coolidge once said Calvin sat through an entire nine-inning Washington Senators baseball game without saying a word except once to ask her what time it was. It should be noted the Washington Senators over the decades were often such a lousy team they left many fans speechless. However, it just so happened under Coolidge, the Senators were the best they ever were, winning the World Series in 1924 and another pennant in 1925.

Indeed, in conformance with a tradition begun by President William Howard Taft in 1910 at a Senators game, presidents ever since, with rare exceptions, threw out a ceremonial first pitch for opening day of the season, or the World Series. Coolidge did so six times at Griffith Stadium in Washington, D.C., four times on opening days during his administration and once each for the 1924 and 1925 World Series.

Mrs. Coolidge apparently was a more serious baseball fan than Cal, attending more games, keeping a box score on her scorecard and listening to games on the radio—that newfangled device—when she could. The Senators featured the great Walter Johnson—the second-winningest pitcher of all time with 417 victories—nearing the end of his career, and when the World Series was captured, the Coolidges contributed to a fund set aside for a gift of a fancy automobile for Johnson.

So, there was some evidence Silent Cal was a sports fan and he seemed happy to greet Jack Dempsey in the Oval Office as a respite from any governing obligation or aggravation.

On February 22, 1924, Dempsey visited President Coolidge, walking through the door of the White House, certainly something as a younger man that never crossed his mind as likely to happen.

At the meeting, Coolidge mentioned to other staff members in attendance, "Here is one who has been before the public even longer than I." Dempsey's friend, and one of his business representatives, Teddy Hayes, also present, said, "Mr. President, the champion can knock people out with a punch that travels only two inches." Coolidge joked around in response to that comment, saying to Dempsey, "That is two inches more of a punch than I would like to get from you."[3]

That was definitely more than two words pulled out of Coolidge's mouth, anyway.

After the Firpo fight, with Kearns always scheming to place Dempsey in advantageous situations, the fighter moved to Los Angeles. Kearns stayed in New York and handled matters from there—except for potential Hollywood deals, which were left to Hayes.

Hollywood proved to be a nice haven for Dempsey—a very important one, not only because he could participate in movies. An actor named Jack Dougherty, who played in Westerns, introduced Dempsey to actress Estelle Taylor, who was filming a picture in the San Fernando Valley.

Some blind date. The air sizzled between Dempsey and Taylor from the start. Dempsey was handsome and muscular, Taylor dark-haired and sultry. The story goes that after Dempsey met Taylor during the day, that night he was dropped off at her home with instructions for a driver to wait to take him back where he was staying—only he never came out all night. This proved to be no casual flirtation.

During the early 1920s, just as Dempsey had, Taylor was moving her way up the ranks and was a rising lady in Hollywood in silent movies, often playing historical figures. Taylor played Moses's sister in Cecil B. DeMille's *The Ten Commandments* of 1923 and played Mary, Queen of Scots, too. And she played Lucrezia Borgia in *Don Juan*. In a quirky arrangement, Taylor and Dempsey both appeared in a Western film called *Manhattan Madness*. Any kind reviews for Dempsey were welcome, but he was not expecting many since he was well aware of his lack of experience.

Even if sparks flew when Dempsey and Taylor first encountered one another, Kearns, being on the other coast, was ill-prepared to accept another Dempsey love interest that might interfere with his boxing career.

It took little time for Dempsey to become fully enamored of Taylor, who was born in Delaware in 1899. He almost never let himself get out of condition, always maintaining a light workout schedule, even with no bout on the horizon. But soon enough, all of his attention was focused on Taylor and he stopped his workouts.

## 25. Doing Everything but Fighting

Teddy Hayes—caught in the middle, pals with Dempsey, working with both him and Kearns—finally told Kearns by telephone that Dempsey was smitten and it was a serious involvement. Kearns blew a gasket and hired a private detective to investigate Taylor's background, presumably to find enough dirt on her to dissuade Dempsey from doing anything foolish—like marrying her.

Which Dempsey fully intended to do. This portended fireworks and they erupted at a posh club in Hollywood when Kearns traveled west. Dempsey, Taylor, Kearns (who was inebriated), Hayes and another friend were at a table when talk turned to business.

Kearns, who had a large ego and no governor on his speech, insulted Taylor, telling her he had enough information on her background to ruin her career. Taylor became infuriated and departed angrily. Dempsey, stunned by the scene, followed her back to her apartment. So did Hayes, seeking to find a way to calm things down. That was not going to happen. When Hayes arrived, he walked through the open door in time to hear, "Fire that slob that insulted me!" from Taylor.[4]

Dempsey, whose ire toward Kearns had been building steadily, initially planned to do just that. First, he offered Kearns the chance to continue managing him, but for 35 percent of the income, not 50 percent. Kearns turned him down, saying they already had a lifetime contract. Instead, what they now had was two remaining lifetimes of animosity and lawsuits bickering over contracts, pseudo-contracts and imaginary contracts. In their case, it really was until death do them part.

This is when Kearns declared that when he first made Dempsey's acquaintance, he was a bum and he would always be a bum. Kearns said Dempsey would be nothing without his guidance.

Taylor was having a dalliance with a power broker at Paramount, who feared her new boyfriend, Dempsey, would demolish him with a single punch. But she was released from that company in 1925, sending her ego into a tailspin and her mind into worry.

Not only was Taylor not employed by a major studio now, but her status also changed as the motion picture industry was beginning to change for good. The first "talkie" movie was *The Jazz Singer*, released in 1927. Although she ended up adapting, Taylor, while being married to Dempsey, was insecure about her future and fearful of being washed up at a young age.

Sure enough, though, the heavyweight champ did marry the Hollywood actress, his second wife. Taylor, with Dempsey by her side reassuring her, did OK during film's transition, continuing in the movies before branching out to become more of a singer a little bit later in her career.

Dempsey, meanwhile, was being pressured by the most famous

sports columnists to get moving with his own career and defend the esteemed heavyweight title—against somebody. Some said he should fight Wills, though there were so many moving parts to making that match happen. Others began advocating for the growing light-heavyweight, Gene Tunney, after he perhaps eliminated one other heavyweight contender.

Tunney did them more than one better. On June 6, 1925, Tunney knocked out Tommy Gibbons, without even financially wrecking a town in Montana, Wyoming or wherever to do so. Dempsey had gone the distance with Gibbons.

While Dempsey was splitting up with Kearns and unifying with Taylor, Tunney also polished off Jack Herman, Bartley Madden, Johnny Risko and Dan O'Dowd, all four of them also in 1925.

Tunney now stood out as the logical top contender beyond the rest. His longtime dream, spanning many years, was about to come true. He was going to fight Jack Dempsey for the heavyweight championship of the world.

# 26

# Red Grange and Notre Dame Meet the Nation

A FASHION ACCESSORY THAT TOOK the 1920s by storm and was linked to sport for a time was the raccoon coat. It became the height of chic for young men on college campuses to dress in the warm furry coats (which had ample room in pockets for illegal flasks) when they took a date to watch their school's football game.

The raccoon coat became a hot fad that was boosted by a song and late in the Roaring Twenties adorned the cover of the *Saturday Evening Post*. A group of college-aged men were portrayed in that issue decked out in their raccoon coats and shouting, quite likely for their alma mater's success on the gridiron.

College football, as did so many other sports, came of age during the Jazz Age, spearheaded in part by Red Grange, "The Galloping Ghost," and Notre Dame, guided by coach Knute Rockne. Grange, like Babe Ruth and Jack Dempsey, became one of the enduring symbols of sport in the 1920s.

Pro football, and the National Football League, were still stumbling their way into the public consciousness, and there was that built-in prejudice against professionalism in most athletics.

The image of college football (boy, would fans of teams back then be astonished by the business aspects of the sport in the 2020s) was of be-true-to-your-school guys suiting up for the pleasure of the alumni and to bring honor to the alma mater.

This was the infancy of large crowds turning out to watch games as the boys did the school proud. Then, the next day, everyone went to church and on Monday the guys went back to school, in their spare time practicing to take on another regional rival.

The sport had bridged the gap between its very rough beginnings when way too many young men died from injuries suffered on the field. Things became so dire that President Theodore Roosevelt, who supported the game, convened a mini-conference to lecture school officials on revamping rules and making the game safer.

After the flying wedge, a culprit in several tragedies, was phased out, the institution of the passing game helped open up offenses and spread players out so they were not all slamming into one another on every play like fleets of dump trucks.

It was one thing to dress up as if it was Halloween with a raccoon coat, waving a little school pennant, and quite another to watch a classmate be clobbered so hard he perished on the field.

Harold "Red" Grange—"The Galloping Ghost" from the University of Illinois—was a huge college football star and then joined the professional Chicago Bears to barnstorm.

By the '20s, that extreme had basically disappeared and the sport matured some. People attended looking for excitement and entertainment, and more than anyone else, the University of Illinois backfield star Harold Grange, who became a man of many nicknames because of his fleet feet and skillful instincts, was the football star of the hour, or really, the decade.

The number 77 became identified with Grange and continued to stand out because later running backs across football were not allowed to wear such high numbers and because Illinois retired his jersey.

Grange, who was marvelously referred to as "The Galloping Ghost" because of his elusiveness carrying the ball, was also called "The Wheaton Iceman." That combined his hometown and his off-season job toting and delivering cakes of ice to homes that did not have freezers. He was faster with the football. In those leather-helmet days of the game, much of American life was more rudimentary than it is today.

Grange, who stood six feet tall and weighed 180 pounds, came of age with the Fighting Illini in 1923 (in his first game he scored three touchdowns against Nebraska), and by his senior season of 1925 his name and face were imprinted all over the football landscape. He was so good, so well-known that he transcended the sport into the average American's mind.

Playing in the Big Ten Conference enhanced Grange's status because those member schools had large stadiums. Even then Ohio State could attract 85,000 people to a game. Once, when Grange and the team returned to campus after a successful road trip, about 20,000 students turned out to fete them.

Early in Grange's senior year, October 5, he appeared on the cover of *Time* magazine, not a common location to be featured for a sports figure. Grange was so popular that a petition was circulated urging him to run for Congress as a Republican—even though he was too young under the Constitution's rules to genuinely consider it.

That was a year after a Grange performance elevated his stature. On October 18, 1924, the Illini were underdogs to defending national champion Michigan, even though they were playing at home in Champaign and breaking in their new Memorial Stadium.

Grange's legendary game lives on. His personal onslaught began on the Wolverines with the opening kickoff. He returned that 95 yards for a touchdown. On offense, within the first quarter, he added touchdown runs of 67, 56 and 44 yards. After the halftime intermission, Grange scored another TD on an 11-yard run and for a change of pace threw a 20-yard touchdown pass. In those days, all players went both ways in the lineup on offense and defense, and Grange also intercepted two passes.

The inability of other teams to tackle Grange because of his shiftiness and speed astounded the sportswriters who watched him during his college days. His achievements left them groping for the appropriate words describing just how good he was.

Damon Runyon, the nationally syndicated columnist, wrote, "This man Red Grange of Illinois is three or four men, and a horse rolled into one for football purposes. He is Jack Dempsey, Babe Ruth, Al Jolson, Paavo Nurmi and Man o' War. Put them all together. They spell Grange."[1]

Surveying the scene, and injecting himself into it, was Cash and Carry Pyle, the sports promoter. He gauged Grange's popularity, made some calculations, put together a plan and enacted it after making Grange's acquaintance by offering an irresistible opportunity he promised would make him rich.

The short version of a long courtship as Grange and Pyle became friendly was that before his senior season, Grange agreed to a national tour of games to show off his talents in a variety of cities around the country where he had never before been seen in the flesh. Pyle said Grange could make anywhere from $100,000 to $1 million from the arrangement. This would have been a pretty good starter salary right out of college.

Pyle wanted to use the vehicle of football to build Grange's name, but he wanted to extend the tentacles of his earnings into other realms, as well. Pyle became Grange's agent, the first to fulfill that role for a college football player.

Grange completed his senior season in one piece and then took Pyle up on his offer. Pyle convinced Chicago Bears owners George Halas and Dutch Sternaman to commit to a months-long swing playing contests with Grange lined up for the pro team.

Unlike some others at the time who really had no interest in pro football, Grange did wish to keep playing after college. Later, he said, he was surprised by Pyle's approach, but added, "Of course, I was flabbergasted, but Charley made good on his word."[2]

In accordance with his mixed reputation as a president who either (A) liked sports or (B) was indifferent to them but believed White House hospitality to the famous was acceptable, there is a well-described Chicago Bears drop-in to see President Calvin Coolidge as the pro team toured.

Ohio senator William McKinley introduced Grange and the Bears to Coolidge. When Coolidge shook hands with Grange, the president said, "Nice to meet you. I always did like animal acts."[3]

These little sports intermissions, throwing out the first pitch for the Washington Senators, chatting up Dempsey and Grange, were nice respites from the major responsibilities of being the leader of the country for Coolidge.

Besides coping with the nonstop political-world swirling and trying to get legislation passed, Coolidge was the unfortunate inheritor of the scandals of the Harding administration, from Teapot Dome to embezzlement, crimes promulgated by Harding cabinet officers that in the immediate years after his death were just becoming public. Although they did not specifically reflect badly on Coolidge, they inevitably had a carryover effect on his Republican party and interfered with governance of the nation.

The tour was a success, but when it was over, Grange and the Bears temporarily went in different directions. Pyle could not cajole what he felt was a suitable salary out of the claws of Halas. So, to showcase

## 26. Red Grange and Notre Dame Meet the Nation

Grange, he went off and started his own pro league. The American Football League (the first one) included a team called the New York Yankees (not affiliated with the baseball club) but lasted just one year.

Grange incurred a career-threatening knee injury in 1927 and was never quite the same player, though he did spend several seasons back with the Bears. Over the years, Grange acted in Hollywood, made public appearances and became a regular voice on nationally telecast football games. Grange joined Halas as one of the inaugural members of the Pro Football Hall of Fame in Canton, Ohio, when it opened in 1963. He died in 1991 at the age of 87.

From the moment he starred in football at Illinois, and with Cash and Carry Pyle's push, Red Grange remained famous and in the public eye for the rest of his life.

Red Grange was the man who wowed the fans on the gridiron. Notre Dame was the team that thrust itself into the forefront of the national college picture year after year.

Notre Dame, the Fighting Irish, began playing football in 1899, but nothing they did really resonated outside South Bend, Indiana, until 1919, when the school won the first of 13 national championships. By then, Knute Rockne, a former player for the school, was the head coach, taking over in 1918.

Under Rockne, who coached through the 1930 season, Notre Dame created a national profile by winning national titles in 1924, 1929 and 1930. Rockne's teams were so good his record was 105–12–5. Talk about never losing. Five of his squads went undefeated.

**Knute Rockne put Notre Dame football on the map by winning national college championships before his untimely death in a plane crash.**

His .881 winning percentage has never been topped in major college football.

While under Rockne's influence, Notre Dame grew from a little Catholic school in a town in Indiana into a national power with a huge national fan following, especially in such cities as Chicago and New York.

As players for ND, Rockne at end and Gus Dorais as quarterback developed some fame in 1913 as a duo that exploited the forward pass with regularity, a new thing, though they were not the absolute pioneers of the throwing offense, as some have suggested.

Early in Rockne's tenure, he coached a colorful running back named George Gipp. Gipp was Notre Dame's first of many All-Americans and gained legendary fame because he died on the job in 1920 with a supposed mouthful of an epitaph on his lips. Gipp, whose illness began as a sore throat and progressed to pneumonia, reportedly gave a farewell speech to Rockne while on his deathbed. The crux of this commentary was that he told Rockne to someday fire up a Notre Dame team when needed to "just win one for the Gipper." This image and these words were further imprinted in lore later when Hollywood made a Notre Dame football movie and the actor uttering them was Ronald Reagan, who later became president of the United States.

The oddest aspect of George Gipp becoming such a powerful symbol of Notre Dame football was that he was a lousy student who enjoyed playing cards and shooting pool more than he did going to class, so was otherwise a poor role model for the student-athlete image. Although he passed away before its heyday, Gipp was better cut out to be a reckless 1920s Jazz Age defier of Prohibition. He seemed a much more likely candidate to have an alcoholic beverage named after him than Gene Tunney.

Notre Dame was blessed with a magnificent public relations arm (though believers simply said Notre Dame was blessed), and in 1924, when the team was again very powerful, the Irish were led by a quartet of heroes, Harry Stuhldreher, Don Miller, Jim Crowley and Elmer Layden.

It was sports columnist Grantland Rice who dubbed the players "The Four Horseman." Rice penned a legendary lead on a game story that employed the metaphor of the four horsemen. On the occasion of Notre Dame besting Army, 13–7, on October 18, 1924, Rice wrote, "Outlined against a blue, gray October sky the Four Horsemen rode again. In dramatic lore they are known as famine, pestilence, destruction and death. These are only aliases. Their real names are: Stuhldreher, Miller, Crowley and Layden. They formed the crest of the South Bend cyclone

## 26. Red Grange and Notre Dame Meet the Nation   163

before which another fighting Army team was swept over the precipice at the Polo Grounds this afternoon as 55,000 spectators peered down upon the bewildering panorama spread out upon the green plain below."[4]

Again, savvy public relations took hold. The four players, all of whom were later selected for the National Football Foundation Hall of Fame, were posed in uniform sitting astride horses. A century later, few fans can name the group individually, but everyone who follows the sport is aware of the Four Horsemen.

One of Rockne's selling points to Notre Dame recruits was telling them the top-ranking trait of a Notre Dame man was "courage. At Notre Dame there are no quitters."[5]

Given Jack Dempsey's stature in boxing, it probably said something about Notre Dame's own rise to a higher status level when Dempsey, with Estelle Taylor on his arm, turned out to greet the Irish football team in a crowd of onlookers when the team disembarked in Los Angeles prior to playing in the January 1, 1925, Rose Bowl in Pasadena against Stanford. Or just maybe Dempsey showed up to greet an old friend. Verly Smith, Dempsey's old boxing camp medical man, was the Notre Dame trainer.

In November 1927, when during the nascent stages of the longstanding Southern Cal–Notre Dame rivalry, the Trojans visited the Fighting Irish, they met at Soldier Field in Chicago for what turned out to be a 7–6 Notre Dame win. Attendance was variously given as 112,000 or 115,000, at the time the largest attendance for a sporting event in Chicago history. Not only was Dempsey present for that game, soon enough he and Gene Tunney were drawing the same type of crowd for a heavyweight title bout there.

College football fans all remember Knute Rockne as one of the greatest coaches of all time. Rockne was the front man for the Notre Dame program as it built its identity across the decade and across the nation. Notre Dame and Rockne were right on time with the backing of an administration thinking big.

Sports fans will probably chuckle to hear that a chief goal of Notre Dame's leadership before Rockne played ball there and became first an assistant coach and then the head coach was stated by university president Andrew J. Morrissey. He wished to build up "the finest library in the whole state of Indiana and the finest Catholic library in the United States."[6] Instead, Notre Dame got the finest college football team and likely none of those same supporters can these days pinpoint where the library ranks.

Rockne established a football dynasty that continued long after he shockingly died at 43 in a plane crash on March 31, 1931. Notre Dame realized how valuable the man born in Voss, Norway, had been by creating this nationwide publicity machine out of thin air. Rockne was followed at the helm of the program for decades by Irish coaches who maintained the school's place among the best football-playing schools in America.

As good as many of those Fighting Irish teams were, it may fairly be said nothing could top the originals of the Roaring Twenties, with Knute Rockne as boss, George Gipp as a star and the Four Horsemen riding to their destiny. At that point, America had never seen anything like it.

# 27

# Dempsey Finally Defends— Tunney Rising

THE INVISIBLE MAN OF BOXING was about to show what had made him invincible. After three years out of the ring, Jack Dempsey was back, preparing to do what he did best—knock the buckwheat out of an opponent that could not stand in against him.

This time the foe, after years of positioning, was a contender who made his case that he was the one with the best chance to end the Dempsey reign as heavyweight champion of the world.

As the calendar flipped from 1923 to 1924 and onward throughout 1925 and into 1926, Dempsey had not fought since his September 14, 1923, showdown with Luis Angel Firpo. It was long past time for him to defend the crown, regardless of all the things taking place in his personal life.

Gene Tunney was getting itchy. He was no longer a novice, no longer merely a light-heavyweight, but someone of superb boxing skills who carried a wallop when he needed it (whether some appreciated it or not) and who made himself into a contender. After Tunney's wars with Harry Greb and his defeat of Tommy Gibbons, he no longer should have been thought of as a far-fetched opponent for Dempsey.

Promoter Tex Rickard recognized the moment was ripe for such a match and was certain that Dempsey was overdue for a bout to excite the populace. Rickard had proved he could read the ticket buyer's mind and he sensed there was a desire percolating to see a big-time fight.

Rickard gathered the interested parties, handed everyone a pen and obtained signatures on a contract for a September 23, 1926, heavyweight championship fight. The real question was where to put it, what city, what stadium could handle such a major event.

Rickard wanted the fight in New York, but as it almost always seemed, the New York athletic commissioners kept presenting obstacles.

A beautiful answer presented itself. Philadelphia was celebrating its Sesquicentennial Exposition, observing the 150th anniversary of the signing of the Declaration of Independence. Philadelphia was going to be party central in 1926. It was going to be a World's Fair with meaning. Not only that, but Philadelphia provided access to one of the largest stadiums in the world.

For this event, the site in South Philadelphia was called Sesquicentennial Stadium. The name was later changed to Philadelphia Municipal Stadium and then John F. Kennedy Stadium before being torn down. Proving how much of an all-in this fair was, constructed for the occasion was an 80-foot-tall replica of the Liberty Bell that spanned Broad Street and was lit with 26,000 light bulbs. It cost $100,000 to build that 42-ton replica bell. If that didn't sing freedom, nothing did.

This built-in opportunity might be said to be a larger-scale version of Shelby, Montana, a community wishing to take advantage of a major sporting event to help promote itself. Some 30 nations were attending as participants and amusements sprinkled the very large grounds. There was a patriotic stage pageant and religious events, political speakers and nods to history of the United States and Philadelphia's role in gaining independence.

Organizers promised 35 million people would clog the gates. How could anybody lose with such a wide-ranging gala of events? Well, they did. Depending on statistic keepers, either 6.5 million or 10 million people were counted entering the gates between June 1 and December 1. The Exposition was a money-losing failure, sold the Bell for scrap metal and a year later declared bankruptcy.

Not the boxing card's fault, however. Jack Dempsey was a huge draw and his finally returning to the ring and putting his heavyweight title up for grabs was an irresistible attraction. It would have been even in the hands of clumsy handlers, but Rickard was the most accomplished promoter in the sport. At least this time he did not have to supervise the construction of temporary wooden grandstands.

It is not as if Dempsey had failed to pay attention to the boxing world while he was in Hollywood, splitting up with Doc Kearns and marrying Estelle Taylor, but if he had an image in his head of Gene Tunney's ring capabilities it was probably of a slick boxer who presented minimal danger to him. Even Rickard, who was theoretically neutral but was close to Dempsey, thought similarly of Tunney. Tunney was a superb boxer and he had scored well playing to that strength. But he was stronger, more experienced and could hit harder than before.

Tunney was not viewed as a big bruiser of a basher like Jess Willard or Firpo. Those types of knockout artists were crowd favorites. Fans as a group seemed to have a better appreciation for a big-punch fellow than

## 27. Dempsey Finally Defends—Tunney Rising

for a defensive sharp mover and jabber. That was one reason they so loved Dempsey's style. If a careless foe ventured too close to Dempsey's iron hands, he was going to get bopped. Recalling the myth that the heavyweight champ was the toughest man in the world, that explosiveness helped define the sport, and especially the heavyweight division. That's what people wanted to believe. They wanted to see cannon fire that devastated.

To put it simply, when it came to the fight game, and particularly the heavyweights, the public liked to identify with a brute. While personally, away from the ring, Dempsey was nothing like that, he carried the image of brutishness well.

When Dempsey began boxing and no one knew who he was, for a time he wore the nickname of "Kid Blackie." It was basically meaningless and struck fear in the hearts of zero opponents. Somewhat later, after he came under the sway of Kearns, and the manager was conducting a publicity blitz, or that ballyhoo, he upped the ante on a Dempsey nickname.

"Doc now referred to me as 'Jack the Giant Killer,'" Dempsey said, "'The Man-Eater,' and similar names his fertile mind invented. This time people listened.'"[1]

Dempsey did not mind such portrayals. He had a strong sense of self and morality, he liked boxing and he was proud of his accomplishments. He could fill out a nice suit in public appearances at the White House, at banquets or in Hollywood and handle himself in conversation politely.

It was Tunney who seemed to be more of an enigma. Even though Tunney had embraced boxing passionately as a career after service during World War I, the wheels always seemed to be turning in his head and he confounded people. Tunney was certainly a tough guy, but not with a tough veneer.

Going back to his childhood habit of reading, devouring words on a page in thick books, in classic books, Tunney had never really changed. He loved to read and he was not shy about discussing what he read. He gulped down knowledge, was all about improving his mind, soaking up new facts and fictional stories. He ate Shakespeare for lunch.

Rather than relay an appreciation of this thirst for knowledge to fans, to write favorable stories about Tunney's quest to inhale the written word, sportswriters of the time, the star scribes of the Roaring Twenties, seemed to take offense that here was someone who wanted to better himself.

Tunney was criticized for putting on airs, for being an elitist, for trying to be something he was not. If someone only read the sports pages, Tunney would emerge as someone who felt he was better than other boxers just because he was well-read. It was a bit on the daft side, especially when those wielding the pens were Grantland Rice, Ring Lardner and Damon Runyon, not men born with a silver spoon in their mouths, either, but who worked their way up to a status based on words.

What was undeniable was Tunney's newfound popularity with younger fans, and especially female fans. His good looks and chiseled body, gaining so much more attention in the lead-up to the fight, meant he became the object of letters from women, who also sent photographs of themselves, presumably to entice him into a date, or more. Tunney even grudgingly admitted that some of the mail included comments that "might be considered proposals." He referred to them as marriage proposals, though perhaps he was merely being polite about what kind of proposals they really were. "When I am ready to get married," he said, "I don't want a girl to propose."[2]

Most of the big-name columnists and boxing writers from the New York newspapers not only picked Dempsey to win, but they also felt he would KO Tunney. Tunney was not perturbed by this lineup of prognosticators going the other way. He gave an interview to a different sportswriter and expressed why he thought he was the better man at this point in their careers.

"What has Dempsey done since he fought Bill Brennan back in 1920?" Tunney said. "I think I can say without boasting that I am a better boxer than Dempsey, who must have been close to his best six years ago."[3]

On the eve of the fight, why would Tunney change his tune? He had been focused on meeting Dempsey for the big prize for years, had trained for it, aimed for it and had even repeated that it would happen more as a sure thing than as a casual comment.

And then the day before the fight, Tunney went out and played 18 holes of golf at the Shawnee Country Club, which was located not far from his training camp.

"The laugh of the twenties was my confident insistence that I would defeat Jack Dempsey for the heavyweight championship of the world," Tunney said later. "To the boxing public, this optimistic belief was the funniest of jokes. To me, it was a reasonable statement of calculated probability, an opinion based on prize-ring logic."[4]

Dempsey was never preoccupied with Tunney the way Tunney was with him. In the time leading up to the bout with Tunney, Dempsey stayed out of training, gained weight, brooded about his breakup with Doc Kearns and focused on his young marriage.

This was a chance, or at least his bargaining stance, to make $500,000,

### 27. Dempsey Finally Defends—Tunney Rising

even as Taylor's movie career temporarily lost its moorings. Still, she would have been happiest if Dempsey retired from the ring. She worried he was going to get seriously hurt boxing. The fallout with Kearns prompted the vindictive manager to besiege Dempsey with lawsuits seeking money. Although most of Kearns's claims were not legitimate, they wore Dempsey down and he spent considerable funds paying lawyers to fight off Kearns.

All of this while Dempsey should have been single-mindedly preparing for his first fight in three years and be thinking about almost nobody else in the world besides Gene Tunney. There were so many distractions for Dempsey that at one point Rickard suggested postponing the fight. Dempsey turned down the offer.

The fight was on.

# 28

# DEMPSEY AND TUNNEY FIGHT AT LAST

ONE REASON THE SESQUICENTENNIAL celebration in Philadelphia fizzled in 1926 compared with what organizers anticipated was the rain. It rained all of the time. Over a 184-day period, it rained 104 days. It rained enough to refill the Schuylkill River all over again.

One of the days it rained was September 23, the date when Jack Dempsey put his heavyweight title on the line against Gene Tunney. While it could not have been comfortable for the boxers, who were in the open, they were too busy with their fists to pay more than passing notice.

Others paid big bucks to get soaked. Nearly a hundred years later, the turnout for the first Dempsey–Tunney bout remains one of the largest crowds ever assembled for a sporting event in the United States that was not the Indianapolis 500 or a stock car race.

The connection between the fighters, the promotion, the stadium and even the city of Philadelphia was a hit from the start. As the men prepared for battle, on one day about five weeks before the match, it was estimated 2,000 people turned out to watch Tunney spar for free. Elsewhere, on the same day, 1,000 other people paid $1 apiece at Saratoga Springs, New York, to watch Dempsey spar.

Attendance for the day of the fight was officially (based on tax records) 120,557. Adding in ushers and concession workers, sportswriters and those who avoided paying to enter, the overall crowd was approximately 135,000. With the exception of the Indianapolis Motor Speedway, the largest sports venue in the world, and a mix of NASCAR sites, only the Kentucky Derby exceeded that level of paid admissions. Plus, more recently, the expansion of college football stadiums has resulted in numerous games approaching that mark.

Not only did Tex Rickard know what he was doing as a promoter, but the absence of activity in the heavyweight division and Dempsey's name as one of the most prominent sporting individuals of his time

The program from the first Jack Dempsey–Gene Tunney heavyweight title fight in Philadelphia in 1926 when Tunney won a decision to gain the title (author's collection).

also brought out the fans, rain be damned. Also, demonstrating how in only a few years radio had become a fixture for many Americans, it was said 39 million people listened to the blow-by-blow of the fight, in living rooms or in public places where crowds gathered. It was covered for NBC by Graham McNamee, the first widely known sportscaster, and Phillips Carlin.

As has often been the case over the subsequent decades, when gossip rags took note, or a roving camera jostled people to spy celebrities, this one attracted big names who wanted to see these fisticuffs up close. President Calvin Coolidge did not make the trip from the White House, but many other well-known individuals were ringside. Other politicians en route included Vice President Charles Dawson, governors and senators.

The saturation newspaper coverage included polling prominent folks about whom they picked to win the bout. Baseball player extraordinaire Ty Cobb, New York Giants manager John McGraw, tennis star "Big Bill" Tilden and billiards champion Willie Hoppe all picked Dempsey to win. Doc Kearns was even asked his opinion, and he picked Dempsey, maybe the only kind words he spoke about his former client for years.

Babe Ruth made sure to attend, as did actor Charlie Chaplin, as did many who were rich and famous from the financial world. Plenty of the glitterati, though it made no difference to Dempsey and Tunney. They had eyes only for each other.

Dempsey had done his preliminary training in Saratoga Springs, then moved his training camp to Atlantic City, roughly 60 miles from Philadelphia, with plans to take the train into the big city on the day of the fight.

As part of his prep work, Dempsey was experimenting with a fresh angle to his diet, drinking olive oil. As part of his entourage, Dempsey now had a bodyguard named Mike Trent, who regularly gave Dempsey that juice. On the morning of the fight, Trent vanished and didn't turn up by the time the group was headed to the Broad Street Station in Philly.

On the train, Dempsey became ill. Manager Gene Normile, nominally the replacement for Kearns, although Dempsey was sort of representing himself, and others became alarmed at Dempsey's weakness and appearance.

At one point Dempsey held himself up by leaning against a door, closed his eyes and failed to recognize Normile. When challenged about how he felt, Dempsey said, "It's nothin' I can't lick. Just a funny feeling's all. Here. And here. 'I pointed to my belly and my head.'"[1]

He was not OK. Dempsey might well have contracted a bug from fighting in the rain in this fight, but he apparently already had one percolating in his system beforehand. The last stretch of the journey was by car and several times Dempsey stopped the driver, jumped from the auto and threw up.

Dempsey was still woozy in his dressing room, so it was borderline

## 28. Dempsey and Tunney Fight at Last

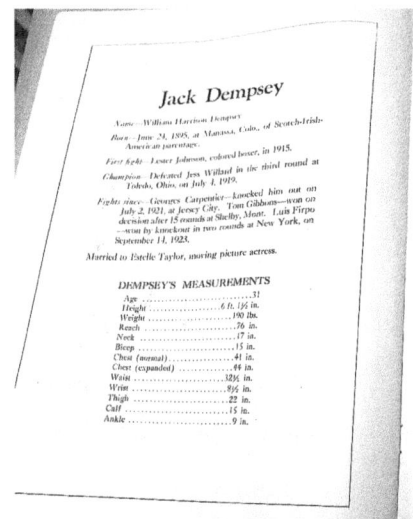

Jack Dempsey, as he was shown and touted in the pages of the official program for his meeting against Gene Tunney in Philadelphia in 1926. In addition to Dempsey's photograph, the program shared information including his full name, date and location of birth, notable fights, marital status and measurements (author's collection).

insanity for him to continue with a boxing match where his opponent was going to try to knock him woozy. Neither Dempsey nor Normile, though, made a public move to postpone the bout, which would have been basic common sense. It was only later, when all of this became publicly known, that there were some suggestions maybe the fix was in on the result. Trent never turned up and by insinuation he took the rap for something—poisoning the olive oil, or some other nefarious action—causing Dempsey's circumstances.

This all was a pretty big deal on the cusp of a huge physical challenge and it is surprising Dempsey went ahead with the fight and didn't make more of the issue until sometime later.

While Dempsey was riding a train to Philadelphia, Tunney utilized a different mode of transportation, one that not only was not popular yet but was viewed with some suspicion. He was flown into town from his training camp, fairly secretively. Flying? Tex Rickard almost had a conniption when he heard Tunney was risking his life in this manner. There was a glitch with the flight plan, but stunt pilot Casey Jones got Tunney to his destination whole.

By fight time, Dempsey was ambulatory and moving on his own for "The Battle of the Century." Of course, Rickard was pleased to anoint

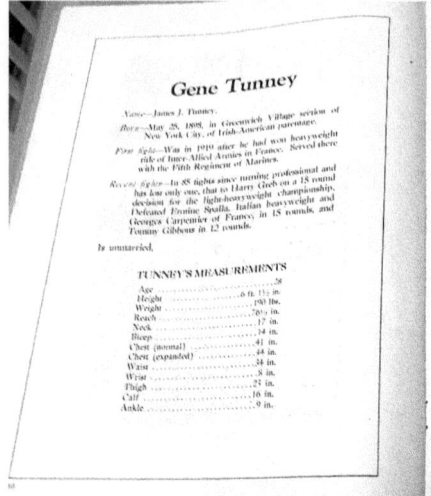

Gene Tunney, the challenger, as he was portrayed in the pages of the program for his shot at the heavyweight title against Jack Dempsey in 1926. In addition to Tunney's photograph, the program shared information including his full name, date and location of birth, notable fights, marital status and measurements (author's collection).

his promotion in that manner. He hoped it would become the first $2 million gate, but the receipts fell short, totaling $1,875,000.

Dempsey felt the rain was coming down so hard it drowned out the sound of the typewriter keys being pounded by the sportswriters he knew at ringside. But it did not drown out the loud roaring of the crowd, full-throated even before the match began. "Lights aimed in my face and I sweated," Dempsey said, "knowing damned well I didn't have my former fighting spark."[2]

Tunney looked pretty fit and trim to Dempsey, who took note that Tunney was wearing a bathrobe with a Marine symbol on the back. Dempsey said he felt lousy. "Tunney was in fine shape and looked completely at ease, while I felt sick and nervous, half-expecting a process server to pop up with another summons [as part of the harassment from Kearns]."[3]

Dempsey, who for many was viewed as the greatest heavyweight of all, may have spoiled some fan adulation by being inactive. When he and Tunney entered the ring and were introduced, Tunney was cheered and Dempsey was booed. In the middle of the ring, the combatants met—and spoke briefly. Tunney simply addressed Dempsey as a champion and Dempsey said hello to Tunney by his first name.

And then it began. It rained in a downpour and the punches rained.

Perhaps within the first minute of action, Dempsey may have realized he was wrong to ignore advice from those close to him urging him to take a tune-up bout before facing Tunney. He had this image in his head, fortified by others' views, that Tunney was an appropriate challenger but whose strength was boxing, not punching, and he could not hurt him or knock him out.

"He's just a boxer, Jack," Rickard said. "I could lick him myself. He's not a puncher like you."[4]

Somewhat unexpected when they stepped on the scales, Dempsey weighed 190 pounds, perfectly fine given false rumors he had bloated up during his time off, but Tunney did, as well. For those used to Tunney climbing between the ropes closer to the light-heavyweight maximum of 175 pounds, this was proof he had gradually bulked up to heavyweight.

Rickard's downplaying Tunney did Dempsey no good at all. He grossly underestimated Tunney. Generally speaking, those who train and work out with a big-time fighter build his ego as they build his fitness, but instilling a belief in invincibility is a common trend. There should always be at least one person in the corner who tells a fighter the truth, and not just when time is running out in the ring. But Dempsey's group lacked that component.

The match was scheduled for 10 three-minute rounds, and that had always given Dempsey plenty of time to KO a foe. He could go the distance if he had to, but he was used to taking out opponents much earlier, and his fans had come to expect it. Not this time.

The fight would be staged on Tunney's terms, with the challenger dictating the pace, controlling the contact, jabbing and flinging hard shots at Dempsey's head without the champion being able to duck them. It was like that from the start, stunning onlookers, and Dempsey rarely got the chance to unleash his offense the way he so often had.

Tunney, the literate man who recognized and nurtured his talent, never pretended to be a knockout artist the way Dempsey was. He understood his own strengths and brought his own approach into battle. "It was argued that I was a synthetic fighter," Tunney said. "That was true. They said I lacked the killer instinct, which was also true. I found no joy in knocking people unconscious, or battering their faces. The lust for battle and massacre was missing. I had a notion that the killer instinct was really founded in fear, that the killer of the ring raged with brutality because deep down he was afraid."[5]

During the training period, a sportswriter visited Tunney and wrote about his allegiance to Shakespeare, whom he had been reading since he was 13. Reading about this in a newspaper, one of Dempsey's supporters waved the story at his fighter of choice and shouted, "Hey, champ! It's in the bag! The sonofabitch is up there reading a book."[6]

Talk about misreading a situation. It wasn't as if Shakespeare steered away from blood and guts, either. Many of his characters come to ill-fated endings, 155 of them, it is said in 38 writings, with stabbing, beheading and poisoning common causes. There are some that die of shame, as well, and when this event concluded it might almost be said Dempsey fell into this category. Shakespeare provided plenty of drama—and so did Tunney. Dempsey, too, though mainly by staying on his feet.

If some chose a silly approach in belittling Tunney as a bookworm, he didn't much care. He said he didn't like playing pinochle, so he read. "It became part of my training routine to read during the five hours between the road work, breakfast sequence, and the ring stints in the afternoon," he said.[7] Focusing on the stories he read kept his mind occupied so he didn't worry constantly about his upcoming fight.

In the ring, Tunney was all focus on Dempsey from the opening bell. Harry Greb kept telling everyone to bet on Tunney because he was going to take Dempsey easily. He was scoffed at and ridiculed. But he was right. Babe Ruth was wrong when he said he expected Dempsey "to murder the bum."[8]

In the first round, the men met in mid-ring and each landed some serious blows, Dempsey clipping Tunney with a left to the jaw that pushed him back but Tunney retaliating with a big right after a Dempsey body punch. Tunney said his score was so hard Dempsey's knees sagged and that if he had been able to capitalize, he may have stopped the champ in the first. Dempsey later admitted to being shaken by Tunney's success.

The second round was similar and so was the third. Tunney was the one in charge. He peppered Dempsey's face, dodged trouble from Dempsey's big mitts and was stunning the huge crowd. Not many expected Tunney to win, never mind dominate.

In his corner, after Jerry the Greek, one of his seconds, applied smelling salts, Dempsey gave himself a pep talk, told himself to get his act together and go get Tunney. Yet he couldn't catch up to him. Tunney backpedaled smoothly when he needed to and kept Dempsey off-balance with the punches that took the starch out of his legs.

Only a few times did Dempsey hit Tunney with big enough punches that seemed to threaten the challenger, at the beginning of the fourth round and with a couple of hooks in the sixth. But they were not payoff punches with long-lasting effects.

It wasn't as if Tunney was hurling big bombs at Dempsey. He pecked

## 28. Dempsey and Tunney Fight at Last

away, landing far more punches, then clinched when Dempsey charged and slipped away from him. If Tunney was not swinging for the fences, Dempsey couldn't get the right angle to try to swing for the fences.

Round after round the fight proceeded the same way. Dempsey could not get traction and Tunney controlled the action. He kept piling up points and Dempsey knew it. The title was fading away and he knew that, too, feeling as time passed that the only way for him to stay champion was to put Tunney down. But he wasn't the Dempsey of old, who was the king of knocking guys down.

Each round Tunney scored well, the points accumulating toward an undisputed, easy decision. Dempsey was bleeding from a cut above his left eye and had swelling over his right eye, and his face was swollen in several areas. When the ball rang concluding the highly anticipated fight, there was no surprise when scores were read and the title changed hands, no dispute about the result.

Dempsey did not fool himself about the reality of what happened. He lost and knew it. "I kept plodding toward him, trying to land a telling blow," Dempsey said, "but Tunney refused to carry the fight to me. He let me do the attacking. That was sound ring strategy. He was well ahead and taking no chances of being knocked out. I was still trying to get home a blow that might save the title. I wasn't able to do it. The old legs wouldn't take me in there fast enough."[9]

Once the decision was read, Dempsey made his way to Tunney's corner to congratulate him as the new champ. Then he was surprised when fans began cheering him, cheering his effort, cheering his seven-year reign. Forgotten, it seemed, were the slings that stung when he was called a slacker and had to beat such charges in court.

"The people were cheering for me, clapping for me, calling out my name in a way I never heard before," Dempsey said. "I never realized how I hungered for a sound like that, and now here it was on the night I blew my title. Losing was the making of me."[10]

Of all things, somehow Tunney was perceived as the villain of the piece, with fans jeering him for winning, for capturing the crown, for living out his dream. That was likely a function of his uneasy relations with the writers, who portrayed him as an oddball for reading all of those books, and for being "different" in the sense he did not conform to stereotypes of boxers. Tunney, who did not easily pal up to the sportswriters, resented that.

Both men were polite in the immediate aftermath of the bout, Tunney saying that Dempsey fought like a true champion, the champion he had been. He did use the past tense, adjusting to that description quite swiftly.

Dempsey's wife, Estelle Taylor, did not attend the fight. He had urged her to remain in Los Angeles, where she had some movie business. He was glad she did not see him immediately after the fight. He spent the night after the contest in his room in the Adelphia Hotel nursing his many facial wounds.

The betting odds, which shifted a few times approaching fight night, had been between 4-to-1 and 7-to-1 on Dempsey, and the writers, with few exceptions, had chosen Dempsey as the likely winner. Discussion of Dempsey being out of shape and rusty took hold and comments on the bad weather appeared in writers' analysis. Tunney was getting little credit for his accomplishment. With no actual proof, Ring Lardner even wrote in a letter that he believed the fight was fixed.

Tunney had meticulously planned and trained for years for his moment, but he was not showered with glory as might have been expected. Instead, more alibis for Dempsey appeared in print than positive notices for Tunney's star turn.

Both Tunney and Dempsey were insulted by the prose describing them. Even Damon Runyon, Dempsey's old friend, seemed particularly harsh in his accounting of why Dempsey lost than in explaining why Tunney won. In part, he wrote, "They all go the same way. Another once-great champion joined the big parade of the has-beens, the never-ending parade."[11] He was blunt in stating Dempsey was washed up. Those types of stories gave Dempsey more pain than his cuts.

Only a day after the fight, Taylor arrived to see Dempsey, aware that he lost the fight and title, but she took it badly seeing him battered. When she asked Dempsey what happened, Dempsey uttered one of the greatest sum-it-up replies in history. "Honey," he said, "I forgot to duck."[12]

The title had changed hands and it had been appropriated forcefully and decisively. But Dempsey remained a big name. He lost by decision, not knockout, and there were no other obvious challengers lined up for the right to beat Tunney.

Naturally enough, with money man Rickard behind it, talk began fairly quickly about a rematch, a Dempsey–Tunney II. It made sense from a business and boxing standpoint.

# 29

# Let's Do It Again—Maybe

For the first time in seven years, Jack Dempsey was not the heavyweight champion of the world and someone else was walking around the United States wearing the mantle of the title. After at least seven years of fixating on Dempsey as the man standing between him and his career goal, Gene Tunney was the heavyweight champ.

Being dethroned after being told you are the world's greatest for so long can be hard on the psyche, and Dempsey felt the loss of the crown keenly. Looking in the mirror to read the pummeling he took from Tunney was a book whose pages he didn't wish to flip through. But the evidence was omnipresent and strong. He said aloud he was disgusted with himself for his showing.

Tunney had every reason to be pleased and satisfied. He had planned and trained and worked and fended off doubters to make the reality of his mind the reality in the world. He earned the title, step by step, and deserved it. If Tunney shocked much of the boxing world, the sports world and the world at large, that was very much the story often enough in sport, where upsets happened with regularity, where the underdog succeeded against popular mindsets and betting odds.

Dempsey needed time to heal and time to determine if he would take a shot at regaining the heavyweight belt, which no one had done before. Tunney needed time to bask and to figure out how he would defend the crown.

Tex Rickard, the promoter of the Dempsey–Tunney fight, and the promoter of the moment in the fight game, did not think the bout would turn out this way. He felt Dempsey could handle Tunney and continue on as champion.

The multipronged career of Rickard, faro dealer and saloon dealer in the Klondike, rancher in South America, boxing showman and the man behind the construction of the latest incarnation of Madison Square Garden, had it in his head he would oversee the building of such sports palaces in many cities. He did preside over the construction of the Boston Garden, for many years the home of the Boston Bruins and Boston Celtics, before it was replaced.

Reading the reaction of the multitudes, Rickard promptly saw the possibilities in promoting a second Dempsey–Tunney fight with built-in storylines as the former champ strove to regain the crown and the current champ wished to prove his ascension was no fluke. He also recognized it was critical for Dempsey to prove himself all over again with another big bout before going after Tunney again.

Initially, as would be expected, Dempsey fell into a depression over the loss, even if the fans were courteous enough to give him a post-match shout-out. He truly thought about retiring. One day during this down period, especially in the beginning when he was well-marked and Estelle cried at the sight of him, Dempsey was in California with his wife.

Tex Rickard, one of the greatest boxing promoters of all time, organized both of the Jack Dempsey–Gene Tunney heavyweight title bouts in the 1920s (author's collection).

The slow-motion official legal dissolution of his relationship with Jack Kearns was bleeding Dempsey financially and mentally and Kearns kept serving him with legal papers. Finally, in 1927, things were as resolved as much as they ever would be.

An old friend dropped by unexpectedly while Dempsey was sorting through things in Los Angeles. It was Babe Ruth, who had just finished wrapping up a movie and was in a contract dispute with the Yankees, holding out for more money.

"What a guy," Dempsey wrote in his autobiography years later, "egg-shaped and boisterous, a connoisseur of booze, food and dames." Dempsey recounted Ruth's appearance and their conversation when he had just about chosen retirement. "Listen, Jack, you lost your crown when you were still on your feet," Dempsey recounted Ruth saying. "Sure, it's tough, but don't you think you owe yourself and your fans one more crack?"[1]

It was a logical argument, but Dempsey was moping, at a low ebb at that point and insisted he was finished.

"Awright, then, sit on your ass and feel sorry for yourself," Ruth continued. "You know, pal, it's guys like us who just can't back off from the spotlight."[2] When Dempsey insisted Ruth's situation was different because he had not lost a step, Ruth said that every time he came up to bat it was as if he was batting zero. That may have been an exaggeration, but in baseball, where if someone collects a hit three tries out of 10, he is a star, there was truth in Ruth's statement.

At the time of Ruth's visit, Dempsey had been pretty much acting a recluse in California, far removed from Broadway, or anyone in New York. Rickard had repeatedly sought to reach Dempsey directly to talk turkey, but Dempsey kept ducking him.

"People are asking where you're holin' up and what you're doin'," Ruth said. "Pals of mine say that letters are pouring into sports desks all around the country for you. And here you are, walkin' sideways and bumping into yourself, for Chrissakes."[3]

The Babe delivered an impassioned plea, from one superstar of the Roaring Twenties to another, essentially on behalf of sports fans. Ruth's comments were emotional as much as based on logic, but they made an impact on Dempsey. After that, Dempsey began thinking comeback, and when Rickard reached out by telephone after his telegrams had gone unanswered, Dempsey listened.

He told Rickard he was finished, but when Rickard said he understood because no boxer wanted to lose to the same man twice, Dempsey bristled, saying Tunney wasn't all that tough. Rickard began his sweet-talking act, urging Dempsey to start training again, that maybe a tune-up would be helpful, and they would just see what played out as time went on.

Now that Gene Tunney was the surprise heavyweight champ in the eyes of the press, the sportswriters wanted him to act like previous heavyweight champs, particularly Dempsey, who reveled in the glory of owning the title. Dempsey went on vaudeville tours, fought exhibitions, signed up for public appearances of all kinds and, even though he really had no talent for it, made himself available in Hollywood. He was very much a public champion, even during his hiatus when he was between fights.

Tunney did a little bit of Hollywood, but he did not expose himself to the masses, or the newspapermen, in the same way. Oh, Tunney met with sportswriters, but he didn't obligingly give them what they wanted. He was more reserved, preferred to discuss the books he was reading, yes, still some Shakespeare, but also George Bernard Shaw, an Irish playwright who was a political activist.

Shaw had been an amateur boxer and followed the fight game. In London, he was one of the early seers who picked Tunney to beat Dempsey because of his ability as a scientific boxer. Eventually, Tunney and Shaw met, hit it off and became friends. In fact, one of Tunney's sons, Jay, later wrote a book about the unlikely connection between the two famous men.

This was something boxing people and the sportswriters could not fathom. The writers especially employed it as evidence Tunney was stuck-up, full of himself, and was masquerading as an elitist, forgetting his hardscrabble background in Greenwich Village as a youth. Or maybe they overlooked the type of guy Tunney had been all along. Tunney did not always reveal his innermost thoughts they wanted to hear and didn't always pose for photos as the journalists wanted him to do.

Paul Gallico, who was part of the in-crowd of sportswriters at the time before he left newspapers to write novels such as *The Poseidon Adventure*, critiqued Tunney from this overall perspective. "I think Tunney has hurt his own game with this cultural nonsense," Gallico wrote in a New York paper.[4]

When Tunney was gaining fame and babes were writing letters hoping to make his acquaintance, he did tell sportswriters the mail was running that way. Unlike Dempsey, who was in the midst of a high-profile marriage with a Hollywood starlet, and who had not been previously shy about much of his dating, Tunney kept his love life under wraps.

Tunney had become heir to the heavyweight title, but he also acquired a heavyweight heiress in his travels. He did not talk about his bride-to-be, did not offer a hint he was going to be married sometime soon, never mind to whom. The whom was of great interest not only because of Tunney's prominence.

Tunney was involved with Mary Josephine "Polly" Lauder, a woman of social standing in Connecticut who had the kind of money in the bank that would have made Rickard envious. She was an heiress to the United States Steel fortune and her great-uncle was Andrew Carnegie. By the time she and Tunney married in 1928, he had his own fortune by the measurement of the times, earned with his sweat in the boxing ring. Tunney wasn't marrying for money and neither was Lauder. Their relationship remained a secret for a while after Tunney became the heavyweight champion.

## 29. Let's Do It Again—Maybe

Rumors began surfacing—which were denied. Then, on August 8, 1928, the Lauder family announced the young woman's engagement. When the couple married, they did so in Rome, across the Atlantic Ocean, and all members of the press were banned from attending. Although there was a near riot by paparazzi equivalents of the era, Tunney said if he caught anyone snapping pictures, he would break the camera.

This was already late in the fight game for Tunney, who was keeping other secrets by then, such as when he might defend the title again. Before that, however, Rickard's creativity teamed up with Tunney's overall plan and Dempsey's desire to plan for a second Dempsey–Tunney bout—as long as Dempsey conducted himself well in another bout versus a worthwhile opponent. Babe Ruth's exhortations aside, he had to show he still had the goods.

They found someone. Dempsey agreed to fight Jack Sharkey, a dangerous contender, as an intermediate step to meeting Tunney for a second time. Sharkey was of Lithuanian heritage and was born Joseph Paul Zukauskas in 1902. Although he was born in Binghamton, New York, Sharkey was mostly a Bostonian after that. When he began boxing, he realized the sport was Irish-dominated in the area and he assumed the name Jack Sharkey.

On his way to positioning himself to fight Dempsey, Sharkey won a bout from Harry Wills on a disqualification and in 1926 scored a technical knockout over Mike McTigue shortly after he relinquished the light-heavyweight title. The confrontation with Dempsey came with the promise that if Sharkey won, he would get a heavyweight crown shot against Tunney.

Dempsey–Sharkey was scheduled for 15 rounds on July 21, 1927, at Yankee Stadium. This was a fight of convenience for Sharkey, for sure, who considered Dempsey to be his boxing idol. Still, he was willing to knock him off his personally made pedestal if it would advance his career, one of many examples of boxing making strange bedfellows. The fans liked the matchup and seemed eager to watch Dempsey fight again, though steely-eyed oddsmakers had Sharkey the 7–5 favorite. How soon everyone was dismissing Dempsey.

The spectators turned out 82,000 strong and produced another million-dollar gate of $1,083,530. Yes, Rickard seemed to have the magic promotional touch.

Sharkey fought with heart and guts and Dempsey came after him aggressively. Dempsey could not put Sharkey down, and Sharkey appeared to be hurting Dempsey with better blows. Through the first six rounds, Dempsey built a slight lead on scorecards.

However, in the seventh round, Sharkey made the most fundamental mistake in boxing. Fighters are told to protect themselves at all times. Sharkey was distracted by what he claimed was a low blow from Dempsey. He started to complain to referee Jack O'Sullivan, dropped his hands from their protective stance and ill-advisedly turned his head, taking his eyes off Dempsey.

That was the fatal error. With the clock running, action unfolding and having no idea what Sharkey was doing besides making himself vulnerable, Dempsey unleashed a powerful left to Sharkey's jaw. Down went Sharkey.

This was what Jack Dempsey was known for—the blockbuster punch that finished an opponent with a single strike. Sharkey fell face-first onto the canvas and was counted out.

Dempsey had the victory, a fresh credential on his record, and he was lined up to face Tunney for a second time. He believed the man who outboxed him could be outfoxed and polished off with the same type of heavy-duty punch that crushed Sharkey. It was time to regain the heavyweight championship of the world from the man who tested and bested him in 1926, and who had that glitzy title only on loan.

# 30

# CHARLES LINDBERGH

OF ALL THE CHAMPIONS AND famous sportsmen of the Roaring Twenties, of all the fresh achievements recorded in a changing world, no one's worldwide acclaim and no one's accomplishments exceeded in value what Charles Lindbergh did by flying solo across the Atlantic Ocean.

Gene Tunney should have waited another year to fly to his fight against Jack Dempsey. The populace would have had more confidence in his safety once Lindbergh pulled off the feat that titillated the world and took a giant step for mankind and aviation.

Dempsey and Tunney collected boxing crowds like no others. Babe Ruth reinvented the home run and changed baseball. Bobby Jones and Walter Hagen transformed golf and Bill Tilden, Suzanne Lenglen and Helen Wills made tennis an attention-getter as the National Football League and Red Grange took the public on broken-field runs.

Lindbergh not only pulled off a death-defying feat, but also he instigated changes in aviation that made the skies friendlier and essentially jump-started the industry of flight. At a minimum, Lindbergh was embraced by the masses as loudly and enthusiastically as if he had broken through as a new kind of sports hero, even if fun and games was not on his to-do list.

Born in Detroit in 1902, Lindbergh was 25 years old when he made the breakthrough solo flight from New York to Paris on May 20 and 21, covering 3,614 miles in 33½ hours as the world did hold its breath in wishing for his survival and success.

Lindbergh, whose father was a Minnesota member of Congress, was a U.S. Army Service cadet, a stunt pilot and a mail pilot, earning his wings through those experiences. When a $25,000 prize was offered to the person who became the first to fly between the two major cities, he decided he wanted to win it. Lindbergh meticulously planned and carefully calculated the carrying capability of his plane, the *Spirit of St. Louis*, and the physical challenges he would face by undertaking the challenge.

**Charles Lindbergh became a hero to millions when he made the first solo airplane flight across the Atlantic Ocean from New York to Paris in 1927.**

In 1923, Lindbergh bought his first airplane, a Jenny, and made his first solo flight in the World War I surplus plane. At times, Lindbergh billed himself as a "daredevil" pilot as he performed stunts, and four times he had to parachute to safety from planes as he performed more complicated midair stunts.

When Lindbergh began thinking of how hard it would be to fly from New York to Paris, he took many things into consideration. One thing he concluded was that he had the experience flying in bad weather—delivering the mail in winter—to cope with just about any conditions he might encounter.

What Lindbergh did not have was the cash to build a plane to his specifications that could succeed, nor a big enough reputation of any kind that might induce someone to fully sponsor him. He was very particular about the kind of plane he believed he needed and thought it would cost around $10,000 to obtain and modify. That was in 1920s dollars, money he certainly lacked.

As the wheels in his brain turned, Lindbergh made an appointment to visit with a wealthy man named Earl Thompson, to whom he had provided with flying lessons. He wanted to pick his brain, he said, but really, he inwardly hoped Thompson could support him with cash and as an intermediary maybe round up some other Saint Louis businessmen to back him, as well.

When Lindbergh met with Thompson, he talked about the value of a solo flight in the big picture. "It would show people what airplanes can do," Lindbergh said. "It would advance aviation and it would advertise St. Louis."[1]

To some extent, Lindbergh's comments were, as in the parlance of the day, all "ballyhoo," as Tex Rickard and Jack Kearns put it in the fight game. Lindbergh was doing public relations, for sure. But what he said was also true. Eventually, through lobbying, talking, flying and planning, Lindbergh sold his idea of being worthy of support, even as others, some more well-known, announced their own initiatives to take on a similar challenge flight.

When Lindbergh sorted everything out to take his shot, really only then did anyone take seriously his attempt to fly the Atlantic. When the newspapers mentioned him, he was called "Lindy" for the convenience of headline writers.

Will Rogers, who was best-known for his wit but also delved into social commentary (sometimes melding both at the same time), took note of Lindbergh when he was in flight, writing in a syndicated newspaper column, "A slim, tall, American boy is somewhere over the Atlantic Ocean, where no lone human being has ever ventured before. He is being prayed for to every kind of Supreme Being that had a following. If he is lost, it will be the most universally regretted loss we ever had."[2]

Ironically, the heavyweight boxing world was unfolding on the ground, in New York, that very night, May 20. Jack Sharkey scored a fifth-round technical knockout over Jim Maloney in a scheduled 15-round bout in Yankee Stadium. It was the victory that propelled Sharkey into his dramatic match against Dempsey two months later.

Rogers was right. Ring announcer Joe Humphreys had the 40,000 fans at ringside pray for Lindbergh. All around the country, at public gatherings, those at podiums asked their listeners to do likewise.

One challenge of the flight for the pilot was staying awake. Lindbergh, who traveled as light as he possibly could, including carrying minimal food, battled fatigue and hallucinations. He probably did not see Yankee Stadium and Sharkey on his takeoff.

As Lindbergh shrugged off sleepiness, and combated being surrounded by fog at times, the world awaited word of his progress. When the moon was bright, he flew as high as 5,000 feet. When visibility was slight, he dropped to as low as 100 feet above the water. When the *Spirit of St. Louis* was sighted off the coast of Ireland, the frenzy was on. Word spread faster than Lindbergh could fly that he was on his way. Lindbergh, who had barely strayed from his planned course, realized he had reached France when he flew over Cherbourg.

Lindbergh spotted the Seine River and the Eiffel Tower but at first could not identify the airfield. That should have been easier than it was because some 150,000 people were there waiting for him. Boy, he did notice them when he flew into the lights of night.

Mobs cheered. Police tried to hold them back as he landed but could not. Lindbergh was greeted as if he was an alien from outer space, which in a sense he was. The reception in France offered the hint of what was to come, Lindbergh welcomed wherever he went in the near future as if he had walked on water, not flown over it.

The protective ring of police and military that had been carefully arranged collapsed promptly, and a few quick-thinking men, some of them pilots, encircled Lindbergh and shoved him through the crowd to a building where he could be fed and treated for any medical needs. This would be only the first time Lindbergh was in danger of being loved to death. The plane, too. After being spirited away, Lindbergh wanted to obtain some items from the airplane, but when he finally got back to it was shocked to see it had been mauled, the crowd ripping pieces off to keep as souvenirs.

That was only the beginning of the international fever over Lindbergh and his achievement, which went on and on once he returned to the United States. When Lindbergh appeared at the Washington Monument, about 250,000 people turned out. In New York, at the Battery, it was estimated 300,000 people showed up and perhaps four million people attended a ticker-tape parade.

Lindbergh was honored with another parade in Saint Louis, attended by about 500,000 people. He received 3.5 million letters in Saint Louis, 100,000 telegrams and 14,000 packages. When he participated in writing a quick-turnaround book, Lindbergh went on an 82-city tour of 22,350 miles and was seen by three million more people.

Courtesy of newspapermen, Lindbergh was mostly referred to as "Lucky Lindy" forevermore after his flight. But the rest of his life was not always so lucky. A baby he had with wife Anne Morrow Lindbergh was kidnapped and murdered. He became a controversial figure because of his political stance saying the United States should stay out of World War II, though he eventually flew 50 missions in the Pacific as a civilian consultant, and he was ripped apart by critics for making anti–Semitic statements.

## 30. Charles Lindbergh

Throughout his life, Charles Lindbergh, who died at 72 in 1974, was revered for his solo flight across the Atlantic and praised for working with airlines to improve safety and offering innovations that could upgrade air travel.

He very much lived a complicated life, though through the rearview mirror of history he will always glow as the aviator who mastered the unknown with one bold stroke.

# 31

## Dempsey–Tunney II Is On

**W**HERE TO PUT IT. Once promoter Tex Rickard had the circumstances fall his way and he had secured the agreement of Jack Dempsey and Gene Tunney to fight for a second time, the next issue to be determined was where the best venue was to hold it.

Philadelphia was a one-off because of the dearly departed Sesquicentennial celebration. What was learned from that experience, however, was that there was a desire from the ticket-buying public to see these men make war on each other. There was a big-time hunger for another Dempsey–Tunney bout. If round one could attract 120,000, or whatever the genuine count was, a stadium of equal size would be demanded to quench the curiosity of the masses for a second bout.

That ruled out Rickard's Madison Square Garden, puny by these standards. Even the Polo Grounds might not accommodate the demand. Or Boyle's Thirty Acres in Jersey. Should Rickard find a willing location and construct his own monstrosity of an arena, as costly as that would be?

Then there was Chicago, with Soldier Field, more than anywhere else a seemingly perfect locale. There was just one issue. Chicago was the home of supreme gangster Al Capone. Capone was not only a boxing fan but a Dempsey fan. There was a strong undercurrent in the atmosphere that the powerful mobster might interfere in the result, somehow fixing the fight so Dempsey would win.

That type of suspicion was not the kind of black eye boxing needed. Nor was it what Dempsey wanted to hear. He was an honorable man, bitterly disappointed about losing his heavyweight championship to Tunney in 1926, but he wanted everything to be on the square. Such talk made Dempsey uneasy.

Many years later, in his autobiography, Dempsey offered an account of what he said transpired between him and Capone, whom he admitted admired his fist-fighting. "Chicago's Al Capone, to whom I was still The Hero, let the word out that he had enough dough and influence spread

Heavyweight champion Gene Tunney (middle), in a headdress, was honored by Native Americans after he claimed the title from Jack Dempsey (Library of Congress).

around to make sure I would win," Dempsey said.[1] Imagine the power of the man, or arrogance.

Capone made it known he was betting $50,000 on a Dempsey

victory. He believed Dempsey was his kind of tough guy, and perhaps through newspaper reading about Tunney and his close, personal relationship with Shakespeare, thought of him as not manly enough to be the heavyweight champ. Capone once called Tunney "a f ... ing pansy."[2] Big Al apparently favored heavy hitters over boxers when it came to style.

Dempsey continued: "Not wanting Scarface to do anything I might regret, I sent him a short, handwritten note asking him to lay off and let the fight go off in true sportsmanship."[3] Sports memorabilia collectors of today would probably pay $100,000 for possession of such a note, but if it is out there anywhere it is on the QT.

Dempsey said he never received a direct response to his note to Capone, but a day later he got the answer he sought in a different way. A massive arrangement of flowers, an estimated $200 worth, showed up at his home delivered to his wife, Estelle, with a card reading, "To the Dempseys, in the name of sportsmanship."[4]

Dempsey took that to mean as far as Capone was concerned, the fight would be on the up-and-up. That also indicated perhaps Dempsey had wiggled out of a tight spot. He had put distance between himself and Capone's idea without insulting him. No one wanted Capone mad at them.

Whatever Capone was truly thinking, there might well have been some members of his outfit who didn't get the same message Dempsey received. The referee assigned to the Dempsey–Tunney rematch was Dave Miller, but when he was out eating in a restaurant one day leading up to the bout, he said he was approached by a group of menacing men who told him to remember who "the boss" was.[5]

That implied Capone and that implied he might not be keeping his hands off. Miller withdrew from the fight and was replaced as the third man in the ring by Dave Barry. Not that anyone could read the future at this moment, but in this fight it would very much matter who the referee was.

Meanwhile, Dempsey tried to drum up a nefarious scenario from his first match against Tunney, writing a guest story in the *Chicago Herald and Examiner* urging Tunney to come clean about his relationship with a Philadelphia strongman named Max "Boo Boo" Huff, from whom he had borrowed $20,000. The convoluted tale touched on gambling and a desire to fix the first fight with a certain referee who would disqualify Dempsey for low blows.

One of those involved was supposed to be the old boxer Abe Attell, besmirched in the Black Sox Scandal, who supposedly had so much faith in Tunney's ability he wanted to manage him even after he lost to Harry Greb.

Tunney's verbal answer to sportswriters at his training camp, and in an open letter, was, "Utter trash. At best, a cheap appeal for public sympathy." Also true to his image, Tunney dismissed the reporters by saying, "I have more important things to do. I am currently reading 'Of Human Bondage' and I am going to return promptly to Mr. [Somerset] Maugham's excellent work."[6] Then Tunney said he was off to the library.

Maxine Rickard, wife of promoter Tex, joked about Tunney's image of that ilk, saying that when he was asked a question, his answer covered the history of boxing from the Roman gladiators to that moment and his comments were all in four-syllable words.

Dempsey was still being bombarded by lawsuits from all angles filed by his old partner, Jack Kearns, serving as distractions. Wife Estelle was depressed because the first talking motion picture had arrived and she wondered if she had a future. And Tunney was now being hit with lawsuits from "Boo Boo" Hoff and New York Giants owner Tim Mara, both of whom stated he owed them hundreds of thousands of dollars. They were outrageous claims. In the land of free speech—and free access to the court system—anyone could say anything.

Anyone could also bet any which way he wanted. If Capone, the powerhouse gangster of the Prohibition world in Chicago (this was a home game for him), could lay down big bucks on Dempsey that he could afford from the millions he made, then a counterbalance could be put forth on Tunney. Hoff was on Tunney's side and anted up major dollars with bookies backing his thinking.

For a guy with a connection, loose as it was, with Al Capone, Dempsey was frantically worried about Tunney's ties to Hoff and the Philadelphia mob. He even wanted to meet Tunney face-to-face to gain assurances this was going to be a fair fight. Tunney would not agree to such a tete-a-tete. Officially, Tunney was a 7-to-5 favorite. That seemed reasonable. Those who set the line had processed what they saw the year before in Philadelphia and applied it to their calculations.

Meanwhile, things were not going so great for Dempsey in sparring. His partners in the ring kept opening old scar tissue, causing him to bleed. That was a bad look if the writers saw what was happening. If he was that susceptible to cuts, that may have indicated Dempsey had stayed around too long. Tunney had beat a tattoo on Dempsey's face the year before and it took more than bandages that time to cover the damage. Was he going to be vulnerable to the same type of assault?

All of the back-and-forth, the hullabaloo or ballyhoo, whatever was being said in Dempsey's allegations or Tunney's replies, pleased one man. Rickard had to be happy. The more the fight was in the limelight—in the newspapers—the more it worked on boxing fans' minds.

The more questions raised, the more true believers in Dempsey who felt the first meeting was a fluke, the more new believers in Tunney who felt he would handle him again, all of that was good for the gate.

"Now they're hating each other," Rickard said to his wife. "I think I'll have some more tickets printed."[7]

It was a big event, another Battle of the Century. You had to be there and Tex Rickard was ready to accommodate you at Soldier Field, another sporting stadium that could hold well over 100,000 people.

# 32

# The Long Count

There are not very many boxing matches that have nicknames such as the Battle of the Century or the "Thrilla in Manila," and even fewer individuals rounds.

The rematch of Jack Dempsey and Gene Tunney for the heavyweight championship on September 22, 1927, carries both the appellation of "The Long Count Fight" and the phrase "The Long Count," applied to the three-minute seventh round when all hell broke out, confusion reigned and a century later likely remains the most significant round in history.

More than 100,000 fans (some sources round it off, others state it was 104,943) filled Soldier Field in Chicago for the scheduled 10-round fight pitting Dempsey against Tunney for a second time. For a second time, when the night was over, the men left the ring with Tunney holding tight to the championship belt. Even if all of those fans did not completely understand what they saw.

Whether any bookies or gangsters got their way, not all of them could, with a result tinged by controversy forevermore. The men in the contest were two of the most famous heavyweights of all time. All of American society of the period seemed touched by insanity and somehow insanity made its way into the ring.

This was a classic showdown between a slugger in Dempsey and a boxer in Tunney, who almost exactly a year earlier lifted the crown from seven-year champ Dempsey with a dominating display of boxing, cutting the strong man up and dancing out of the way of his big blows. There was no debate about who won the decision.

Whether it was the entreaties of his pal Babe Ruth, his promoter Tex Rickard, both or a clamor from other sources, Dempsey, who originally intended to retire, agreed to an attempt to regain the title. He defeated Jack Sharkey in an elimination match and there was Tunney again, now the owner of the sport's biggest prize.

Rickard, always proud of the massive crowds his matches attracted,

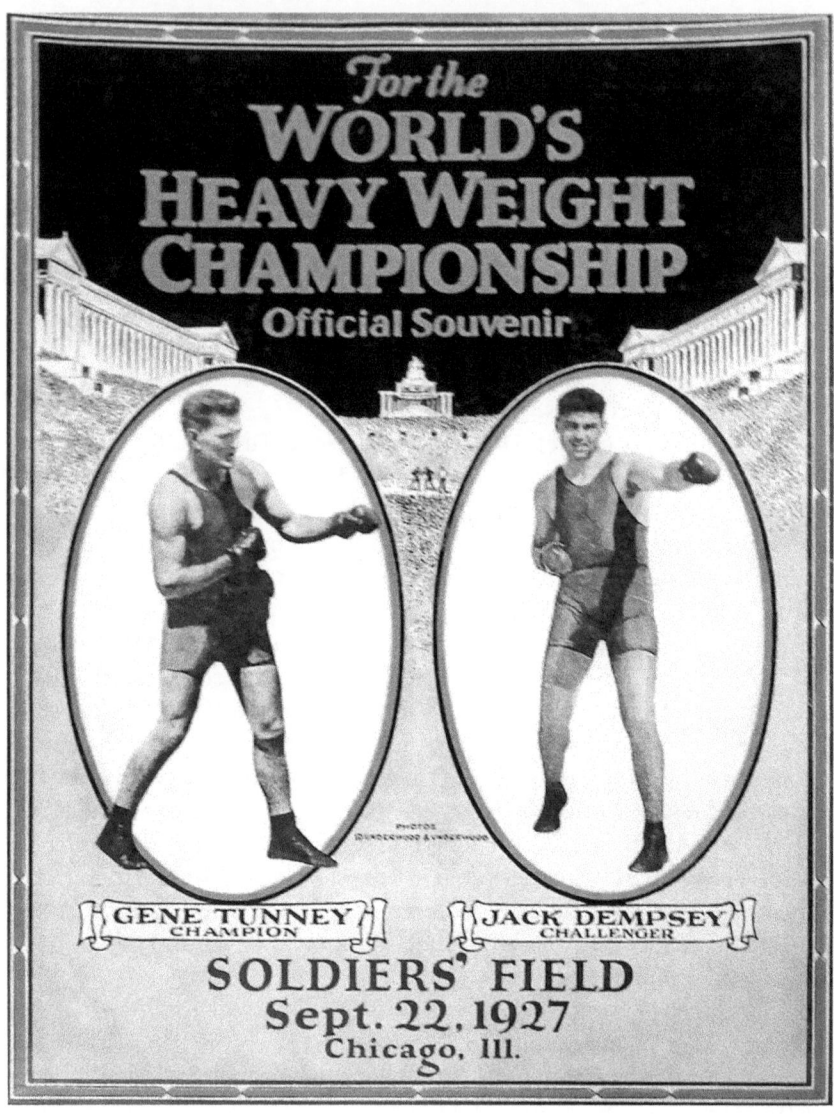

The program sold to fans for the second Jack Dempsey–Gene Tunney heavyweight fight in Chicago in 1927, when Tunney held the crowd, was a glossier, fancier magazine-type keepsake than the one from the Philadelphia fight (author's collection).

glanced at the huge throng before the bout's start and commented on how the rich and famous had made Soldier Field the place to be. "Kid," Rickard said to a sportswriter, "if the earth came up and the sky came down and wiped out my first 10 rows, it would be the end of everything.

## 32. The Long Count

Because I've got in those 10 rows all the world's wealth, all the world's brains and production talent. Just in them 10 rows, kid. And you and me never seed anything like it."[1]

The last was a favorite expression of Rickard's, who was always given to hyperbole, but this was no exaggeration. Dempsey–Tunney II was the first $2 million gate ever (close to $2.7 million) and Rickard knew it since he had promoted boxing's first $1 million date with Dempsey against Georges Carpentier.

It was calculated that $2.7 million was worth more than $46 million in 2023 dollars. As another view, in the 2020s baseball's minimum salary for members of its 25-man roster is $740,000.

"The money from boxing dwarfed baseball in the 1920s," said Hall of Fame boxing promoter J. Russell Peltz of Philadelphia. "Dempsey was bigger than Babe Ruth."[2]

Some current-day baseball players collect as much as $40 million for their season. Some team totals in the 1920s did not exceed $250,000.

What Rickard could not know at that point was, in its own way, the sky was about to fall on the sport and it wasn't rain as it was in Philadelphia.

Winners of the first match between two boxers always think the rematch will go as the first bout did. Losers of the first match always believe the rematch will go their way, that this time they will be better than they were, luckier than they were or the other guy won't be as good as he was.

Sometimes, the clearheaded, independent thinkers who analyzed the first showdown come to their own conclusion. They review the data and remind themselves what they saw and, putting their rooting interests and hearts aside, vote with their brains. They show up for a second show—for all the talk—with the belief it might play out exactly the same way as the first one.

For the first six rounds in Chicago, that is what happened. Dempsey could not change his stripes and Tunney was not inclined to change his. So, Dempsey came out of his corner from the first round on seeking to penetrate Tunney's defenses, seeking to unload with the big punch he was so famous for delivering and scoring with over the years. Tunney came out of his corner at the opening bell with the same strategy that worked so well for him in Philadelphia. Such a boxing style is often called stick-and-move. Tunney stayed a safe distance away from Dempsey's charges and whenever he saw an opening, he flicked a jab or a straight shot at Dempsey's head.

Tunney's blows, as they had in the first fight, made a difference when he cut up his foe's face and almost closed both of his eyes. The performance may not have been as decisively one-sided, but it was obvious to witnesses that Tunney was accumulating points and if the bout went to a decision at the end, he was going to be ahead again.

There was one major difference for the second Dempsey–Tunney fight. Between their first bout and this one, a new rule had been promulgated. One reason Dempsey had piled up so many victories and so many knockouts over the years was his ability to put down opponents with knockdowns over and over again.

Under the old system, just because one fighter's fists knocked down his foe, he did not have to back off as the man struggled to rise to his feet again. The opponent may have beaten the 10-count of a referee, but the foe who put him on the canvas would be right there, standing over him, ready to pounce all over again while he was trying to recover. Luis Angel Firpo was a victim of such a situation. Dempsey would blast him, Firpo would fall, then immediately after Firpo got up, Dempsey smashed him again and he hit the dirt again.

What had changed was this: now if a fighter knocked a man down, the person who threw the punch had to back off to a neutral corner (not one manned by either his or his foe's seconds) before the referee began counting. That provided the guy who was knocked down a little bit more unofficial recovery time before the fighter with the upper hand could get back to him and fling more punches at his head.

There was a careful explanation of the new rule to the fighters before the Dempsey–Tunny fight began to make sure the key players understood it. This may have seemed to be an innocuous rule change in the interests, at least, of better safety, and except for a basic issuance of the way things changed, it was not dwelled upon in the press, or by trainers and managers with their fighters.

Fundamentally, with their minds racing, the pressure mounting, attention on the attendance and focus on the opponent, there was no reason to believe that either man spent extra time reading up on the rule book. This rule that was fresh and, has been institutionalized for the nearly 100 years since, changed everything.

As became commonplace, not only was there a huge live turnout of spectators, but big events such as this turned out to be the kind of thing the new medium of radio coveted. Once again, broadcasters Graham McNamee and his partner, Phillips Carlin, did the talking, and their words were sent out to 60 NBC stations. That meant just as those on hand would be confused by the happenings, listeners could be.

The crux of the fight, the controversy and history played out in the seventh round when Dempsey finally broke through Tunney's protective cocoon. Dempsey, as he had long sought to do, in both fights, trapped Tunney against the ropes and when he did, he was able to capitalize.

Dempsey, a solid puncher with both hands, connected with two rights and two lefts, combinations that wobbled Tunney. Then Dempsey delivered four more blows and dropped him to the canvas. Tunney was down and opportunity screamed out to Dempsey. This was the only time in Tunney's career he was knocked down.

Dempsey was supposed to back off to a neutral corner, but he did not move, instead standing over Tunney ready to smack him again when he stood up, just as he had done in all of his previous fights. But it was no longer legal. Referee Dave Barry, who remembered the new rule well, kept yelling at Dempsey to head to a neutral corner, but he stayed in one spot menacing.

Until Dempsey got out of the way, Barry did not begin his 10-count. In the heat of this battle, Dempsey had forgotten all about the rule. Tunney was down and he was slow to rise. He would clearly have been out since easily another three to five bonus seconds had passed (some even say eight) beyond the 10-second limit. Barry himself guided Dempsey to a neutral corner.

While this element of drama was taking place, Paul Beeler, the official timekeeper at ringside, was counting over the knockdown and had reached five. However, Barry then began the count all over again from one.

Dempsey's gaffe resulted in Tunney, who appeared dizzy and out of it, gaining extra time to clear his head, just enough for him to beat the delayed count. Never mind 10 seconds, Tunney was down for anywhere between 13 and 18 seconds. Dempsey should have scored a knockout and regained the heavyweight title right then and there. Hence, the Long Count.

To at least one sportswriter, Tunney reported that he had been out on his feet. To others, he said he was ready to stand at a count of two and stayed down until nine merely to rest. "Who really knows, if he could have gotten up?" Peltz said nearly a hundred years later. "It wouldn't be the story of it."[3]

Dempsey's best chance to become champ again evaporated. In the eighth round, a round later, a rejuvenated Tunney, relishing his survival, landed a big shot on Dempsey and knocked him down. Peculiarly, after all of the to-do of the previous round, Barry began counting over Dempsey before Tunney moved to a neutral corner. That sounds like an inconsistency, but much more was made of the seventh-round brouhaha then and over time.

Almost bizarrely, Dempsey's popularity rose after he lost twice to

Tunney. He had endured slurs of being a slacker during World War I, even as he had tried to enlist and he had dominated the heavyweight division for years. Yet there was something in the nobility of his struggles against the younger Tunney and the weirdness of losing on a long count that freshly endeared Dempsey to a public that had looked at him with a certain skepticism during his fallow periods when he went years without defending the crown.

The sportswriters gave Dempsey a fresh look and liked what they saw. Perhaps because they thought of him as a down-to-earth guy who was always straight compared with Tunney and his public flirtations with Shakespeare. There was no internet and there was no television, so the newspapers, aided by radio, were the sources of news and opinion-forming for the famous. Paul Gallico, one of those New York sportswriters who had been up and down on Dempsey over the years, wrote that Dempsey was considered to be the "greatest and most beloved sports hero the country had ever known."[4]

Maybe, even overlooking Babe Ruth. Yet it only shows that even a century ago the public was as fickle as it is in the 2020s.

In his autobiography, decades after the fight, Dempsey recalled the legendary Long Count. "Round seven was the round that made the fight, the round I shall never forget simply because it created more than 50 years of controversy [now about 100]," Dempsey said in the early 1970s.

"I forgot the rules. I lost my head and couldn't move as referee Barry shouted, 'Get to a neutral corner.' I stayed put. The count had already started when I was pushed toward a neutral corner, already having lost valuable seconds. I was the jungle fighter so completely set in my ways I couldn't accept new conditions. I was used to standing over my opponents to make sure that when I pounded them down, they stayed down."[5]

Dempsey recalled the count starting all over and Tunney ducking away successfully. He said he growled at his opponent, "Come on and fight."[6] When the final bell sounded, Dempsey knew he had lost and he said he knew right then he should retire. He was 32 years old and said he felt much older than that, no longer the youthful up-and-comer who had dreamed of fighting his way to the top.

When Tunney, the champion going in and coming out, talked to Rickard about collecting his paycheck, he was informed it came to $990,445. The Fighting Marine thought it would be a neat thing to be paid $1 million for a single night's work so he brought Rickard a check for about $10,000 so the promoter could write him one for a million bucks.

Although Tunney was asked many times about how quickly he

could have climbed off the canvas, right after the fight, and for years after the fight, he often fine-tuned his response. Once, he spoke in depth about what he likely really thought. "Realizing, as do all professional boxers, that the first nine seconds of a knockdown belong to the man who is on the floor, I never had any thought of getting up until the referee said nine," Tunney said. "Only dazed boxers who have momentarily lost consciousness and 'show-offs' fail to take the nine seconds that are theirs."[7]

Of course, there was some analysis stating Tunney appeared to fit that very description of momentarily losing consciousness.

Boxing experts and observers of the modern era note that Dempsey and Tunney's fights might have faded from memory or been more overshadowed—except for the Long Count.

Steve Farhood, once editor of *KO* magazine *The Ring* and a Showtime television boxing expert, said the only excuse Dempsey had for his mistake was not heeding the change requiring the pause in the neutral corner. "It was a brand-new rule," Farhood said. "The rule is a 10-count. There have been a lot of counts [picked up by refs from timekeepers]. Would Dempsey have stopped him? We don't know."[8]

That is the heart of the matter, the mystery of the entire Long Count kerfuffle. Did Jack Dempsey really knock out Gene Tunney and not get credit for it because of an arithmetic error? Or did Dempsey lose the heavyweight title because he didn't pay attention in school when the teacher was lecturing?

## 33

## That's All, Folks

**I**T WAS OVER. JACK DEMPSEY realized it before he left the ring as the loser for a second time to Gene Tunney in Chicago. His long boxing career was finished. Not even the combined wooing of Babe Ruth, Ty Cobb, Walter Johnson and Lou Gehrig could persuade him to fight again. And don't think Tex Rickard didn't try.

For the increasingly vocal Dempsey boxing fans, that was a sad time. Much like the transition of power in a country, there was a new standard-bearer in Tunney, so there was no vacuum at the top. But it felt different. Change always does. Even with his defeat the year before, Dempsey was still around, still in the hunt, pointing toward redemption in Dempsey–Tunney II.

People who had been mean to Dempsey over the World War I issue were still going to miss him. Tunney just did not have the same widespread appeal to the masses as Dempsey and he did not really seek it out. Indeed, he pretty much had an otherwise secret life going on away from the spotlight. He dropped one hint that no one really picked up on in the moments after he survived the Long Count and radio announcers gave him the microphone.

Tunney sent a shout-out to his friends in Greenwich, Connecticut. In case listeners with only half an ear cocked to the sound, or thought his message was half-dropped, they heard correctly. Tunney was not saying hello to his old neighborhood of Greenwich Village, but his new neighborhood in Greenwich.

That was where the love of his life, Polly Lauder, had her own radio turned on to listen to his progress in the battle against Dempsey. Tunney was sending a private message to his supporters in the monied town that most sportswriters, if any, were unaware he had any connection.

For Tunney, winning the heavyweight championship from Dempsey in 1926 was a goal achieved. Defending it successfully, controversy aside, in 1927 was validation. His valor and his fists—and don't

# 33. That's All, Folks

After defeating Jack Dempsey twice in heavyweight championship boxing matches, Gene Tunney married Polly Lauder, a Connecticut heiress, and entered the business world (Library of Congress).

underestimate his brainpower—had carried him to a second triumph over one of the greatest fighters who ever lived.

What did that mean now? When Dempsey thought ahead, he wondered what he might do with the rest of his life since he was just 32 years old. He just knew he had no desire to strap on the gloves again. Tunney was quietly looking forward to marriage and raising a family.

After counting the receipts and gazing out at the massive sea of faces focused on the ring in Chicago, promoter Rickard thought otherwise about both men's futures. Dollar signs whirred in his eyes as one would see on a cartoon character. True, Tunney had beaten Dempsey twice, but both times Dempsey finished on his feet. Dempsey had knocked Tunney down in that wild seventh round in the second bout, engendering the Long Count that remained a topic of national discussion.

Rickard even guaranteed Dempsey—the challenger—a million-dollar payday if he would assent to a third fight with Tunney. Rickard was that sure a third match between the two men would become the biggest moneymaking fight of all time.

This, however, proved the point that there are some things more important than money. While it is believed pride was somewhat involved in Dempsey's decision because he could not imagine losing to the same man three times in a row, there was another element at work that was priceless. Doctors had warned Dempsey that if he continued to fight, he might lose his sight. There was already damage and if he continued to box his vision might seriously and irreversibly deteriorate. That was the clincher for Dempsey.

Transitioning from Dempsey to Tunney in the heavyweight division was not exactly a bloodless coup since there had been blood spilt, most of it belonging to Dempsey. But it was time to move on. There are times in the evolution of sport that the stars align and greatness overlaps. There are other times when greatness dominates. And there are still other times when the cupboards are bare. Tunney was indeed the undisputed king. But there was no new, younger Tunney lurking to challenge him the way Tunney had stalked Dempsey and spent years working his way into the No. 1 contender spot.

Rickard lamented that there was no one at all on the horizon to produce a decent match for Tunney that would excite the public into buying tickets in droves the way they had for those two humongous turnouts of Dempsey–Tunney I and Dempsey–Tunney II.

With no Dempsey around, Rickard had to work with pumping up Tunney, and he dived in. "There is no denying that Tunney is not only a champion, but a great champion. I believe that he is one of the greatest champions the class has ever seen," Rickard said.[1]

Rickard could promote anything. He could hype anything. But artificiality went only so far in drumming up business. To produce a credible opponent for Tunney, Rickard oversaw a series of elimination bouts featuring those whom he felt were worthy of inclusion.

Some of those involved had been waiting a long time for a chance, and some had lost to Dempsey. For them, this was likely a last chance to grab at the garland of roses. Tom Heeney of New Zealand was pitted against Bostonian Jim Maloney at Madison Square Garden. Little was known about Heeney in New York at the time, but he overwhelmed Maloney, knocking him out at one minute, 17 seconds of the first round.

Rickard next matched Heeney with Jack Sharkey, who was probably the best known and appreciated of those vying for the crown. Sharkey was favored, but the fight went the distance, 12 rounds, and was scored a draw, a result that pleased no one.

While more than half the observers felt Sharkey won, Sharkey was not bragging afterward. He summed up Heeney as a very tough foe, who was "like a stone wall. You hit one of those guys flush on the lug and he keeps coming at you and you say to yourself, 'How do I get out of this ring? Where's the exit? The hell with trying to knock him out, I'm just busting my hands.'"[2]

Rickard did not give up on Sharkey and he put him in the ring with veteran Johnny Risko. Only Risko won a split decision. Heeney, meanwhile, overcame Jack Delaney in a 15-round crowd-pleaser. Delaney, who was born in Canada, though he eventually became an American citizen, won the world light-heavyweight championship and had a legion of fans, many of them vocal females who admired his form.

Delaney then faced Sharkey. But secretly, Delaney had a severe drinking problem. He got himself blotto out of public view on benders and when he showed up to meet Sharkey he was not in shape. Sharkey knocked him out in the first round.

Tunney had already signed a contract with Rickard to promote his first defense with a guaranteed payday of $525,000. Rickard took a deep sigh and was ready to throw in the war horse Sharkey as a more advantageous foe for the public than Heeney. Only Tunney vetoed it. He insisted on Heeney as the opponent. Rickard sighed again.

Heeney's following, if he really had one, was an ocean or two away. He had worked professionally as a plumber and even been awarded a medal for rescuing two women who were in danger of drowning. Heeney, then 30, had tried out London but got lucky with his inclusion into the boxing elimination tournament out of New York. All of which was nice but couldn't truly be counted on to sell tickets.

What Heeney had was punching power, though at just five-foot-nine he was short for a heavyweight. The man did not back off and Damon Runyon called him "The Hard Rock from Down Under."[3]

By then, Tunney, turning 31 in 1928, had decided that this was going to be his last fight. He was going to marry his sweetheart and go into the business world.

As the fight drew closer, the reality of promoting was as Rickard feared. This match was short on ballyhoo. Heeney's lack of name recognition was not helping the gate. Tunney may well have been as terrific a fighter as Rickard said he was, but he lacked the charisma of a Dempsey.

Although compared with his recent successes this Broadway show was not a major financial hit, the Tunney–Heeney bout drew 45,890 fans to Yankee Stadium. Those in attendance did not know it, but they were witnessing Gene Tunney's last boxing match.

There was no doubt Heeney was playing up his heritage for the occasion. When he stepped into the ring, he displayed a native Maori robe advertising the phrase "Be strong, be active, be brave," sent to him to wear by the widow of a New Zealand government official. It was good theater.

Whether he brought the ultimate confidence to the fight after downing Dempsey twice, whether he was relaxed because he knew this was the end, or Tunney was simply at the top of his form, many said his handling of Heeney was his best showing ever.

Not only did Tunney demonstrate his always-reliable slick boxing style, but unlike in the Dempsey fights, he unleashed more powerful right-hand connections than ever and the boxer even showed he could take a good punch—several of them—from a slugger.

Tunney won by technical knockout, the referee stopping the fight with eight seconds remaining in the 11th round. Some believe, for Heeney's overall health, it should have been halted a round sooner. As it was, Tunney's punches did the same kind of job on Heeney's face as they had done on Dempsey's, leaving the opponent cut up and mirror shy for a while afterward.

Runyon was especially graphic in his description, writing, "It was all just about as expected, the man from New Zealand wading in bravely to certain destruction. Blood dripping from his nose, blood dripping from cuts along the creases of his strangely old-looking face. One eye partly closed."[4]

It was only days after the bout that Tunney sent Rickard a note informing him that he planned to retire from boxing and had no intention of defending his title again. Only a couple of days after that, Tunney was honored at a New York luncheon and presented with *The Ring* magazine's most valuable boxer trophy.

He thanked everyone and then stunned the gathering of supporters and sportswriters by announcing that he was officially retiring, going on to the next chapter of his life. Tunney had reached the pinnacle of his profession, the top of the world, it might be said, accomplished the ambition that drove him for years, and gotten rich in the process. To him, it was time to walk away, even if in their own way, the writers were just saying hello.

With Tunney, conqueror of the great Dempsey, departed from the scene, the two best-known fighters of the time ended an era in the sport. However, it went further than that. Although no one could have predicted such a thing with precision as late July turned to August in 1928, America was about to conclude its Roaring Twenties era.

The grandiosity that had burst upon the scene was about to dissolve, the prosperity that followed the end of World War I was about to dissipate.

In the boxing world, the legends of Jack Dempsey and Gene Tunney lived on, far beyond their life spans.

# 34

## Things Unravel

They got Al Capone by coming through the back door. If the police in Chicago and Cicero in Illinois were not going to corral the gangster and shut off the flow of booze and blood, the feds would find a way.

The Saint Valentine's Day Massacre was the signature crime of the Roaring Twenties and it was too much for many. It was one thing to set up glasses of booze when it was illegal, because, after all, whom did that really hurt? But it was another thing to embarrass Chicago nationally with wanton murders. There was no hard proof, but everyone believed Capone was at fault, even if the king of the mobsters was vacationing in Florida at the time holding press conferences while stating, "Who, me?"

This was also a heavyweight matchup, without the aid of Tex Rickard. Compared with this issue, Jack Dempsey–Gene Tunney was tame, though with many more witnesses in the end. Big Al's Chicago Outfit, representing the Italians, sent a message to George "Bugs" Moran's Irish North Side gang to butt out of their territory in the booze-running business.

The event that inspired the nation and has endured as one of the best-recalled crimes in American history involved the murders of seven associates of the North Side operation on February 14, 1929. Happy Valentine's Day to you.

Victims were lured to a warehouse in the Lincoln Park area of Chicago at 10:30 a.m. and met by a well-dressed quartet of men, two wearing suits and ties and the other two dressed as police officers, who it could be said confused their holidays thinking it must be Halloween. The fake police and their cohorts wiped out all seven men, several with bullets from Thompson submachine guns.

Moran was not among the deceased. When real police responded to the scene, one of the Moran associates was still alive, despite having been shot 14 times. He refused to identify the killers and died a few hours later.

## 34. Things Unravel

**The nation did tire of Prohibition, and by the time it was repealed in 1933, union laborers were marching in the streets chanting to be rid of it.**

No one was charged in the massacre, so called by newspapers with blaring headlines. It remains unsolved despite the suspicion it was a revenge killing by Capone for Moran's hijacking of some of Big Al's Canadian whiskey and attempts to muscle in on his business. The lure for bringing in Moran's men—it was anticipated he would be among them and was the probable main target—was a promised sale of discount booze.

As part of the overall ruse, apparently to satisfy initial public curiosity after the loud blasts from the guns, the two "policemen" guided the other two villains in street clothes out the warehouse door. They exited with hands in the air, giving the impression to outdoor passersby that arrests had been made. Then they all scampered away. It was a slick scheme. Besides the drastically wounded Moran gang member who died later that afternoon with his lips sealed was a dog named "Highball." The dog did no ratting either.

This high-profile multi-person slaying seemed to outrage the populace, but local law enforcement authorities were not going to buck the booze runners. The federal government could enforce Prohibition violations but had no jurisdiction in a local murder case. The new Federal Bureau of Investigation was probing, however, trying to find a way to get Capone off the street, somehow, some way.

It took years of pursuit and creative prosecution away from the state and local court system in Illinois, but a special federal unit, led by Eliot Ness, eventually charged Scarface with 22 counts of federal tax evasion. It was discovered that Capone had not filed his federal taxes for four years. To some, it may have seemed like charging a vicious killer with parking violations, but in the end, this ended Capone's reign in 1931.

Capone was indicted that year, and when the case went to trial in 1933, he was convicted and sentenced to 11 years in federal prison. Capone went to prison, where he was soon showing signs of declining health from syphilis. However, Capone was free when he died of a heart attack in 1947.

Long before that, also in 1933, the poorly planned, ill-thought-out constitutional amendment known as Prohibition had been repealed. The wild, wide-open days of booze running presided over by Capone and similar-oriented mobsters was over.

Although Dempsey and Tunney had both retired, leaving a vacancy at the top of the heavyweight division, promoter Rickard was always on the lookout for new frontiers. Only his heyday was also over. In a startling and sudden development, the colorful and hugely successful promoter who had lifted boxing to new heights was stricken by an attack of appendicitis.

Rickard spent Christmas at home in New York and then, on December 26, 1928, he traveled to Miami on business. He was seeking to arrange a boxing contest between Jack Sharkey and Young Stribling. While in South Florida, for amusement, Rickard attended the grand opening of the Miami Beach Kennel Club.

He began feeling poorly, then worse. Taken to a hospital, Rickard underwent an appendectomy, which was only supposed to lay him up for a short time. However, something went wrong and he began showing complications from the surgery. Shockingly, within days, what began as a casual diagnosis of indigestion ended with Rickard's death. When Rickard passed away on January 6, 1929, at the age of 59, Dempsey was present in his hospital room, it was said holding his hand as he expired.

Rickard's body was flown north and actually lay in state at Madison Square Garden, as if he had been a former president of the United States. Dempsey could not hide his tears.

President Calvin Coolidge, who had been in a position of governmental power basically for the entire Roaring Twenties, as vice president first and as president since 1923 by succeeding Warren Harding at his death, and after winning his own election in 1924, decided he had had enough.

Although eligible to represent the Republicans in the 1928 election, and after presiding over a grand period of economic prosperity for the United States, Coolidge yielded to a yearning to return to a quieter life in New England.

Silent Cal made clear his intentions of not running for another term, but typical of his nature, when he announced his game plan, he did not issue a flowery, lengthy commentary. In fact, even more typical of his nature, Coolidge did not utter the words of his announcement but wrote them on a piece of paper.

While visiting his summer White House in the Black Hills of South Dakota, Coolidge wrote out a statement reading, "I do not choose to run for president in 1928," and handed it to his secretary, Everett Sanders, preparing for release at a press conference on August 2, 1927. Over the years, the statement, both in seriousness and in joking fashion, joined the American lexicon, but usually in truncated fashion of simply, "I do not choose to run." In a quirky bit of behavior, at the press conference, Coolidge had copies of the statement cut into small strips of paper and handed out to the news people, then said he had nothing to add, took no questions and adjourned for the day.[1]

Coolidge's choice set off a free-for-all in the Republican Party. His vice president, Charles Dawes, jumped into the race. So did Herbert Hoover, Coolidge's secretary of commerce between 1923 and 1928. Poor Hoover won the nomination and the election. Unanticipated was the coming collapse of the U.S. economy and the descent into the Great Depression that ruined any hope he had for a meaningful presidency. The economic freefall completely altered the mood and daily life of the country so soon after the wonderful days of the earlier 1920s.

By September of 1929, the stock market appeared shaky. On October 24, Wall Street experienced its largest sell-off of stock shares in its history. On October 29, the day labeled Black Tuesday, the stock market endured "The Great Crash," negating the years-long bull market that had been a booming highlight of American economic well-being. Get out, get out, get out was the theme at the New York Stock Exchange. But it was too late. The good times were over and the bad times were going to be very bad.

The problems began with a bang and worsened with steady erosion. Jobs evaporated, as unemployment, which was virtually nil when the Depression began, climbed to more than 25 percent nationwide in 1933, although worse in many areas. Men left their families to travel the roads and railroads seeking jobs. Banks locked their doors, devouring Americans' savings and thrusting families into poverty.

Discretionary income evaporated. There was no money for fun stuff, and, for many, not enough cash for food. Government services provided emergency rations and people stood in long lines to receive sustenance for themselves and their families. It was as bleak an overall era as most Americans ever lived through and it scarred many for life.

Only months earlier, and for years before that, the United States as a society was living the high life, acting wild and carefree, frenziedly dancing the Charleston, illegally imbibing, a partying lifestyle punctuated by nights out on the town to watch the biggest of prize fights up close, the home baseball team make a run for the pennant or Red Grange and the Chicago Bears on tour. People didn't chat about the heavyweight championship belt. They tightened their own belts. For so many, the brakes had been put on taking advantage of such enjoyments.

As the last months of the 1920s ticked off, and the 1930s dawned, it was no longer the Roaring Twenties, but the Whimpering Twenties, on its way to the Depressing Thirties.

# 35

# DEMPSEY AND TUNNEY TOGETHER FOREVER

JACK DEMPSEY NEVER STOPPED BEING a fighter and a celebrity for the rest of his life. Gene Tunney tried to give up being a fighter and a celebrity five minutes after he retired from the ring.

They both lived long lives and they both had what might be termed happy long-term existences for the remainder of those lives. Their exploits in the ring never faded, nor did their rivalry, and in the minds of boxing fans and historians, their names have been linked forever. No one talks about one without talking about the other.

Dempsey won the heavyweight crown in 1919 from Jess Willard and kept it for seven years. He completed his boxing career with a record of 58 wins, six losses and nine draws.

Tunney won the heavyweight crown in 1926 from Dempsey and kept it for two years. He completed his boxing career with a record of 79 wins, one loss and four draws. The sole loss came to annoying nemesis Harry Greb.

The two men engaged in pioneering matches a year apart in the 1920s, each drawing live attendance of more than 100,000 people, and together their rivalry produced the first $2 million gate, in Chicago. They came to prominence at a good time for Americans to appreciate them and to be able to afford tickets to watch them. And they benefited from the foresight and acumen of Tex Rickard, one of the sport's greatest promoters of all time.

Dempsey took over the public consciousness first and is still remembered that way a hundred years after he burst onto the scene. "He was part and parcel of the era," said Don Majeski, a well-known boxing writer and historian. "It was the moveable feast post-war era. He made other fighters famous."[1] Just by fighting him. Would anyone remember Luis Angel Firpo, Georges Carpentier or some other opponents if they hadn't had their moment in the spotlight with Jack Dempsey?

Not only was Dempsey one of those human symbols of the 1920s, but it also helped that Dempsey was very good at what he did, outstanding, with the word *greatness* applied to him at his best in the ring. It has always been so, dating at least to Dempsey, that the true-blue boxing fan admires most the man who can be that toughest guy in the world.

"He should've been the only heavyweight anybody ever thought of when they thought about the greatest heavyweight champion," said legendary trainer Ray Arcel, who worked with 18 world champions. "I mean he had everything. He could punch, he could box. He was mean and determined."[2]

Monte D. Cox, a boxing writer, said of Dempsey, "Jack Dempsey was a sure killer. A fighter with great killer instinct and the ability and will to finish a hurt fighter." John Lardner, who followed father Ring Lardner into journalism, wrote, "Bobbing and weaving is a phrase that will probably be associated with Jack Dempsey until the end of time."[3] Actually, bobbing and weaving became part of everyday boxing lexicon, but it suggested that not only could Dempsey hit with devastating power, but he could also avoid getting hit most of the time.

Gene Tunney had a hugely successful boxing career, but many sportswriters portrayed him in print as an elitist who put on airs and tried to appear as a different kind of man from what he was (Library of Congress).

Although people love to do it across the sports world, it is almost impossible to compare luminaries across the decades. The late Bert Sugar, a historian who later edited *The Ring* magazine and *Boxing Illustrated*, called Dempsey the best pound-for-pound heavyweight champ. Nat Fleischer, the founder of *The Ring*, rated him fourth all time among all heavyweight champs into the 1970s. Fleischer died in 1973.

Dempsey was shocked and aggrieved by Rickard's untimely death. The men were in a joint partnership at the time to promote the

Sharkey–Stribling fight in Florida. At the urging of others, Dempsey carried through with the bout. Before his own troubles mushroomed, Al Capone, who bet on Sharkey, showed up for the fight.

Dempsey engaged in other business opportunities, but like most in the Depression, he was slammed financially by the crunch. To have an income, he took to touring and fighting exhibitions. His name, as did his hands, carried clout and his first swing through 13 cities in a month earned him $250,000. In a one-year period, Dempsey calculated he faced 175 would-be boxers and knocked out 100 of them.

For the first time, he entertained the notion of a serious ring comeback. To test himself, he engaged in a four-round exhibition with Kingfish Levinsky, but when the younger man thoroughly outboxed the old champ, then 37, he shelved that idea. As if he had not realized it in all starkness before, Dempsey recognized his boxing prime was in his rearview mirror.

What Dempsey learned from this phase of his life, annunciated by historian Majeski so many years later, was that he "was a professional celebrity."[4] That is not a bad thing to be if it keeps the person living a comfortable lifestyle, and that worked well enough for Dempsey.

In sports, an individual's dominance, being so much better than those competing against him or her, can create such a figure. That stature can be enhanced with the addition of a rivalry to the mix. Dempsey had both. He had his own achievements that gave him a reputation and he had the Tunney matches on his résumé, too.

When the United States entered World War II, Dempsey, perhaps seeking a do-over from earlier in life, tried to enlist but was rejected because he was too old. However, the government called on him to operate a physical training program. Then he was sent to the Pacific Theater, where he was supposed to stay out of the line of fire.

Yet when a unit he worked of men half his age was sent to attack Okinawa on April 1, 1945, Dempsey, then 49, insisted on joining them for the sea assault on the beach. In a moment of reflection later, the ex-champ said he was portrayed as a slacker in World War I and a hero in World War II and he observed that the commentators were incorrect both times.

Dempsey really never stopped shining to the public.

"He was a huge star and he was a hard hitter," said Nigel Collins, the one-time editor of *The Ring* magazine who is in the International Boxing Hall of Fame in Canastota, New York, as are Dempsey and Tunney. "Dempsey fit in so well with the Roaring Twenties. In some ways, he was a romantic figure."

That "hard hitter" summation is not to be underestimated as an important element in the Dempsey legend and his enduring respect.

"He was what the people thought a heavyweight champion should be," Collins said. "I think people like the guys who give them exciting fights."

And Tunney was not that guy. His being a boxer instead of a slugger brought a different style to the ring and it felt wrong to some that a slick guy could handle a powerful guy. Then there was the Tunney image of being aloof, that deep commitment to reading literature. "He was a strange bird," Collins said. "He was a snooty guy."

Collins, in his 70s, met Dempsey in person once, though it was not for a long visit. He was attending the New York Boxing Writers' banquet and the ex-champ was there. "I just went up to him and we just shook hands," Collins recalled. "He looked good."[5]

Tunney took his earnings from boxing, roughly $1.5 million from the last couple of bouts alone, and rode off into the sunset. He did not fight exhibitions. He went to tony Greenwich, Connecticut, first; married the love of his life; and had four children, including one son, John, who became a United States senator from California.

The Fighting Marine became a businessman who entered and thrived in the corporate world, simultaneously serving as a member of the board of directors of numerous companies. His name recognition from being the heavyweight champion did him no harm in opening doors. Ironically, given it was perceived as a liability in the fight game, Tunney's reputation as someone who was an avid reader of high-class literature, definitely including Shakespeare, found this trait enhanced his image in this other realm. It seemed to prove to those hiring that he was no simple palooka who could talk only with his fists.

Tunney proved quite versatile in the corporate world, becoming president of a distillery, dealing in rubber products and becoming the boss of a construction company, among other roles. Tunney, who had been a late entry in World War I and did his fighting with his fists in the ring then, played a very different role during World War II. Given the rank of captain, Tunney was appointed to lead a physical fitness program for the U.S. Navy between 1941 and 1945.

Essentially emphasizing how Tunney mostly removed himself from boxing was how he reacted to being invited to attend major bouts. In the earliest years of his retirement from the sport, and for some time across the 1930s, 1940s and 1950s, Tunney did attend big matches.

As is typical and traditional even today, as a luminary of the sport, his presence was announced to the crowd. He climbed through the ropes, waved and smiled. That was the role expected of former champs in such settings. Eventually, though, he tired of it.

"They're always inviting me to major fights, with all expenses paid for my wife and I, but I have no interest in going," Tunney said in the 1960s. "And when I turn down the invitations, they seem to hold it against me. I just don't see any point in me being introduced in the ring before a fight. After all, I haven't fought in more than 30 years."[6]

Tunney made an exception to his rule of not attending big matches when Muhammad Ali and Joe Frazier fought in 1971. He showed up to watch. There is no question Ali–Frazier is the biggest rivalry in the history of boxing and Tunney was not crazy enough to skip the bout.

History has been kinder to Tunney than the public was at the zenith of his accomplishments. Experts laud his growth and improvement over time as he went from a light-heavyweight to heavyweight and twice handled Dempsey.

In 1979, *Boxing Illustrated* felt compelled to publish an article headlined "A Tribute to Tunney," analyzing him as being underrated. "For a boxer who suffered only one defeat in his professional career—a loss he later avenged—James Joseph Tunney was never given his just due as heavyweight champion," the story read.[7]

Basically, it could be said Tunney's stature in boxing history was colored by image as much as substance, a picture painted of him as someone who was more dilettante than one to be viewed seriously despite the reality. Tunney invested as much energy into improving his brain through reading as he did in improving his boxing through workouts but was mostly ridiculed for that behavior.

That affected his image for all time's sake, during his fight days, throughout the rest of his life, until death at 81 in 1978, and beyond.

He seemed to always be defending his ability to think, actually, or be interested in subjects that did not involve bashing another man. Tunney once pointed out that Jem Mace, a long-before bare-knuckle champ, played the violin and another 19th-century fighter, Jem Ward, became an artist. Ward also played the flute and violin and sang in concerts. "Because a man is a boxer, it doesn't follow that he has to be illiterate," Tunney said in a so-there manner in citing those two examples.[8]

Tunney really should not have had to ever defend his record in the ring. "He was accepted as a great fighter, but as underrated for a long time," Majeski said of Tunney. "He was a phenomenal fighter."

Tunney was not a phenomenal personality to fight fans, though. Many years after the Dempsey–Tunney bouts Majeski approached both men to gather autographs for a cause. Dempsey, he said, asked, "How many autographs would you like?" For Tunney's signatures, he had to go to a corporation office and leave a card in the waiting room. He did get the autographs, though. To Majeski, the situation seemed to illustrate the difference between the two men.[9]

Certainly, Dempsey was more of a people person, more at ease with fans. Dempsey was more famous as a champion than Tunney, with longevity on his side, and is better remembered even though he lost twice to him.

Dempsey was royalty in the Roaring Twenties and it was his name that drove the ticket sales for the first fight with Tunney in 1926. There have been other great rivalries in the sport, said Steve Farhood, the boxing magazine editor, but what elevates Dempsey–Tunney beyond so many others is the Long Count.

"The Long Count keeps it going," Farhood said of memories of Dempsey–Tunney. "Could Tunney have gotten up in time? We don't know. When you add things up it really makes it a remarkable rivalry."[10]

Any discussion of Dempsey and Tunney inevitably comes back to the Long Count. Collins makes a rare and intriguing point. When interpreting the rules, he noted, they read that a knockout is determined when the referee counts to 10. "In the rules," Collins said, "it says the count of 10. It's not 10 seconds. You could count really fast or really slow."[11]

Of course, the referee, the timekeeper, the sportswriters, the fans sitting at ringside shouldn't be able to count to 14, 15 or 18. Occasionally, at times in the aftermath, Dempsey said he got robbed because of the Long Count. As he aged, he seemed to mellow somewhat, resigned to the idea that he just got beat.

Dempsey was divorced from Estelle Taylor in 1931, though he married twice more over the years.

Even as he weathered the Depression better than most, though at first losing a lot of money, Dempsey aged out of boxing completely, moving away from knocking out faux fighters in exhibitions. But he was able to still trade on his name.

Probably the most accessible heavyweight champion of all time (in contrast to Tunney being perhaps one of the least accessible), the fan-friendly Dempsey had a perfect forum for image burnishing, even if that was not the fundamental purpose.

In 1935, Dempsey opened Jack Dempsey's Broadway Restaurant in mid-town Manhattan with his name on the marquee in bright lights and handy to the foot traffic from nearby Times Square and, eventually, the latest Madison Square Garden.

Dempsey was an on-site greeter much of the time at what became a landmark New York institution. The restaurant served mountains of cheesecake and welcomed and fed boxing fans from around the world. The cheesecake became such a famous menu item that Dempsey could tout French president Charles de Gaulle as a customer who ordered from overseas several times a year.

## 35. Dempsey and Tunney Together Forever

For nearly 40 years after his retirement, from the mid–1930s to the mid–1970s, Jack Dempsey presided at his popular mid-town Manhattan establishment called Jack Dempsey's Broadway Restaurant.

"Dempsey's restaurant was pervasive," Majeski said. "You go to Dempsey's. You went to Dempsey's. It was a ritual. You took fighters there. And Dempsey was there, and he told stories."[12]

The restaurant was in New York and the champ was there, live and in person, the famous former heavyweight champion of the world.

"He outlived his contemporaries, he was in New York," Majeski said. "If there was a Mount Rushmore of boxing, he would be on it."[13]

In 1950, Dempsey wrote a book that was supposed to serve as an instructional manual for anyone wanting to pick up boxing pointers. However, in the introduction, and occasionally elsewhere in the pages, Dempsey offered reflective comments.

He mentioned that when Jess Willard took off his "bathrobe" in the ring in Toledo, Dempsey truly felt he was a giant. "Moreover, he was a perfectly proportioned giant," Dempsey wrote. "He was every inch an athlete. In comparison, I shaped up like an infant or a dwarf."[14] At least that's how Dempsey remembered the situation more than 30 years later.

Another notable remark he made was about Gene Tunney. "Incidentally," Dempsey wrote, "don't let anyone tell you Gene Tunney can't punch. Many fight fans have that wrong impression today."[15]

Indeed, when they were no longer in danger of facing one another in the ring ever again, the men became friendly as they aged.

Although Dempsey helped pen a couple of books, he did spend more time selling cheesecake in his ring retirement.

The restaurant was the perfect sinecure for Dempsey. It gave him income. He was the star of his own show. He chatted up the people there. In a hurry-up, what-have-you-done-for-me-lately society, the restaurant—no underestimating the value of the name in lights—prevented his name from fading from the limelight and memory.

Jack Dempsey's Broadway Restaurant did not close its doors until 1974, after a run of nearly 40 years, longer than any nearby playing Broadway show. Dempsey's run closed in 1983 when he was 87. Perhaps it was only really then that the Roaring Twenties ended.

Before that, when he was 15 years old, J. Russell Peltz met Jack Dempsey at the restaurant. Peltz, a member of the International Boxing Hall of Fame for his work as a fight promoter, grew up a boxing fan and was a newspaper boxing writer before turning to the business end of the sport.

Peltz was on a class trip to New York City from his Philadelphia-area school and the monitors had not chosen a place for lunch. Peltz lobbied hard for the meal at Dempsey's and won the argument.

Even better than the food was the presence of Jack Dempsey himself (no one in the group appreciated that more than Peltz). On that day in 1962, the wide-eyed teen not only met the immortal fighter but also got the chance to take a photograph with him. It was one of those schmaltzy boxing public relations–type pics, where each man places a closed fist on the other's jaw.

But for Peltz, it was the souvenir of a lifetime, especially for someone who spent a lifetime in boxing. "I still have it," Peltz said of the framed photo in his home.[16]

*The Ring* later published a copy of the picture. It was one way of keeping the Roaring Twenties alive.

# Chapter Notes

## Preface

1. Lucy Moore, *Anything Goes: A Biography of the Roaring Twenties* (New York: The Overlook Press, 2011), p. 17.
2. Jack Cavanaugh, *Tunney: Boxing's Brainiest Champ and His Upset of the Great Jack Dempsey* (New York: Random House, 2006), p. 302.
3. Moore, p. 294.
4. John L. Sullivan, *I Can Lick Any Sonofabitch in the House* (London: Proteus Books, 1979).

## Chapter 1

1. Jack Dempsey and Barbara Piatelli Dempsey, *Dempsey* (New York: Harper & Row, 1977), p. 8.
2. Roger Kahn, *A Flame of Pure Fire: Jack Dempsey and the Roaring Twenties* (New York: Harcourt Brace, 1999), p. 6.
3. Dempsey and Dempsey, p. 17.
4. Dempsey and Dempsey, p. 23.
5. Dempsey and Dempsey, p. 45.
6. Dempsey and Dempsey, p. 58.
7. Dempsey and Dempsey, p. 60.

## Chapter 2

1. Sudiksha Kochi, "Fact check: Theodore Roosevelt's eyesight was permanently damaged by military aide during boxing match," *USA Today*, Nov. 5, 2021.
2. John Jarrett, *Gene Tunney: The Golden Boy Who Licked Jack Dempsey Twice* (London: Robson Books, 2003), p. 7.
3. Jarrett, p. 16.
4. Jarrett, p. 25.
5. Jarrett, p. 29.

## Chapter 3

1. Robert Ecksel, "What's Up, Doc Kearns?" *Boxing Noir* (blog), April 13, 2009.
2. Ecksel.
3. Ecksel.
4. Jack Dempsey and Barbara Piatelli Dempsey, *Dempsey* (New York: Harper & Row, 1977), p. 65.
5. Dempsey and Dempsey, pp. 81–82.
6. Frederick Lewis Allen, *Only Yesterday* (New York: Perennial Library Classics, 2000), p. 13.

## Chapter 4

1. Edward Behr, *Prohibition: Thirteen Years That Changed America* (New York: Arcade, 2011), Frontispiece.
2. Behr, p. 3
3. Behr, p. 113.
4. June Allen, "A President's Ill-fated Trek to Alaska: What Did Kill Warren G. Harding?" *Ketchikan* [Alaska] *Daily News*, July 23, 2003.
5. Mark Will-Weber, "A Complete List of Every President's Favorite Drink," *New York Post*, January 1, 2018.
6. Minute Bartender website, https://minutebartender.com/bourbon-based-cocktails/gene-tunney-recipe/.
7. Minute Bartender.
8. Minute Bartender.

## Chapter 5

1. John Jarrett, *Gene Tunney: The Golden Boy Who Licked Jack Dempsey*

*Twice* (London: Robson Books, 2003), p. 35.
  2. Jarrett, pp. 34–35.

## Chapter 6

  1. Biography (No byline), "Jack Johnson," https://www.biography.com/athletes/jack-johnson, May 13, 2021.
  2. Roger Kahn, *A Flame of Pure Fire: Jack Dempsey and the Roaring Twenties* (New York: Harcourt Brace, 1999), p. 269.
  3. Colleen Aycock and Mark Scott, *Tex Rickard: Boxing's Greatest Promoter* (Jefferson, North Carolina: McFarland, 2012), p. 174.
  4. Kahn, p. 45.
  5. (No byline), "Jack Johnson," https://iloveancestry.net/post/88183705611/blackedu-blackhistory-john-arthur-jack.

## Chapter 7

  1. Arly Allen (assisted by James Willard Mace), *Jess Willard: Heavyweight Champion of the World* (Jefferson, North Carolina: McFarland, 2017), p. 135.
  2. Roger Kahn, *A Flame of Pure Fire: Jack Dempsey and the Roaring Twenties* (New York: Harcourt Brace, 1999), p. 21.
  3. Kahn, p. 46.
  4. Kahn, p. 50.
  5. Kahn, p. 32.
  6. Allen, p. 176.
  7. Grantland Rice, *The Tumult and the Shouting* (New York: A.S. Barnes, 1954), p. 117.
  8. Kahn, p. 91.
  9. Kahn, pp. 97–98.
  10. Kahn, pp. 98–99.

## Chapter 8

  1. Bill Crawford, *All-American: The Rise and Fall of Jim Thorpe* (Hoboken: John Wiley & Sons, 2005), p. 212.
  2. Crawford, p. 194.
  3. Crawford, p. 226.
  4. George Halas Pro Football Hall of Fame induction speech transcript of video, 1963, Canton, Ohio.

## Chapter 9

  1. John Jarrett, *Gene Tunney: The Golden Boy Who Licked Jack Dempsey Twice* (London: Robson Books, 2003), p. 30.
  2. Jarrett, p. 33.
  3. Jarrett, p. 36.

## Chapter 10

  1. Frederick Lewis Allen, *Only Yesterday* (New York: Perennial Library Classics, 2000), p. 78.
  2. Lucy Moore, *Anything Goes: A Biography of the Roaring Twenties* (New York: The Overlook Press, 2011), p. 54.
  3. Moore, p. 58.
  4. Timothy Egan, *A Fever in the Heartland: The Ku Klux Klan's Plot to Take Over America and the Woman Who Stopped Them* (New York: Viking, 2023), p. 340.
  5. Egan, p. 340.

## Chapter 11

  1. Roger Kahn, *A Flame of Pure Fire: Jack Dempsey and the Roaring Twenties* (New York: Harcourt Brace, 1999), p. 102.
  2. Kahn, p. 103.
  3. Kahn, p. 206.
  4. Jack Dempsey and Barbara Piatelli Dempsey, *Dempsey* (New York: Harper & Row, 1977), p. 136.

## Chapter 12

  1. *Sports Center* Flashback: "The Chicago Black Sox Banned from Baseball," ESPN, November 19, 2003.
  2. Kevin Baker, *The New York Game: Baseball and the Rise of a New City* (New York: Alfred A. Knopf, 2024), p. 211.
  3. Robert Weintraub, *The House That Ruth Built* (New York: Little, Brown, 2011), p. 257.
  4. Craig Muder, "Making of a Legend," National Baseball Hall of Fame website, https://baseballhall.org.

## Chapter 13

  1. Thomas Brennan, *The Million Dollar Man* (Berkeley: Regent Press, 2017), p. 145.

# Chapter Notes

2. Grantland Rice, *The Tumult and the Shouting* (New York: A.S. Barnes, 1954), p. 118.
3. Rice, p. 118.
4. Roger Kahn, *A Flame of Pure Fire: Jack Dempsey and the Roaring Twenties* (New York: Harcourt Brace, 1999), p. 263.
5. Kahn, p. 266.

## Chapter 14

1. Frederick Lewis Allen, *Only Yesterday* (New York: Perennial Library Classics, 2000), p. 228.
2. Daniel Okrent, *Last Call: The Rise and Fall of Prohibition* (New York: Scribner, 2010), p. 252.
3. Okent, p. 321.
4. Lucy Moore, *Anything Goes: A Biography of the Roaring Twenties* (New York: The Overlook Press, 2011), p. 43.
5. George Pendle, "The Improbable Prohibition Agents Who Outsmarted Speakeasy Owners," https://www.history.com, March 28, 2023.
6. Okrent, p. 258.

## Chapter 15

1. John Jarrett, *Gene Tunney: The Golden Boy Who Licked Jack Dempsey Twice* (London: Robson Books, 2003), p. 43.
2. Jarrett, p. 49.
3. Jarrett, p. 52.
4. Jack Cavanaugh, *Tunney: Boxing's Brainiest Champ and His Upset of the Great Jack Dempsey* (New York: Random House, 2006), p. 118.

## Chapter 16

1. Roger Kahn, *A Flame of Pure Fire: Jack Dempsey and the Roaring Twenties* (New York: Harcourt Brace, 1999), p. 305.
2. Kahn, p. 306.
3. Thomas Brennan, *The Million Dollar Man* (Berkeley: Regent Press, 2017), p. 162.
4. Jack Dempsey and Barbara Piatelli Dempsey, *Dempsey* (New York: Harper & Row, 1977), p. 154.
5. Dempsey and Dempsey, p. 154.
6. Dempsey and Dempsey, pp. 154–155.

7. Cade Menter, "Shelby will host Dempsey vs. Gibbons centennial celebration," KRTV news, June 1, 2023.

## Chapter 17

1. Wendy Knickerbocker, "Billy Sunday," Society for American Baseball Research, and *Sunday at the Ballpark: Billy Sunday's Professional Baseball Career* (Lanham, Maryland: Scarecrow Press, 2000).
2. William G. McLoughlin, Jr., *Billy Sunday Was His Real Name* (Chicago: University of Chicago Press, 1955), p. xix.
3. Lucy Moore, *Anything Goes: A Biography of the Roaring Twenties* (New York: The Overlook Press, 2011), p. 260.

## Chapter 18

1. Bill Paxton, *The Fearless Harry Greb: Biography of a Tragic Hero of Boxing* (Jefferson, North Carolina: McFarland, 2009), p. 119.
2. Paxton, pp. 122–123.
3. Jack Cavanaugh, *Tunney: Boxing's Brainiest Champ and His Upset of the Great Jack Dempsey* (New York: Random House, 2006), p. 140.
4. Cavanaugh, p. 141.
5. Cavanaugh, p. 142.

## Chapter 19

1. Celeste Moore, "History of Man o' War," Man o' War: Racing Icon, https://www.manowar.info/history.html, 2017.
2. Moore.
3. Moore.
4. Kevin Baker, *The New York Game: Baseball and the Rise of a New City* (New York: Alfred A. Knopf, 2024), p. 219.
5. Ron Rapoport, *The Immortal Bobby: Bobby Jones and the Golden Age of Golf* (Lincoln: University of Nebraska Press, 2021), p. 57.
6. Rapoport, p. 70.

## Chapter 20

1. Roger Kahn, *A Flame of Pure Fire: Jack Dempsey and the Roaring Twenties* (New York: Harcourt Brace, 1999), p. 279.

2. Kahn, p. 281.
3. Kahn, p. 291.
4. Kahn, p. 297.

## Chapter 21

1. Arly Allen (assisted by James Willard Mace), *Jess Willard: Heavyweight Champion of the World* (Jefferson, North Carolina: McFarland, 2017), p. 209.
2. Colleen Aycock and Mark Scott, *Tex Rickard: Boxing's Greatest Promoter* (Jefferson, North Carolina: McFarland, 2012), p. 147.
3. Thomas Brennan, *The Million Dollar Man* (Berkeley: Regent Press, 2017), p. 157.
4. Brennan, p. 175.
5. Brennan, p. 176.
6. Jack Dempsey and Barbara Piatelli Dempsey, *Dempsey* (New York: Harper & Row, 1977), p. 160.
7. Dempsey and Dempsey, pp. 161.

## Chapter 22

1. Gay and Laney Salisbury, *The Cruelest Miles* (New York: W.W. Norton, 2003), p. 173.
2. Salisbury and Salisbury, p. 225.
3. Salisbury and Salisbury, p. 248.

## Chapter 23

1. Jack Cavanaugh, *Tunney: Boxing's Brainiest Champ and His Upset of the Great Jack Dempsey* (New York: Random House, 2006), p. 175.
2. Nat Fleischer, *Gene Tunney, the Enigma of the Ring* (New York: The Ring Publishing, 1931), n.p.
3. Cavanaugh, p. 177.
4. John Jarrett, *Gene Tunney: The Golden Boy Who Licked Jack Dempsey Twice* (London: Robson Books, 2003), p. 80.
5. Jarrett, p. 81.
6. Bill Paxton, *The Fearless Harry Greb: Biography of a Tragic Hero of Boxing* (Jefferson, North Carolina: McFarland, 2009), p. 160.
7. Paxton, p. 162.
8. Nick Bond, "On This Day: Harry Greb dishes out one of boxing history's most savage beatings," *Boxing News*, May 23, 2018, https://www.boxingnewsonline.net.author/nbond.

## Chapter 24

1. Frank Deford, *Big Bill Tilden: The Triumphs and the Tragedy* (New York: Simon & Schuster, 1975), p. 20.
2. Deford, p. 45.
3. Deford, p. 45.
4. Deford, p. 76.
5. Larry Engelman, *The Goddess and the American Girl* (New York: Oxford University Press, 1988), p. 241.
6. Engelman, p. 252.
7. Engelman, pp. 255–256.

## Chapter 25

1. Roger Kahn, *A Flame of Pure Fire: Jack Dempsey and the Roaring Twenties* (New York: Harcourt Brace, 1999), p. 349.
2. Amity Shales, *Coolidge* (New York: HarperCollins, 2013), p. 221.
3. Kahn, p. 353.
4. Kahn, p. 365.

## Chapter 26

1. Damon Runyon, "Penn Trampled Under Flying Feet of Red Grange," *Tampa Tribune*, November 1, 1925.
2. Chris Willis, *Red Grange: The Life and Legacy of the NFL's First Superstar* (Lanham, Maryland: Rowman & Littlefield, 2019), p. 102.
3. Robert D'Angelo, "At 84, NFL savior Red Grange prefers baseball," *Chicago Tribune*, September 13, 1987.
4. Grantland Rice, "The Four Horsemen," fightingirish.com, October 19, 1924.
5. Jim Lefebvre, *Coach for a Nation: The Life and Times of Knute Rockne* (Minneapolis: Great Day Press, 2013), p. 268.
6. Lefebvre, p. 183.

## Chapter 27

1. Jack Dempsey and Barbara Piatelli Dempsey, *Dempsey* (New York: Harper & Row, 1977), p. 77.

2. Jack Cavanaugh, *Tunney: Boxing's Brainiest Champ and His Upset of the Great Jack Dempsey* (New York: Random House, 2006), p. 267.
3. Cavanaugh, p. 275.
4. Isabel Leighton, *The Aspirin Age, 1919–1941* (New York: Simon & Schuster, 1949), p. 45.

## Chapter 28

1. Jack Dempsey and Barbara Piatelli Dempsey, *Dempsey* (New York: Harper & Row, 1977), p. 199.
2. Dempsey and Dempsey, p. 240.
3. Dempsey and Dempsey, p. 201.
4. Roger Kahn, *A Flame of Pure Fire: Jack Dempsey and the Roaring Twenties* (New York: Harcourt Brace, 1999), p. 389.
5. John Jarrett, *Gene Tunney: The Golden Boy Who Licked Jack Dempsey Twice* (London: Robson Books, 2003), p. 142.
6. Jarrett, p. 144.
7. Jarrett, p. 145.
8. Jarrett, p. 187.
9. Jarrett, p. 199.
10. Jarrett, p. 202.
11. Jack Cavanaugh, *Tunney: Boxing's Brainiest Champ and His Upset of the Great Jack Dempsey* (New York: Random House, 2006), p. 309.
12. Cavanaugh, p. 311.

## Chapter 29

1. Jack and Barbara Piatelli Dempsey, *Dempsey* (New York: Harper & Row, 1977), p. 207.
2. Dempsey and Dempsey, p. 208.
3. Dempsey and Dempsey, p. 208.
4. Peter Carlson, "Gene Tunney Hits It Off with George Bernard Shaw," https://www.history.net, May 10, 2017.

## Chapter 30

1. A. Scott Berg, *Lindbergh* (New York: Berkley Books, 1998), p. 92.
2. Berg, p. 121.

## Chapter 31

1. Jack Dempsey and Barbara Piatelli Dempsey, *Dempsey* (New York: Harper & Row, 1977), p. 217.
2. Roger Kahn, *A Flame of Pure Fire: Jack Dempsey and the Roaring Twenties* (New York: Harcourt Brace, 1999), p. 412.
3. Dempsey and Dempsey, p. 217.
4. Dempsey and Dempsey, p. 217.
5. Thomas Brennan, *The Million Dollar Man* (Berkeley: Regent Press, 2017), p. 241.
6. Kahn, p. 414.
7. Colleen Aycock and Mark Scott, *Tex Rickard: Boxing's Greatest Promoter* (Jefferson, North Carolina: McFarland, 2012), p. 187.

## Chapter 32

1. Roger Kahn, *A Flame of Pure Fire: Jack Dempsey and the Roaring Twenties* (New York: Harcourt Brace, 1999), pp. 418–19.
2. J. Russell Peltz, personal interview, May 17, 2024.
3. Peltz.
4. Thomas Brennan, *The Million Dollar Man* (Berkeley: Regent Press, 2017), p. 253.
5. Jack Dempsey and Barbara Piatelli Dempsey, *Dempsey* (New York: Harper & Row, 1977), p. 219.
6. Dempsey and Dempsey, p. 219.
7. Jack Cavanaugh, *Tunney: Boxing's Brainiest Champ and His Upset of the Great Jack Dempsey* (New York: Random House, 2006), p. 368.
8. Steve Farhood, personal interview, May 22, 2024.

## Chapter 33

1. John Jarrett, *Gene Tunney: The Golden Boy Who Licked Jack Dempsey Twice* (London: Robson Books, 2003), p. 252.
2. Jarrett, p. 252.
3. Jarrett, p. 254.
4. Jarrett, p. 258.

## Chapter 34

1. "Unusual Political Career of Calvin Coolidge, Never Defeated for an Office," *New York Times*, January 6, 1933.

## Chapter 35

1. Don Majeski, personal interview, June 2, 2024.
2. Monte D. Cox, "Jack Dempsey, The Manassa Mauler—The Greatest Rough and Tumble Fighter Who Ever Lived," https://coxcorner.tripod.com/jdempsey.html, no date.
3. Cox.
4. Majeski.
5. Nigel Collins, personal interview, May 3, 2024.
6. Jack Cavanaugh, *Tunney: Boxing's Brainiest Champ and His Upset of the Great Jack Dempsey* (New York: Random House, 2006), p. 394.
7. Greg Nolan, "A Tribute to Tunney," *Boxing Illustrated*, February 1979.
8. Lisa Kerr, "Heavyweights: When F. Scott Fitzgerald Met Gene Tunney," *Literary Traveler*, November 29, 2007.
9. Majeski.
10. Steve Farhood, personal interview, May 22, 2024.
11. Collins.
12. Majeski.
13. Majeski.
14. Jack Dempsey, *Championship Fighting: Explosive Punching and Aggressive Defense* (New York: Simon & Schuster, 1950), pp. 7–8.
15. Dempsey, p. 10.
16. J. Russell Peltz, personal interview, May 17, 2024.

# BIBLIOGRAPHY

## Books

Allen, Arly (assisted by James Willard Mace). *Jess Willard: Heavyweight Champion of the World*. Jefferson, North Carolina: McFarland, 2017.
Allen, Frederick Lewis. *Only Yesterday*. New York: Perennial Library Classics, 2000.
Aycock, Colleen, and Mark Scott. *Tex Rickard: Boxing's Greatest Promoter*. Jefferson, North Carolina: McFarland, 2012.
Baker, Kevin. *The New York Game: Baseball and the Rise of a New City*. New York: Alfred A. Knopf, 2024.
Behr, Edward. *Prohibition: Thirteen Years That Changed America*. New York, Arcade, 2011.
Berg, A. Scott. *Lindbergh*. New York: Berkley Books, 1998.
Brennan, Thomas. *The Million Dollar Man*. Berkeley: Regent Press, 2017.
Cavanaugh, Jack. *Tunney: Boxing's Brainiest Champ and His Upset of the Great Jack Dempsey*. New York: Random House, 2006.
Crawford, Bill. *All-American: The Rise and Fall of Jim Thorpe*. Hoboken: John Wiley & Sons, 2005.
Deford, Frank. *Big Bill Tilden: The Triumphs and the Tragedy*. New York: Simon & Schuster, 1975.
Dempsey, Jack, and Barbara Piatelli Dempsey. *Dempsey*. New York: Harper & Row, 1977.
Egan, Timothy. *A Fever in the Heartland: The Ku Klux Klan's Plot to Take Over America and the Woman Who Stopped Them*. New York: Viking, 2023.
Engelman, Larry. *The Goddess and the American Girl*: New York: Oxford University Press, 1988.
Fleischer, Nat. *Gene Tunney, the Enigma of the Ring*. New York: The Ring Publishing, 1931.
Jarrett, John. *Gene Tunney: The Golden Boy Who Licked Jack Dempsey Twice*. London: Robson Books, 2003.
Kahn, Roger. *A Flame of Pure Fire: Jack Dempsey and the Roaring Twenties*. New York: Harcourt Brace, 1999.
Lefebvre, Jim. *Coach for a Nation: The Life and Times of Knute Rockne*. Minneapolis: Great Day Press, 2013.
Leighton, Isabel. *The Aspirin Age, 1919–1941*. New York: Simon & Schuster, 1949.
McLoughlin, William G., Jr. *Billy Sunday Was His Real Name*. Chicago: University of Chicago Press, 1955.
Moore, Lucy. *Anything Goes: A Biography of the Roaring Twenties*. New York: The Overlook Press, 2011.
Okrent, Daniel. *Last Call: The Rise and Fall of Prohibition*. New York: Scribner's, 2010.
Paxton, Bill. *The Fearless Harry Greb: Biography of a Tragic Hero of Boxing*. Jefferson, North Carolina: McFarland, 2009.
Rapoport, Ron. *The Immortal Bobby: Bobby Jones and the Golden Age of Golf*. Lincoln: University of Nebraska Press, 2021.

Rice, Grantland. *The Tumult and the Shouting.* New York: A.S. Barnes, 1954.
Salisbury, Gay, and Laney Salisbury. *The Cruelest Miles.* New York: W.W. Norton, 2003.
Shales, Amity. *Coolidge.* New York: HarperCollins, 2013.
Sullivan, John L. *I Can Lick Any Sonofabitch in the House.* London: Proteus Books, 1979.
Weintraub, Robert. *The House That Ruth Built.* New York: Little, Brown, 2011.
Willis, Chris. *Red Grange: The Life and Legacy of the NFL's First Superstar.* Lanham, Maryland: Rowman & Littlefield, 2019.

## Personal Interviews

Nigel Collins
Steve Farhood
Don Majeski
J. Russell Peltz

## Magazines

Boxing Illustrated
Literary Traveler
The Ring

## Newspapers

Chicago Tribune
Ketchikan [Alaska] Daily News
New York Post
New York Times
Tampa Tribune
USA Today

## Online Sources

Biography
Boxing Noir
Boxingnewsonline.net
Coxcorner.tripod.com
ESPN
Fightingirish.com
History.com
History.net
Iloveancestry.net
KRTV News (Montana)
Minute Bartender
National Baseball Hall of Fame
Pro Football Hall of Fame
Society for American Baseball Research

# INDEX

Adelphia Hotel 178
Affirmed 111
Africa 15, 132
Akron Pros 53
Alaska 29, 30, 47, 75, 131, 132, 135
Alaska Railroad 29
Alaska-Yukon Gold Rush 23, 47, 131, 132, 179
Aldrin, Harold 60, 64
Alexander, Grover Cleveland 70
Alhambra 63
All-Alaska Sweepstakes 132, 133
Allegheny Athletic Association 52
Allen, Whitey 35, 36, 58
Ali, Muhammad (Cassius Clay) 3, 11, 68, 217
Alydar 111
American Civil Liberties Union 103
American Football League (1920s) 161
American League 72, 73, 114
*American Mercury* (magazine) 84
American Revolution 26
Anchorage 132, 133
Anderson, Ole 58
Anson, Adrian (Cap) 100, 101
Anthony, Susan B. 26, 27
*Aquitania* (ship) 120
Arcel, Ray 214
Argentina 120, 123, 125, 127, 130
Armstrong, Louis 62
Army (football) 162, 163
Asia 15
Asinof, Eliott 71
Associated Press 147, 153
Atlantic City 143, 172
Atlantic Ocean 183, 185–187, 189
Attell, Abe 109, 192
Augusta, Georgia 117
Augusta National Golf Club 118
Australia 38
Austria-Hungary 15

Bagley, Frank "Doc" 33, 86, 109, 110
Baltimore 72, 84, 85, 112
*Baltimore Sun* 84, 103
Balto 134, 135
Barnum, P.T. 148
Barry, Dave 192, 199, 200
Barrymore, John 105
Battery Park (New York) 188
Bayonne, New Jersey 34, 35
Beeler, Paul 199
Belgium 120
Bellows, George 124, 128
Belmont Stakes 112
Benjamin, Joe 120
Benton Harbor, Michigan 69
Bering Sea 132, 133
Berlin 121
Big Ten Conference 159
Billings, Montana 23
Binghamton, New York 183
Black Hills (South Dakota) 211
Black Sox Scandal 70, 71, 109, 192
Blue Mountain, Mississippi 104
Bonds, Joe 23
Bone, Scott 29
Borgia, Lucrezia 154
Boston 40, 73, 183, 205
Boston Bruins 180
Boston Celtics 3, 180
Boston Garden 180
*Boston Globe* 146
Boston Marathon 18
Boston Red Sox 3, 72, 79, 114, 115
Bow, Clara 105
Bowe, Riddick 11, 43
*Boxing Illustrated* 214, 217
Boyle's Thirty Acres 76, 126, 190
Braddock, James J. 81
Brennan, Bill 24, 69, 75, 125, 150, 168
British Open Golf Tournament 116, 117
Broad Street (Philadelphia) 166

229

Broadway 63, 121, 181
Brooklyn, New York 81, 86
Brooklyn Dodgers 125
Brooks, Louise 61
Brown University 54
Bryan, William Jennings 104
Budge, Don 146
Buenos Aires 124, 125
Buffalo Bill's Wild West 46
Burke, Jack 88, 89
Burns, Ken 42
Burns, Tommy 8, 38
Butler Act 103
Butte, Montana 94

California 30, 98, 122, 149, 180, 181
Canada 23, 38, 80, 82, 87, 90, 132, 149, 205
Canastota, New York 34, 215
Cannes, France 150
Canton, Ohio 52, 161
Canton Bulldogs 53
Capone, Al 6, 28, 80–85, 190–193, 208–210, 215
Carlin, Phillips 171, 198
Carlisle Indian Industrial School 53, 54
Carnegie, Andrew 182
Carpentier, Georges 34, 65, 76–79, 87, 88, 90, 94, 102, 108, 109, 121, 123, 148, 151, 197, 213
Central Park, New York 135
Champaign, Illinois 159
Champions Park, Shelby, Montana 93, 95–99
Chaney, Lon 105
Chaplin, Charlie 104
Charleston (dance) 63, 83, 131, 212
Charleston, South Carolina 63
Cherbourg, France 188
Chicago 3, 62, 80, 82–84, 92, 131, 162, 163, 190, 195–197, 202, 204, 208, 213
Chicago Bears 2, 3, 50, 53, 55, 158, 160, 161, 212
Chicago Cardinals (Arizona Cardinals) 53, 55
Chicago Charities College All-Star Game 55
Chicago Cubs 102
*Chicago Herald and Examiner* 192
Chicago Outfit 82, 208
*Chicago Tribune* 55
Chicago White Sox 7, 70–72
Chicago White Stockings 100, 101
Chicago World's Fair 42
Churchill Downs 111
Cicero, Illinois 82, 208
Cicotte, Ed 70, 71

Cincinnati Reds 7, 70
Citation 111
Civil War 63
Cleveland 141
*Cleveland Plain-Dealer* 134
Cleveland Zoo 135
Clifford, Jack 58, 89
Cobb, Ty 7, 70, 172, 202
Collins, Bud 146
Collins, Eddie 70
Collins, Nigel 215, 216, 218
Colorado 3, 11, 148
Connecticut 182, 203
Cook County 83
Coolidge, Calvin (president) 30, 31, 152–154, 160, 172, 210, 211
Coolidge, Grace (wife) 153
Cooperstown, New York 7
Corbett, James J. 8, 16
Cordova, Alaska 30
Cotton Club 63
Cox, James 64
Cox, Monte D. 214
Crowley, Jim 162
Cruickshank, Bobby 119
Curran, County Kildare, Ireland 10

Danzig, Allison 146
Darrow, Clarence 103, 104
Darwin, Charles 103, 104
Davenport, Iowa 100
Davis Cup 64, 144, 146
Dawes, Charles 211
Dawson, Bobby 19
Dawson, Charles 172
Dayton, Tennessee 103, 104
Dayton Triangles 53
Decatur Staleys 53
Declaration of Independence 166
De Gaulle, Charles 218
Delaney, Jack 205
Delaware 154
DeMille, Cecil B. 154
Dempsey, Bernie (brother) 9–12, 15
Dempsey, Estelle Taylor (wife) 154–156, 163, 166, 169, 178, 180, 192, 218
Dempsey, Hyrum (Hiram, father) 9, 11
Dempsey, Jack (Manassa Mauler, Kid Blackie, Harry) 2–5, 8–16, 20, 22–24, 26, 27, 33, 36, 37, 40, 41, 43, 44, 46–51, 57–60, 62, 65–69, 73, 75, 77–79, 85–87, 90–95, 97–99, 102, 104–106, 108, 116, 120–131, 142, 143, 147, 148, 151–157, 159, 160, 163, 165–182, 184, 185, 187, 190–192, 194–208, 210, 213–220

## Index

Dempsey, Mary Celia (mother)  9, 12
Dempsey, Maxine (first wife)  14, 66, 121
Denali (Mount McKinley)  132
Denver  131
Detroit  82, 185
Detroit Tigers  102
Dickerson, Ray  112
diphtheria  131, 133
Dorais, Gus  162
Dougherty, Jack  154
Dundee, Johnny  64

Eagan, Eddie  20, 21
Earp, Wyatt  47
Ebay  99
Ebbets Field  125
Egypt  1
Eiffel Tower  188
*Eight Men Out* (movie)  71
Einstein, Isadore  83, 84
Ellington, Duke  62
Ely, Nevada  13
England  15, 120, 121, 144
Ertle, Harry  79
Europe  5, 15, 62, 120
Evansville, Indiana  64
Evert, Chris  150

Faber, Red  70
Fairbanks, Douglas  105
Fairbanks, Alaska  30, 134
Farhood, Steve  202, 218
FBI  209
Feustal, Louis  113
Firpo, Luis Angel  120, 123–130, 151, 152, 154, 165, 166, 198, 213
Fitzgerald, F. Scott  1, 62
Fitzgerald, Zelda  62
Fitzsimmons, Fred  8, 38, 43
Fleischer, Nat  66, 122, 138, 214
Florida  80, 81, 215
Forbes Field  60
Ford, Henry  26
"The Four Horsemen of Notre Dame"  162–164
Foxx, Jimmie  74, 115
France  15, 16, 19, 20, 34, 49, 76, 78, 109, 120, 121, 144–148, 188
Frazier, Joe  3, 217
French Open (tennis)  147, 150
Fullerton, Hugh  71
Fury, Tyson  43

Galena, Alaska  135
Gallagher, Johnny  128, 129
Gallico, Paul  182, 200

Galveston, Texas  38
Gans, Joe  41
Garbo, Greta  105
Garden, Mary  147
Garrick Theatre  12
Gehrig, Lou  74, 115, 202
George Halas Drive  55
Georgia  118
Germantown, Pennsylvania  144
Germany  5, 15, 22, 120, 121, 146
Gettysburg Address  152
Gibbons, Gerard  98
Gibbons, Michael  98
Gibbons, Ryan, Jr.  98
Gibbons, Tommy  90–99, 108, 123, 151, 156, 165
Gibson, Billy  33, 139, 140
Gipp (The Gipper), George  2, 162, 164
Gleason, Scoop  14
Glenwood, Iowa  100
*Golf Magazine*  118
Golovin, Alaska  134
Grand Rapids, Michigan  86
Grange, Red (Galloping Ghost, The Wheaton Iceman)  2, 157–161, 185, 212
Great Britain  8
Great Depression  1, 55, 211, 218
Great Falls, Montana  93, 95, 98
Great Migration  63
*The Great White Hope* (movie)  42
Greb, Harry  69, 86, 89, 106–110, 121, 122, 137–143, 151, 165, 176, 192, 213
Greb, Mildred  138, 139
Green, Willie  18
Green Bay Packers  3, 52, 55
Greenberg, Hank  54
Greenwich, Connecticut  16, 202, 216
Greenwich Village  16, 35, 58, 86, 109, 182, 202
Gregory, Tristan  98
Griffith Stadium  153
*Guys and Dolls*  14

Hagen, Walter  116–118, 185
Halas, George  53–56, 160, 161
Haley, Patsy  138, 140
Harding, Florence (first lady)  29, 30
Harding, Warren (president)  28–31, 64, 152, 160, 210
Harlem  63
Harper, Frances Ellen Watkins  26
Hart, Marvin  8
Havana, Cuba  39, 45, 125, 149
Hayes, Teddy  154, 155
Heeney, Tom  205, 206
Heffelfinger, William (Pudge)  52

# 232 Index

Hemingway, Ernest 1, 62, 121
Herman, Jack 125, 156
Hibbard, Jim 125
Hoff, Max (Boo Boo) 192, 193
Hollywood 1, 123, 149, 154, 155, 161, 181, 182
Hooper, Harry 115
Hoodwink 113
Hoover, Herbert (president) 211
Hoppe, Willie 172
Houck, Leo 58
Hughes, Langston 63
Humphreys, Joe 138, 187

Iditarod Trail Sled Dog Race (Last Great Race on Earth) 132, 134, 135
Igoe, Hype 129
Illinois 208, 210
Indiana 63, 127, 162
Indianapolis 42
Indianapolis 500 3, 170
Indianapolis Motor Speedway 170
*Inherit the Wind* (movie) 104
International Boxing Hall of Fame 22, 34, 215, 220
International Olympic Committee 54
Inwood, New York 119
Inwood Country Club 119
Iowa 100
Ireland 10, 16, 22, 98, 188

Jack Dempsey's Broadway Restaurant 218–220
Jackson, Joe (Shoeless) 70, 72
Jacobs, Billy 33
Jazz Age 1, 62, 83, 157, 162
*The Jazz Singer* (movie) 155
Jeffries, James J. 38, 39, 43, 48, 126
Jenny (airplane) 186
Jerry the Greek 176
Jersey City, New Jersey 34, 126
Jesus Christ 101, 102
Jim Crow 63
Jockey Gold Cup 112
Johnson, Floyd 126
Johnson, Jack 8, 38–43, 45–48, 67, 76, 122, 126, 127
Johnson, James Weldon 63
Johnson, Walter 70, 153, 202
Jolson, Al 159
Jones, Casey 173
Jones, Robert Tyre, Jr. (Bobby) 2, 116–119, 147, 185
Jones, Soldier 87
Juneau, Alaska 29, 134
Jungle Jim 115, 116

Kaasen, Gunnar 134, 135
Kansas 125, 126
Kansas City 42, 46
KDKA 60, 64
Kearns, (Doc, John Patrick Leo McKernan) Jack 15, 22–24, 33, 36, 40, 41, 43, 47, 49–51, 66, 67, 75, 90–96, 98, 99, 120–122, 127, 130, 152, 155, 166–169, 172, 174, 180, 187, 193
Keaton, Buster 104
Kelly, Gene 104
Kelly, John Edward (The Nonpareil, Jack Dempsey) 10, 11
Kelly, Sammy 33
Kelso 113
Kentucky Derby 111, 170
Kentucky Horse Park 113
Ketchikan, Alaska 29, 30
Kid Ory's Original Creole Band 62
Kiernan, John 3
King Tut 1
Kinley, Ed 58
Knights of Columbus (France) 20
*KO Magazine* 201
Koerner, Paul Sampson 58
Kramer, Jack 146
Ku Klux Klan 1, 63, 64, 127

Lajoie, Napoleon 7
Lake Placid, New York 135
Lake Shore Drive (Chicago) 83
Lambeau, Curly 52
Landis, Kenesaw Mountain 71, 72
Langford, Sam 40, 41
Lardner, John 214
Lardner, Ring 48, 71, 168, 178
Latin America 47
Lawrence Realization 113
Layden, Elmer 162
League of Nations 5
Leavenworth Prison 41
Lenglen, Charles 147
Lenglen, Suzanne 2, 145, 147–150, 185
Leonard, Benny 138, 139
Levinsky, Battling (Barney Lebrowitz, Barney Williams) 24, 46, 76, 88, 89
Levinsky, Kingfish 215
Lewis, Lennox 11, 43
Lexington, Kentucky 113
Liberty Bell 166
Lincoln, Abraham 152
Lincoln Park (Chicago) 208
Lindbergh, Anne Morrow 188
Lindbergh, Charles 1, 185, 186, 188, 189
Liston, Sonny 18
London 182, 205

Long, John 18
Long Count 195, 199–202, 204, 218
Long Hill, New Jersey 77
Los Angeles 154, 163, 178, 180
Los Angeles Lakers 3
"Lost Generation" 62
Louvre 121

Mace, Jem 217
Madden, Bartley 156
Madden, Jeff 58
Madison Square Garden 34, 45, 47, 69, 86, 88, 108, 110, 125, 126, 137, 141, 149, 179, 190, 205, 210, 218
Maine 135, 139
Majeski, Don 213, 215, 217, 219
Major League Baseball 3, 7, 60, 71, 74, 82, 101, 114
Mallory, Mola 149
Maloney, Jim 187, 205
Manassa, Colorado 9
Manhasset, New York 77
*Manhattan Madness* (movie) 154
Man O' War 2, 111–113, 116, 159
Mann Act 39
Maori (tribe) 206
Mara, Tim 55, 193
March, Fredric 104
Marias Fairgrounds, Shelby, Montana 98
Marquis of Queensbury Rules 8
Martin, T.T. 104
Mary, Queen of Scots 154
Massachusetts 103, 152
Massillon Tigers 55
Masters Golf Tournament 117, 118
Mathewson, Christy 7
Maxted, Tom 125
Maynard, George 133, 134
McAuliffe, Jack II 125
McCabe, Billy 20
McCann, Joe 125
McCarthy Era (Sen. Joseph McCarthy) 104
McGraw, John J. 54, 172
McKinley, William (senator) 160
McNamee, Graham 171, 198
McPartland, Kid 109
McTigue, Mike 183
Meehan, Willie 46
Meighan, Charles 138
Memorial Stadium (Illinois) 159
Mencken, H.L. 84, 85, 103, 104
Meredith, Burgess 139
Metlakatla, Alaska 29
Mexico 42

Mexico City 125
Miami, Florida 210
Miami Beach Kennel Club 210
Middle East 15
Miles, Charles E. 138
Miller, Dave 192
Miller, Don 162
Miller, Henry 62
Minnesota 68, 185
MinuteBartender.com 31, 32
Miske, Billy 24, 46, 68, 69, 75, 123, 150
Mississippi River 62
Molumby, Loy J. 92
Monahan, Jim 58
Montana 92, 94, 151, 156
Montreal 2, 42
Moore, Daniel T. (Colonel) 18
Moran, Dan (Dumb) 88
Moran, Frank 45, 46
Moran, George (Bugs) 208, 209
Morris, Carl 46
Morrissey, Andrew J. 163
Morton, Jelly Roll 62
Muldoon, William 140
Muncie Flyers 55
Murphy, Billy 12

NASCAR (stock car racing) 170
Nashville 131
National Baseball Hall of Fame 7, 71, 74
National Basketball Association 3
National Football Foundation Hall of Fame 163
National Football League (American Professional Football Association) 2, 50, 52–56, 157, 185
National Hockey League 2, 47
National League 7, 100, 114
Navratilova, Martina 150
NBC (broadcasting) 64, 171, 198
Nelson, Bud 58
Nenana, Alaska 30, 133, 134
Ness, Eliot 210
Nevada 47, 48
New England 135, 211
New Jersey 34, 47, 58, 76, 86, 87, 92, 125, 127, 190
New Orleans 40, 45, 62
New York Boxing Writers 216
New York City 14, 16, 19, 34, 45, 48, 57, 62, 69, 73, 76, 81–84, 86, 87, 92, 102, 112, 120, 126, 128, 129, 131, 135, 137, 138, 153, 154, 162, 165, 168, 181, 182, 185, 186, 188, 200, 205, 206, 210, 219, 220

# Index

New York Giants (baseball) 54, 172
New York Giants (football) 55, 193
"New York, New York" (song) 14
New York Rangers 47
New York State Boxing Commission (New York State Athletic Association) 41, 139
New York State Senate 34
New York Stock Exchange 211
*New York Times* 3, 140, 146
New York Yankees (Murderers' Row) 3, 53, 79, 114
New York Yankees (football) 161
New Zealand 205, 206
Newark, New Jersey 34, 125
Nollner, Edgar 135
Nome, Alaska 131–135
Normile, Gene 172, 173
North Dakota 23
Notre Dame 2, 157, 161–164
Nova Scotia 40
Noyes, Frank 153
Nulato, Alaska 133, 134
Nurmi, Paavo 159

Oakland 23
Ocean Steamship Company 18
O'Dowd, Dan 156
Ohio 28, 52, 79
Ohio State University 159
Okinawa 215
Oklahoma 42
Olson, Charlie 134
Olympic Arena (Cleveland) 141
101 Wild West Show 46
Orlando 131
O'Sullivan, Jack 184
Ott, Mel 74
Ottoman Empire 5, 15
Oyo Hotel, Shelby, Montana 98

Paraguay 47
Paris 62, 146, 185, 186
Parris Island 19
Pasadena, California 163
Pearce, Bob 35
Peltz, J. Russell 197, 199, 220
Pennsylvania 53
Phelps, Michael 115
Philadelphia 3, 86, 144, 165, 166, 170–173, 190, 193, 196, 197, 220
Philadelphia Phillies 60, 100, 114
Phoenix 131
Pickford, Mary 104
Pittsburgh 60, 79, 86, 89, 107, 137–139, 141

Pittsburgh Pirates 64, 100
*Police Gazette* 12
Polo Grounds 34, 54, 73, 79, 102, 128, 163, 190
Pottawatamie, Kansas 44
Pottsville Maroons 55
Pound, Ezra 62
Preakness Stakes 112
Pro Football Hall of Fame 53, 55, 161
Professional Golf Association 118
prohibition 1, 6, 27–30, 60, 69, 73, 80–85, 101, 102, 131, 146, 162, 209, 210
Pyle, C.C. 148–150, 159–161

radio 1, 60, 64, 79, 103
Ray, Johnny 64
RCA 64
Reagan, Ronald 162
Red Bank, New Jersey 86
Reno, Nevada 13, 39
Rice, Grantland 48, 49, 66, 78, 109, 162, 168
Richardson Highway (Alaska) 30
Rickard, Maxine 193, 194
Rickard, Tex 39, 41, 45–48, 50, 69, 75–79, 88, 90, 94, 109, 122, 123, 125–128, 148, 152, 165, 166, 169, 170, 173, 175, 178–183, 187, 190, 193–197, 200, 202, 204–206, 208, 210, 213, 214
Riddle, Samuel 111–113
*The Ring* (magazine) 40, 66, 108, 122, 138, 201, 206, 214, 215, 220
Risko, Johnny 156, 205
Roaring Twenties 1, 5, 6, 51, 55, 73, 79, 81, 83, 103, 106, 112, 113, 115, 116, 144, 147, 157, 164, 181, 185, 207, 208, 210, 212, 215, 218, 220
Roberts, Al 35, 58, 59
Roche, Billy 33, 57, 59, 86
Rochester, New York 27, 116
Rochester Jeffersons 55
Rock Island Independents 53
Rockne, Knute 2, 161–164
Rockwell, Helen 122
*Rocky* (movie) 18, 139
Rogers, Will 27, 187
Rome 183
Roosevelt, Theodore (president) 17, 18, 47, 52, 158
Rose Bowl 163
Ross, Barney 81
Ross, Luke 119
Rothstein, Arnold 71
Rowlands, Len 139
Royal and Ancient Golf Club 116

# Index 235

Runyon, Damon 14, 120, 121, 148, 159, 168, 178, 205
Rupert, Jacob 73
Russia 5, 29
Ruth, Babe (George Herman) 2, 7, 11, 27, 53, 70–74, 79, 104, 113–116, 127, 131, 145, 147, 157, 159, 172, 176, 180, 181, 183, 185, 195, 197, 200, 202

Sacco and Vanzetti (Nicola Sacco, Bartolomeo Vanzetti) 1, 103
Saint Louis 187, 188
Saint Louis Browns 114
Saint Paul, Minnesota 92, 98, 142
Saint Valentine's Day Massacre 208
Salt Lake City 11, 12
San Fernando Valley (California) 154
San Francisco 14, 15, 23, 29, 30
*San Francisco Bulletin* 14
Sanders, Everett 211
Saratoga Race Course 112
Saratoga Springs, New York 170, 172
Sarnoff, David 64
*Saturday Evening Post* (magazine) 157
Savoy Ballroom 63
Schuylkill River 170
Scopes, John Thomas 103, 104
Scopes Monkey Trial 103, 104
Seabiscuit 111
Seattle 30, 133
*Seattle Post-Intelligencer* 134
Seattle Slew 111
Secretariat 111
Seine River 188
Seppala, Leonhard 133–135, 141
Serum Run (Great Race of Mercy) 131, 134, 135
Sesquicentennial Exposition 166, 170, 190
Sesquicentennial Stadium (Philadelphia Municipal Stadium, JFK Stadium) 166
Seward (city) 29
Seward, William H. 29
Shakespeare, William 3, 88, 167, 175, 176, 182, 192, 200, 216
Shaktoolik, Alaska 134
Shannon, "Wild" Bill 134
Sharkey, Jack 183, 184, 187, 195, 205, 210, 215
Shaw, George Bernard 182
Shawnee Country Club 168
Shelby, Montana 90–92, 94–99, 123, 166
Shieber, Tom 74
Siberian huskies 132
Sisler, George 70

Sitka, Alaska 30
Small's Paradise 63
Smith, Bessie 62
Smith, Gunboat 24, 46, 124, 125
Smith, Moe 83, 84
Smith, Sergeant Ray 58
Smith, Verly 163
Soldier Field 163, 190, 194–196
Soldiers' Orphans Home (Iowa) 100
South Bend, Indiana 161
South Carolina 19
Spalding Sporting Goods 118
Speaker, Tris 70
Spinks, Leon 68
Spitz, Mark 115
*Spirit of St. Louis* 185, 188
Spokane, Washington 23
*Sports Illustrated* 67, 118
Stallone, Sylvester 139
Stanford University 163
Stanton, Elizabeth Cady 26
Staten Island, New York 34, 35
Stein, Gertrude 62
Stephenson, David (Old Man) 63, 64
Sternaman, Dutch 160
Stone, Lucy 26
Stribling, Young 210, 215
Stuhldreher, Harry 162
Sugar, Bert 214
Sunday, Billy 100, 101, 102
Sullivan, KO 58
Sullivan, John L. (Boston Strong Boy) 3, 8, 9, 13, 16
Summer Olympics 20, 53, 68, 115, 147
Swanson, Gloria 105
Sweden 53
Sydney, Australia 38

Tacoma, Washington 15
Taft, William Howard (president) 153
Tarzan 115, 116
Teapot Dome Scandal 28, 160
Tennessee 103
Thompson, Earl 187
Thorpe, Jim 53, 54, 73, 147, 148
Tilden, Bill 2, 144–147, 150, 172, 185
*Time* magazine 159
Times Square 63, 218
Togo 134, 135
Toklas, Alice B. 62
Toledo, Ohio 44, 48, 49, 76, 92
*Toledo Blade* 51
Tonopah, Nevada 13
Torrio, Johnny 81
Tracey, Jim 125
Tracy, Spencer 104

# Index

Travers Stakes 112, 113
Treaty of Versailles 26
Trent, Mike 172, 173
Triple Crown (horse racing) 111
Tunney, Gene (The Fighting Marine) 2–4, 6, 8, 16–21, 26, 27, 31–37, 41, 55, 57–60, 62, 86–89, 104–110, 116, 131, 137–143, 146, 151, 155, 156, 162, 163, 165, 167–171, 173–179, 181–183, 185, 190–192, 194–208, 210, 213, 215–219
Tunney, John (father) 16
Tunney, John (son) 216
Tunney, Mary Josephine (Polly) Lauder (wife) 182, 183, 202, 203
Tunney, Mary Lydon (mother) 16

*Unforgivable Blackness: The Rise and Fall of Jack Johnson* (documentary film) 42
United States 1, 2, 4, 5, 12, 15, 16, 19, 20, 24–27, 29–31, 34, 38, 56, 64, 66, 76, 77, 97, 103, 104, 116, 124, 125, 127, 132, 144, 146, 148, 149, 162, 166, 170, 179, 182, 188, 211, 212, 215
United States Amateur Golf Championship 118
United States Army 185
United States Constitution 26, 159
United States Congress 28, 159
U.S. Open Golf Tournament 116, 118, 119
United States Navy 216
United States Senate 26
University of Colorado 122
University of Illinois 2, 53, 158, 161
University of Michigan 159
University of Nebraska 159
University of Southern California 163
*USA Today* 18
Utah 11, 12, 14, 15, 22, 23

Valentino, Rudolph 104
Vancouver, British Columbia 30
Villagers Athletic Club 17
Volstead Act 27–29, 60, 82, 83, 102
Voss, Norway 164

Walker, Jimmy 34, 35
Wall Street 211
Waller, Fats 62, 83
Ward, Arch 55
Ward, Jem 217
Warner, Pop 54
Washington (state) 15, 22, 23

Washington, D.C. 29, 30, 134
Washington Monument 188
Washington Redskins 50
Washington Senators 153, 160
Wasilla, Alaska 29, 135
Waterloo, Michigan 22
Weaver, Buck 72
Weehawken, New Jersey 48
Weissmuller, Johnny 2, 115, 116
Welch, Dr. Curtis 133, 134
West Virginia 11
Western Open Golf Tournament 118
Westinghouse Electronic Corporation 64
White House 1, 17, 28, 29, 52, 64, 152, 160, 167
Wichita 42
Will-Weber, Mark 31
Willard, Hattie 46
Willard, Jess 8, 24, 36, 39, 44–51, 57, 67, 68, 76, 79, 121, 123, 125–128, 150, 166, 213, 219
Willow, Alaska 29
Wills, Catherine (Helen mother) 149
Wills, Clarence (Helen father) 149
Wills, Harry 39–41, 46, 68, 76, 122, 126, 151, 155, 183
Wills, Helen 2, 145, 147, 149, 150, 185
Wilson, Hack 115
Wilson, Johnny 139
Wilson, Woodrow (president) 5, 24, 26, 28
Wilson Sporting Goods 118
Wimbledon 146, 147, 149, 150
Windsor, Fred 14
Winter Olympics 20, 135
Women's Christian Temperance Union 27
Women's suffrage 6, 26
World Series 7, 70–73, 102, 115, 153
World War I 1, 2, 5, 8, 16, 24, 26, 35, 45, 55, 62, 64, 66, 68, 76, 85, 101, 132, 144, 147, 167, 186, 200, 202, 215, 216
World War II 5, 188, 215, 216
Wyoming 156

Yale University 21
Yankee Stadium (The House That Ruth Built) 73, 79, 125, 126, 183, 187, 206
YMCA 19
York, Dick 104
Young, Cy 7

www.ingramcontent.com/pod-product-compliance
Ingram Content Group UK Ltd.
Pitfield, Milton Keynes, MK11 3LW, UK
UKHW042358021025
463558UK00017B/120